In Praise of *What's Your Call?* From Curlers Like You

We asked a few non-pro yet serious curlers to review our book and see if it would help them. This is what they had to say...

"I don't know what to say other than I absolutely love it! I'll be acquiring copies for each of my regular teammates and stacking up a few copies for future gifts. They will all love it. Using QR codes is a pretty cool idea. It's the first time I've experienced it in a format like this but it really brings the book to life.

As you well know, I have been a big fan of the Daily Curling Puzzle from the day I discovered it. This takes it to a new level and could become biblical for all aspiring curlers.

The level is totally appropriate. In my opinion, every amateur sportsperson believes that they are tactically brilliant – certainly from the comfort of their couches. This provides them real-life, top-class scenarios to test their wits on and it also explains all the reasons why the call was good or bad and explores the other reasonable options. What more could you possibly ask for?

I think you might have created something that could be considered groundbreaking for many. It's unique and exceptional."

-Stephen McClymont, Competitive Club Curler & 2023 Strathcona Cup Team Member, Scotland

"I love this. I really like the way we get to see what the Pro played in the actual game and then read Doug and Mickey's discussion about why they played what they played. It's perfect for my level, and I'm pretty sure it's going to help me beat my husband this year. He won't be getting a copy for Christmas!"

-Leslie Cogill, Improving Club Curler, Toronto, Canada

"As a coach, this book is going to be invaluable. I'm getting one for every player on my teams."

-Allison Earl, Four-time Alberta Champion and Top Coach, Canada

"Overall: Wow! I'm thoroughly impressed. This has 'curling bible' potential. The format (Doug questions, Mickey teaches) works really well, and the principles are really well explained. I love it. Good use of diagrams, good choice of language, good catch-phrases. Well done!"

-Thomas Koch, Competitive Club Curler, Japan

"Normally, I am quite happy to be 'constructively critical', but too be honest I just can't with this. What you and Mickey have achieved is quite remarkable. It is such a fresh way of looking at tactics. Using real game situations, you get to think what shot to call. The video links to real games enable the viewer to see the shot being played and the outcomes thereafter. Reading on, you get a real in-depth understanding of the Pro's thought processes with clear and concise explanations. Your "A Brief Strategy & Tactics Primer" is an excellent guide to the book – and current curling tactics in general. I find the Vic Rauter-style approach by Doug, and the expert Mickey explanations style of discussion, perfect for getting across the main message from each of the situations reviewed. A wonderful informative learning experience to improve your curling."

-John Duff, Longtime Competitive Club Curler & Scotland Over-50s Runner-Up, 2020

"You and Mickey have put together an important addition to curler libraries. You have struck a good balance from beginner to experienced with the use of Club and Pro classifications. I especially like the explanation of how the calls can be so different depending on the shot making abilities of the two groups. Mickey's observations are on point and a good addition to your understanding at a different level. The layout with diagrams works well. I find the QR codes are a very good addition and I found myself referring to the videos more often even than in the Daily Curling Puzzles. They are easy to use and give a clear understanding of the conditions you are laying out. You have collected a diverse selection of situations that skips can find themselves in and have given well thought out responses, as well as a good measure of humour. This book will present new insights into the complexities of our glorious game…"

-Ron Cruikshank, Competitive Club Curler, Brandon, Manitoba

"You may not throw rocks like a pro, have rocks like the pros, nor can sweep anything but your garage floor, but with Doug and Mickey, you can start understanding the pros. You might even improve your curling team's sense of humour. You most certainly will understand the monsters lurking behind your opponent's nefarious plots. Or, at least you will finally understand how solid ends are built to be both flexible and more likely to succeed. Good luck is the residue of good design. Now get out there and good curling!"

-Doug Schmucker, Competitive Club Curler, Oklahoma City, USA

"Reading thru your book a bit in the mornings before work. Love the idea of the QR code to provide the link to what really happened. Will have to watch myself if I want to keep taking the odd 6 off you!"

-Stuart Stark, my friend and probably the luckiest curler in Forfar, Scotland

What's Your Call?

Curling Strategy & Tactics
in 50 Real-Life Puzzles

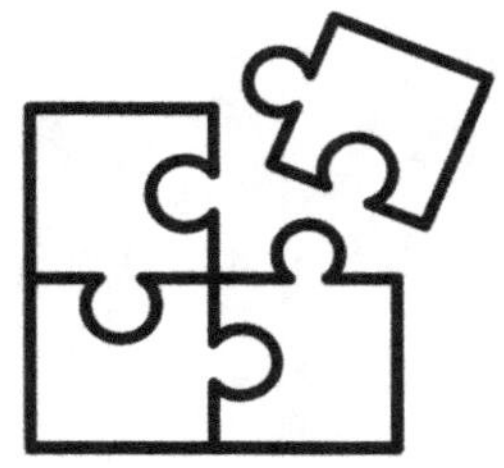

An Interactive Guide by

Doug Wilson & Mickey Pendergast

Foreword with Kevin Koe

What's Your Call?
Curling Strategy & Tactics in 50 Real-Life Puzzles

ISBN: 978-1-7387328-1-4

For my long-suffering wife and kids, Sandy, Abby & Freddie
– who have endured too many hours of curling to count.

For my wife, Debby, one of the top leads in the game in her day;
40 years sharing life and curling.

And our boys, Mark and Joel, who grew up in various curling rinks
and finally fell in love with the game in their 20s.

Table of Contents

Introduction – Doug Wilson

Doug is an Over-50s competitive curler. A native Canadian but living in Fife, Scotland for the past thirty years, Doug came to curling later than most, learning to curl in Scotland in his late 30s. He's had several successes – winning his rink and province championships a few times – all while being almost completely ignorant about anything to do with tactics or strategy!

In the spring of 2020 – just before covid hit – I'd lost two big games: the final of the Scottish Seniors, and the semi-final of the Scottish Pairs (two players, eight rocks thrown, regular rules). Anyway, our tactics were completely screwball; we had no idea what we were doing.

Realizing I needed to improve that part of my game, I went along to a Scottish Curling tactics seminar, hosted by Alan Hannah, former coach of Team Mouat. It was great. We looked at a bunch of hypothetical situations, discussed the calls we'd make, and tried to learn from our peers. Three days later, I sprang out of bed with the idea of using real-life situations, adding the real-life YouTube outcome, and sticking it up on Facebook. The Daily Curling Puzzle facebook group was born!

Essentially, I was trying to crowd-source a curling brain, and over 16,000 mad curlers joined in the effort to educate me. It's been great and we have almost three-hundred puzzles now posted, with detailed discussions of why the pro called what he called. Go on to facebook and search for '*Daily Curling Puzzle*' – you'll find us busy arguing about calls there!

Anyway, one of the guys pitching in kept on calling the exact same shots as the pros, over and over and over again. At first, I thought he was cheating, getting clues from the score and the brushes and the ice markings, figuring out what game it was and finding the shots on YouTube.

So I changed it up, using a graphics tool to diagram the situation in black-and-white, with no ice markings, no player uniforms, no identifying brushes – no anything that would help that guy Mickey find the game situation. And after all that – he still got them right! I threw in the towel, looked him up, and on the basis of can't-beat-em-join-em, started plotting to enlist his help. This book is the result of that plot.

I really couldn't have asked for a better partner in this venture. Not only does Mickey possess a seemingly bottomless reserve of patience – very much needed to repeat the fundamentals over and over and over again

to this relative Newbie – but he seems to have a unique grasp of the principles that underpin a great tactical plan. In reviewing his team's chances in the 2007 Alberta Provincials against the likes of Kevin Martin, Randy Ferbey, Kevin Koe and all the rest that seem to grow on trees out there, the Calgary Herald acknowledged that "no one will outskip" Mickey Pendergast. (*"Pendergast Takes Aim at the Big Boys"*, Calgary Herald, February 6th, 2007).

That skipping ability took him to several Tour wins, a few Tour Championship appearances and several Provincials, including two Alberta finals, losing in 1990 when his last rock picked, and later to Martin in 2000. If he was unlucky that he didn't get over the line in a province where the champion is often odds-on to win the Worlds, I was lucky that he agreed to work with me.

My main curling problem is time. Coming late to the sport after my body broke down playing other stuff, I didn't start curling competitively until I qualified for the Over-50 Senior game in 2014. And so while Ferbey, Martin, Pendergast and co. learned all this stuff by osmosis over decades of play, I don't have that luxury. I need a cheat sheet, someone to break down the basics of tactics and strategy for me, isolating some key fundamental principles and helping me move up the skipping learning curve – fast!

Looking for it, I took coaching courses, expecting some good lessons there. Not so much.

I watched hundreds of hours of curling on TV and YouTube. It was very entertaining, but the commentators talked over my head. I continued to be lost.

Finally, I bought books. Curling for Dummies was a gift from my wife – she said it was written for me! Sadly, almost no tactical tips.

And so this book is our effort at distilling out the key underlying principles of curling tactics in the five-rock era. They codify the game of chess, I reckoned – we should be able to do it in curling.

It has been a tougher challenge than I thought, and maybe that's why not many others have tried. I hope we've advanced the subject matter a bit, and I hope that that helps curlers of all ages and abilities move up the learning curve faster – before they run out of time.

Doug Wilson
September 2022

Introduction – Mickey Pendergast

Mickey is a long-time competitive curler, growing up playing in the curling hothouse that is Alberta. Earning twelve victories on Tour and twice making it to the province final – one game away from the Brier – he credits much of his success to competing against former world champions like Kevin Martin, Randy Ferbey, Pat Ryan, Ed Lukowich and others. "Figuring out how to play against those guys, and sometimes beat them, made us a much better team," he says. Now competing in the Master's category, he's the two-time defending Canadian Masters champion, beating Al Hackner (the Iceman) to win his most recent title.

My connection with Doug started when someone told me I should check out this interesting curling puzzle page on Facebook, so I did. I promptly provided my "solution" to one puzzle and was instantly hooked. Having curled for over 50 years and coached for about 5 years at the time, I've always enjoyed discussing and debating curling strategy, and Doug's Daily Curling Puzzle offered a novel way to do just that. I immediately started sharing my opinions, discussing shots with other puzzlers, and anxiously waiting for the next puzzle to come out so I could do it again. I especially liked the fact that each puzzle was linked to a real game where we could hear their conversations, see why and what they called and watch how it panned out.

Eventually Doug reached out to me to discuss a few puzzles and solutions, and I offered a few others I had run across while watching TV games. We shared some thoughts on how to make the puzzles and the concepts they generated available to more people, which is where the idea of this book began.

What I found interesting while doing the puzzles and discussing them with Doug was how these conversations helped to clarify and crystallize many of the strategy basics that had become instinctual to me through the decades that I've played. By having to explain the rationale behind various calls, I was forced to put into words the ideas and concepts that had become more like gut feelings to me over the years.

And the wonderful thing is there is usually more than one "correct" call, so even though I may have my thoughts on how to approach a given situation and why to choose one shot over another, someone else might prefer a completely different shot and it could work just as well. The idea is to demonstrate how certain calls are more likely to lead to certain types of ends, leading to somewhat predictable situations and outcomes.

I have to correct a misconception that you might get from reading this book. Doug has stolen a leaf from Vic Rauter, the TSN host on Canadian TV who quizzes ex-pro's Russ Howard and Cheryl Bernard about one shot versus another. It works great on TV, drawing out the logic of the play from a former world champion and an Olympic medallist. We've used a similar style here, Doug playing the straight man as Vic does.

And at the outset, I think Doug would admit that he was often genuinely puzzled about the choices the pros made. In fact, that's why he started the whole Daily Curling Puzzle in the first place – to improve his tactical game.

But over the past year and the hundreds of hours we've spent discussing hundreds of situations, I've noticed a huge advance in his tactical understanding. Now, when we talk in-depth about a complex end, he generates as many insights as I do. In fact, by the time we finished writing this book, he was pretty much writing the puzzle solutions for me. So don't be fooled: he takes on (as they say in Scotland) the 'daft laddie' role, just like Vic, but he (now) knows his stuff.

My hope is that those who use this book will also gain the insight and confidence to call a better game. If you work through the puzzles and reflect upon the discussion with each, I am sure you will start to see the patterns in play that the pros use and will start to create the type of ends you want. That can only lead to winning a few more games at whatever level you play – or aspire to play – in this crazy game of ours.

Mickey Pendergast
September 2022

Foreword – Kevin Koe with Mickey Pendergast

Kevin Koe has been such a dominant force in curling over the past twenty-five years, most people forget or never knew he didn't reach his first Brier until he was 35. That was when he won the 2010 Brier final over Glenn Howard and went on to win handily at the World Championships-not bad for a first-timer! He's since compiled a record of ten Brier appearances making it to eight finals and four titles.

He paid his dues trying to get out of Alberta in the Ferbey/Martin era, two teams consistently ranked in the top 3 in the world at the time, and played with a few teams on Tour honing his craft. He played third for me when he first came out of Juniors, then put together a young team with his brother, then joined forces with John Morris trying to find the right combination. Those teams reached several Provincials, won several Tour events including the 2004 Players' Championship, qualified for the Olympic Trials, and many other victories and tough losses along the way where he learned what it takes to win.

I reached out to him to get his general thoughts on strategy in today's game and how his experiences helped him become the pre-eminent strategist and player he is today.

"Well, at the top level most teams call a similar game, so we know what the other guy is planning to do. It comes down to who makes the most shots at the right time. Teams have different preferences, but it still comes down to execution. When we lose a game, it's because we missed shots, not calls.

"But for developing teams, I've noticed they don't always recognize how an end might develop if they call a certain shot, especially if they don't make it perfectly. You can get into big trouble if you don't understand how a bad call early in an end can take you in the wrong direction, and by the time you realize it, it's often too late to bail out. You learn to recognize situations as either risks or opportunities and decide from there.

"Playing all the best Tour teams all those years taught us a lot about how to manage a game and the scoreboard and how good we had to play – consistently – if we wanted to win. And we won lots of events and beat all the best players in the world, so when we finally got to the Brier, we knew we had the game. And so we had the confidence to win.

"But when the rules changed to the 5-rock Free Guard Zone a few years back, old strategies went out the window – that one extra guard for the guy with hammer added a lot of complexity to the game. In order to win, we all had to adapt. In 5-rock, if the team with hammer wants rocks in play, it's pretty hard to keep it clean for a whole game. When it was 4-rock, things only got interesting if both teams wanted to mix it up; it was pretty easy to play defence if you made your peels and a few doubles. You didn't see a lot of deuces, let alone 3-enders, but now we see them both all the time. Up 2 coming home without hammer is not a comfortable place to be.

"Trying to play defence is tough now. Since you can't play peels until it's too late, you have to put your rocks in the right places. Some teams put three on the centre-line, some go top-four then choke the corners, but I don't think anyone really has it figured out yet – except that you have to make your all shots really well.

"So sure, execution is critical, but if you call a good game, you're going to create more good chances to make it count. So it's important to learn how to recognize and plan for certain situations and how to defend and how to create offence. A book like this should help curlers who want to learn that stuff get there faster."

How This Book Works

Aren't Tactics Just for Pros? In a word: no. Sure, those guys can throw all the shots almost all the time, but most of us who play can throw most of the shots some of the time. And so tactics have a place at virtually all levels. *'If you're trying to score, all rocks – even the other guy's – are your friends.'* Or *'Controlling that four-foot area and shrinking down that scoring area is a fundamental defensive principle.'* Or *'Staggered guards: use them or lose them.'* All these ideas apply to all levels of curling. If you aspire to improve your game, this guide is for you.

What's with the Puzzles and QR codes? With this guide, you can test your wits against the best curlers in the world. Read the situation, look at the rock placement, decide your call and then scan the QR code using your phone or tablet to see the actual shot the pros played. Once you've had a chance to jump up and down, shouting that Kevin Koe/Eve Muirhead/Bruce Mouat really have no idea what they're doing, Mickey and I discuss their thought process and try to distil out the key principles at play. *It's very helpful to watch the video first before reading about the tactics. It will make so much more sense!*

FYI, we've also pinned the web links to a post at the top of the Daily Curling Puzzle facebook page. If you prefer to click on a link instead of scanning QR codes, just go there.

(See www.facebook.com/groups/dailycurlingpuzzle)

We should point out that the games our QR codes point to are currently freely available on YouTube and are posted by the Canadian Curling Association (CCA) and the World Curling Federation (WCF). While these games are freely available at the time of writing, we're not able to guarantee that the CCA and WCF will keep them that way. We think they will – in many cases, they've been up for years – but we can't guarantee it. It's beyond our control.

The 'Solution'? In Curling? Really? We refer to solutions in our write-ups, but this is not to say that there is one right call for each situation. In fact, that's rarely the case, and club calls are often different because of ability or risk or whatever. In each 'solution', we try to identify good calls for club and aspiring curlers. Anyway, just be conscious that we are rarely saying there is one correct call.

Order, Order! We begin the book with a few pages to outline the essence of tactics. Next, we move on to ten puzzles we've selected to illustrate some of what I like to call 'USPs' – or Universal Skipping Principles. These are pretty core.

And then we present forty puzzles to see how those fundamentals play out. They kinda increase in complexity as they go, but all of them present challenges.

Rinse, Repeat You'll find that we repeat some concepts in many puzzles. Bear in mind that this is not a textbook in which we cover each concept once – it's a puzzle book in which some concepts apply to many of the situations. Rather than ignoring them in one situation simply because we spoke about them in another, we try to present the whole picture in each, even if we're sometimes repeating ourselves. Besides, you'll get better at spotting them in many various circumstances.

Why So Many Canucks? You'll notice that most puzzles come from Canadian games. This is not by choice, or from a belief that Canadians are inherently more exciting than other curlers. Rather, it's because the WCF limits which geographies can view which games (geo-blocking) while the CCA doesn't. Consequently, we use more CCA games so we can make this guide available to as many as possible.

Out with the Out-Turns You'll see that we've decided to use clockwise and counter-clockwise instead of inturns and out-turns. We'd like to say it's because we're hip, happening, modern guys, but mostly it's because we couldn't decide whether it's in-turn or inturn, out-turn or outturn. In any event, lefties need love too and we've gone with the up-to-date convention. You'll get used to it. Honestly, you will.

Red-Black, Yellow-Clear You'll notice our diagrams show the red rocks as black and the yellow rocks as clear. We know it's not ideal, but printing in black and white is a fraction of the cost of colour, and that helps us keep our price down. Because our aim is to make this book accessible to as many as possible, including Juniors just learning the game, we thought it was a compromise worth making. And besides, if you can't keep straight that red is black and yellow is clear, maybe a book about curling tactics isn't for you. ☺

Layout Finally, we have elected to show the puzzle and its 'solution' on facing pages for a couple of reasons. First, it's useful to be able to refer to the puzzle diagram when we're talking about, say, running R3 back or drawing around Y2. And second, by making use of space below the puzzle and avoiding wrapping over onto the following page, we keep our page count to a minimum and that too keeps the cost down. Anyway, we're sure that you enterprising curlers will figure out a way to avoid looking at the solution until you've come up with your call.

We hope you enjoy it!

A Brief Strategy & Tactics Primer

The goal of this book is simple: to help you win more curling games and enjoy our sport a bit more. We do this by presenting real-life situations, asking you to put yourself in the Skip's shoes and make your call, before then revealing what the pro curler played. And once we do that, we break down the situation, talk about several optional calls and discuss the underlying tactical principles at play. We hope that by focusing upon the principles, you'll be able to apply them to your game whatever your level.

Strategy vs Tactics We should probably first define what we call a strategy and what we call a tactic. In our book, a strategy is a broad approach to the game. If you are a drawing, tippy tappy team who feels comfortable with lots of rocks in play and confident you can out-position, outwit and outshoot the other guys, then your strategy might be to junk it up with hammer and to junk it up without, applying pressure and seeing how they respond. (Think Jennifer Jones and Kevin Koe.) If you're a team that likes to keep it simple and minimize risk, your strategy might be to be patient and keep things clean, pouncing on the odd miss from the other guys to score your points. (Think Brad Jacobs and Rachel Homan.) Anyway, both these styles are examples of strategies or approaches to the game, and both can be successful.

Tactics, on the other hand, are about meeting your objectives for this specific end. For instance, your objective might be to force the other guys to a single here in the 9th. The tactics employed are the shots and choices you make to achieve that specific goal. Strategies: the overall style of play you think will make you more successful. Tactics: the choices and shots you make this end to achieve your goal for this end. In this book, we talk almost exclusively about tactics.

Tactics and Technique It's been said many times that great shooting beats great strategy. However, if you're calling a lot of bad ends, you could be wasting all those well-made shots. In this book, we illustrate how certain calls in real-life situations create favourable (or unfavourable) conditions for winning. The multiple skills you need to execute consistently – balanced delivery, clean release, powerful sweeping, superb weight control, good ice-reading, weight-judging, communication, and so on – are not our focus here. We highly recommend you work on all the above skills, but we're hoping to share some thoughts about how you apply all those hard-earned skills to their best advantage to increase your odds of winning more games.

Phases of an End To win more games, we need to figure out how to *achieve our objectives* in as many ends as we can, both with and without hammer. (Notice we didn't say 'win as many ends as we can'. More on this later!) We think it's important to recognize that an end is played out in three phases, what we call the *Set-Up*, the *Decision Phase*, and the *Finale*. (We're borrowing *finale* from bike racing, the final phase of a race when the long-suffering teammates have finished drafting their leader along, fetching their water, defending other teams' attacks and generally putting them into a great position from which he or she sprints clear, wins the race and takes the glory. We think you'll see the similarities to a curling end.) Anyway, understanding your place in an end can help you call the most appropriate shots.

Phase 1 – The Setup The first few shots are typically ones that determine how the rest of the end develops. Here, we're trying to put our rocks in good positions on our first two or three or sometimes more 'set-up' stones and set up a structure that points towards us meeting our goals for the end. We try to execute our guards, come-arounds, and freezes properly and gain an advantage over our competition. Or, if we prefer a simpler style, we may choose to try to keep it clean, hitting if possible and waiting for an opportunity. In any event, the set-up phase is all about setting the table, trying to construct the shape and conditions that point us in the direction of our ideal or acceptable goals for that end.

Phase 2 – The Decision Phase This is when we assess how things are setting up for us. Are the angles good, protecting our rocks, or are they poor and leave our stones ready to fly out while the other team's remain? Are the guards covering our rocks, or are they helping them cover theirs? Is the shape of this end heading in the right direction? So, here in the decision phase, we decide if it's better to bail out or to keep building on our advantage with our next three or four stones as we try to accomplish our goals.

Phase 3 – The Finale On our last few rocks, we hope to cash in on a good end or find a way to survive a bad one. These are usually the Skip's shots and maybe one or two of the Third's, and they're meant to capitalize upon the work of the preceding shots and achieve your ideal result, or clean up the mess your team has created so you can at least get your acceptable result. (More on these types of results in a moment.)

If we're mindful of what we're trying to achieve in those phases and learn to feel that rhythm as the end plays out, we should be making better decisions, continuing to set-up when we need to score big, or bailing earlier when we need to be cautious or when things are going sideways. Knowing our objectives and understanding this timing will help.

Control of the Four-Foot There are some key principles that successful teams use to stay on track. It's stuff that's been taught in learn-to-curl camps forever, but it's worth repeating. The most basic concept of all is something an instructor described in a junior strategy session Mickey attended about 50 years ago. (We wish we were exaggerating, but that's the real number!) The instructor explained that the key to a winning strategy is to control the four-foot circle. That has never changed and it never will, as long as the rocks closest to the middle are the ones that score. Sounds simple, right?

In those days, "Control the Four-Foot" meant keeping the middle open when you had hammer and clogging it up when you didn't. To be honest, it's not much different today. And although the five-rock free guard zone makes achieving it much more interesting, the principle of making sure you have a way to score when you have hammer (and trying to make that hard for your opposition when you don't) is still the best way to win curling games.

Three Guiding Questions So how do you win an end? First, we have to define what winning an end means and it starts with The Three Guiding Questions – again, not a new concept, but many curlers have never been taught this or have forgotten it if they have. And what it means is that we need to define the following goals for every end we play:

1. Our Ideal Outcome
2. Our Acceptable Outcome
3. Our Unacceptable Outcome

It's important to know what our targets are before we set off. And it's equally important to keep them in mind as the end progresses, especially when things are going poorly and we are looking for a way to survive a bad situation and achieve at least our acceptable result. We can get lost in a confusion of options, but reminding ourselves of what is Ideal, Acceptable and Unacceptable often clears things up. We'll talk a lot more about this later. For now, just know that these three questions are perhaps the most important tool you'll have as a Skip.

Score 2 With Hammer, Force 1 Without Of course, a key principle in winning games is that things work out best if you score 2 (or 'a deuce') with hammer and keep them to 1 when they have last shot. 'Forcing' them to 1 when they have the hammer means you get it back with a minimum of damage to the score line and can then continue your onward march to victory with another deuce – or even more.

But How to Score? In simple terms, your task is to get a rock or two protected in the rings and remove theirs so that two or more of yours count after you throw your last shot. That means that on offence, we're generally keeping rocks in play. The basic strategy for offence is to get your stones into hard-to-remove places, then make them count with your last few shots and score 2 or more.

And the ways you make rocks hard to remove are (i) getting them underneath guards that you or the other team has thrown earlier, (ii) sitting them on top of other rocks and using them as backing, (iii) setting up catchers behind your rocks so they jam if the other team tries to remove them, and (iv) positioning your rocks far apart so there are no doubles for the other guy. All of these are good ways to keep your rocks safely in the rings until you can bring them into score with your last few shots.

The textbook play (there are others – we'll get to those) when you're trying to score a few is to get your corner guards established, get one or two buried underneath as the end develops, and bring those in to score later. But of course, while you're throwing corners, the other team is (usually) sticking them in the centre. So after you set up a corner or two, you'll have to address what's going on in the middle of the sheet and hope to eventually use your guards later.

One sub-plot is that you want to keep the centre of the rings open, not letting them wedge one in the four-foot to frustrate your scoring ambitions – and making sure you have a clear draw to the centre with your last if you need to take your single and avoid the steal. Again, control of that four-foot area is key.

Creating offence became a lot easier with the introduction of the various free guard zones. Sadly, these rules mean that keeping an open path to the four-foot is now that much harder.

One last point about playing offence: the key goal of controlling the four-foot doesn't necessarily mean having your rocks in there. Often, it's quite the opposite, with control meaning that you've kept the four-foot clear of all rocks. You'll often see big ends being scored when the offensive team's rocks are sprinkled around the edges of the house, and they then remove the defending team's rock(s) in the centre to add those sprinkled rocks onto the scoresheet. Open, airy rings are great for offence.

We need to keep in mind that throwing guards isn't generating offence. Throwing guards is setting up a *chance* to generate offence. If you execute well and clear up the centre, then you might get something under those guards and start to point towards a score of 2 or 3. But you need to execute.

How to Defend Now if you're playing offence, the other guys are playing defence and will be trying to 'force' you to 1 or even 'steal' 1 or more points themselves. In the old days, defence was about removing their rocks. But now, with the five-rock free guard zone, it's hard to keep a clean sheet if the team with hammer wants to junk it up, throw guards, and apply pressure. We can't simply focus on removing theirs since we can't do that until we're well into the end. We need to have an additional tactic.

And that tactic is to focus more on dominating the four-foot and 'shrinking that scoring area.' That is, it's hard for them to wedge a few of their rocks in to score when your closest stone is six-inches off the button and protected. You've successfully shrunken the target.

So under the new rules, you see defending teams throw a centre guard or even two, try to get behind them and make the other guys deal with them if they want to score. Of course, defenders will still be looking to remove any opposition rocks which have wandered into the rings and threaten to go on the score sheet. You can see that playing defence now is like walking a tightrope between killing opposition rocks and establishing a position in the four-foot – like rubbing your belly and patting your head at the same time. Tricky to do on ice.

Shapes & Three-Shot Sequences So how does the Skip plot their way through this maze? First off, recognize that a lot of what we have been discussing above has to do with 'shapes': crowded or open four-foot circles, centre guards that clog the middle, open and airy houses, and so on. So a Skip's first job is to try and create 'shapes' or conditions or structures that increase the odds of them achieving their objectives. (This is all kinda abstract here, but we'll discuss this in much more detail later.)

We create these shapes in a series of shot sequences, and we think that looking three shots ahead is a useful planning horizon. Because of the error factor in our game – people miss their shots – nobody can plot out how sixteen rocks will be played. Players miss, the end takes on a different look, and our plans become obsolete. So we think that seeing the game in a 'Rolling Three-Shot Window' is a useful way to look at things. I play this, they play that, and then we have this other thing. If this other thing isn't very appealing, let's look at going down a different path with our first.

Perhaps three shots might be four shots if you're playing at higher levels. But the point is that unless your team – and theirs – are making a very high percentage of their throws, any plans beyond that period probably become useless. Don't waste brainpower looking any deeper into the crystal ball. Set up your structures and conditions using three shots and you'll do fine.

Not (Yet) a Science One of the most interesting (and frustrating) things about making decisions in this crazy game is that there are usually several potential calls that could be made, and often two or three of them could be considered the 'right call'. We have tried to focus upon the factors underpinning the Skip's thinking, and sometimes don't declare a 'right call'. Getting to grips with the fundamental principles will serve you better on the ice than knowing which particular shot to play in a given situation.

This book is intended for curlers who have some skills and experience and want to improve how they approach a game. We doubt if Nik Edin, Kevin Koe or Eve Muirhead is referring to these puzzles for strategy pointers, but players who are aspiring to reach the next level and relish debating strategy will enjoy the discussions and probably pick up a few ideas they may choose to add to their arsenal.

That said, we have tried to discuss calls for both the competitive and the club player, recognizing they may have widely differing ways of solving the same problems. At the end of the day, our goal is always to stimulate conversation, offer suggestions and ideas, provide our rationale for why the curlers called what they did, and why we think it was a good or bad idea. It's up to you to decide if that helps you learn something or convinces you we're totally out to lunch. We're good either way.

*We can get lost in a confusion of options, but reminding
ourselves of what is Ideal, Acceptable and Unacceptable
often clears things up. These three questions are perhaps
the most important tool you'll have as a Skip.*

The Fundamentals:
Ten Puzzles to Illustrate
Key Concepts

Puzzle #1

Remember the good old days when we used to just bash things around, keep it clear, and score our single in 10 to take the game? Sadly Toto, we're not in Kansas anymore. This yellow team wants to mix it up, and with the five-rock free guard rule, they can! Still, you've got a useable rock at the top of the rings, and their yellows are nicely grouped for some of your thermonuclear runbacks. You could manufacture a decent end here. But how? Here's the situation:

- 4th end of 10
- You're red
- You're down by 1
- But you have hammer
- It's your Third's last
- Five-foot swing on good ice

C'mon Skip, give little Toto something to bark about. What's your call – and why?

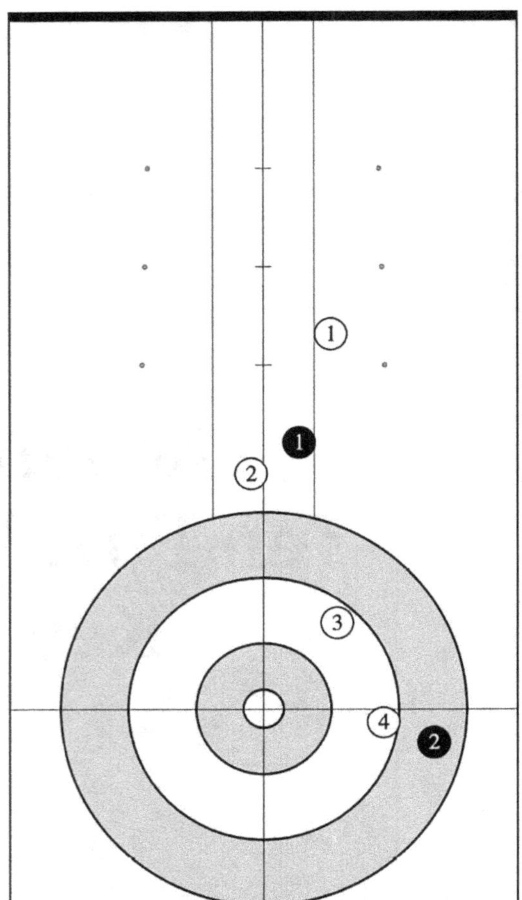

Three Questions to Rule Them All

The most useful tactical advice that Mickey has given me is to keep three core questions in mind: what's my ideal outcome to this end, what's an acceptable outcome, and what's the unacceptable outcome? "Know those when you start the end – and most importantly, keep them in mind as you play the end – and you won't go far wrong," he advises.

Mickey continues. "This is about recognizing that you want to win the game, not the end. Too often at lower-level curling I see teams going hell-bent-for-leather trying to score their deuce or trying to steal in every end, and they get into all sorts of messes when they really don't need to. A key to winning more games is to look at the scoreboard and realize that you don't have to get that ideal outcome all the time. As the end develops, you might see that that ideal result involves a risk of crashing into your unacceptable result – say giving up a steal – and therefore it might be more prudent to pivot towards your acceptable result – maybe a score of 1 or a blank.

"My point is that knowing what is ideal, acceptable and unacceptable helps you make choices throughout the end."

And so it is in this puzzle. Brad Gushue is wrestling with a decision to go for the ideal or take the unacceptable off the table. Down by 1 here in the fourth end, Gushue (red) would ideally like to score a deuce or more. But if that doesn't happen, he probably feels a blank would be just fine, and a force would be acceptable too. The unacceptable outcome? Giving up a steal to go 2-down to a team like Kevin Koe's would be bad. Very, very bad.

We find ourselves in what we call *Decision Time*, and Brad has a choice to make. Mickey explains.

"Given the way the end has developed, Brad must decide whether it's worth pushing for his ideal (a deuce) and risk his unacceptable (a steal), or whether it's more prudent to bail out, settle for his acceptable (a single), level the game and soldier on in the 5th. And that's what he decides to do here.

"The thing is that the calculus will change during the game. In an early end, he might be more willing to go for the deuce and risk the steal than he would later on in a tight game. Or, if he's a few down later on, he might have to go for it, regardless of the risks of giving up a potentially game-ending steal. And if he's leading, he's very likely not going to risk a steal and will be happy to take a single and keep a cushion between himself and Koe."

So what are the risks with going for a deuce, I ask?

"Well, to score, you need some rocks in play. The standard line when you're on offence is that early in an end, all stones – regardless of colour – are your friends, even though they may not be in quite the right spots yet. You can draw around behind them, freeze to them for backing, build pockets with them, all manner of stuff to make your rocks hard to remove and keep them in play.

"But the problem with offence is that their rocks are in play as well as yours. And if your team doesn't execute well, one or two of theirs might end up in hard-to-remove locations, and you might not be able to dig them out later. If you were playing defence the whole time, you would have been knocking theirs out and you wouldn't be at much risk. But of course, you wouldn't be able to develop a situation where you can create much offence either."

So if my goal is offence, then I want lots of rocks in play. But if I leave lots of rocks in play, I make opportunities for them to steal. Risky.

To me, it looks like Gushue has set out to play an aggressive end, but it hasn't quite come off.

"That's right," says Mickey. "He's been trying to generate some offence, but Koe's outplayed them. Kevin's got the strong yellow Y2 sitting on top of the rings, some junk down the right side just off centre (Y1 and R1) that could be used to hide rocks near the four-foot, and some side yellows (Y3 and Y4) that can be used to pick out anything that Brad manages to get into the scoring area. So it's not looking good for red right now."

Have we reached the infamous bail point where risks of unacceptable outcomes exceed the chances of ideal outcomes?

"We have. Sitting at 1-down in the 4th, Brad knows that scoring 1 is perfectly fine. He switches gears, decides to start working to clear a route to at least achieve his acceptable outcome (a single) and take his unacceptable outcome (a steal) off the table. You can hear him thinking aloud, discussing a draw around to top button but worrying that Koe could stick the runback and leave him with no chance to score. 'We gotta open up the scoring area a little bit,' he says, and all the commentators agree.

"He doesn't mind leaving some of that stuff off to the side because maybe it might help him manufacture a 'Skip's deuce' (where the Skip's two rocks end up being the ones that score.) And leaving those rocks to the side doesn't hurt his path to the four-foot, so he's happy enough to leave them there.

"And just before Mark Nichols throws, he talks about a creative option that might leave a setup for a possible deuce while still making sure he's clearing a path to the four-foot. In the end, he figures it might leave Koe an option to get under some staggers and maybe set up a steal so he goes back to a pure bail, cleaning stuff up and hoping for something magical to happen with his last two. If it doesn't, with an open front of the house, he's never giving up a steal."

And at my level, Mickey?

"At club and aspiring curler levels, the same principles apply. You need to know what's acceptable and unacceptable. In this situation, a steal is unacceptable and Y2 is the rock that's going to cause it. You need to get rid of it, or at least replace it with your colour and make them think twice about going around it. The deuce is looking unlikely here, so take your medicine, don't give up a steal and just accept a force."

In the end, there was no Skip's Deuce, but there was a nice, wide-open draw to the four-foot for the Skip's Single – which is just fine for Brad Gushue.

What are the fundamental skipping principles I can apply to my game? First, know my ideal, acceptable and unacceptable outcomes before the end starts.

Secondly, keep those objectives in mind as the end progresses. They are my guiding lights as I make decisions through the end.

And finally, take the temperature after my front-end's rocks and decide how likely I am to get my ideal outcome versus the risk of getting bounced into my unacceptable one. Think about bailing out and shooting for my acceptable.

Mickey's Last Word? "Let your answers to these three questions help you navigate your choices throughout the end. Brad saw that going for his ideal meant opening the door to his unacceptable. He decided that he had to at least set up his acceptable, and then hope for a little magic with his last two rocks."

Puzzle #2

Oh baby, baby. This is really nice! Who would have thought you'd get an opportunity like this so early? And against these guys too, making their way out of one of the most challenging provinces and now gunning for their first Brier title. You've got one fully buried on the button, and their Second just gave you a gift, throwing heavy and bouncing off to give you a chance to hit and lie 2. Should you take it? Here's the situation:

- 1st end of 10
- Score is tied
- You're yellow
- And you have hammer
- It's your Second's first shot
- Five feet of swing on good ice

C'mon Skip, don't look a gift horse in the mouth. What's your call – and why?

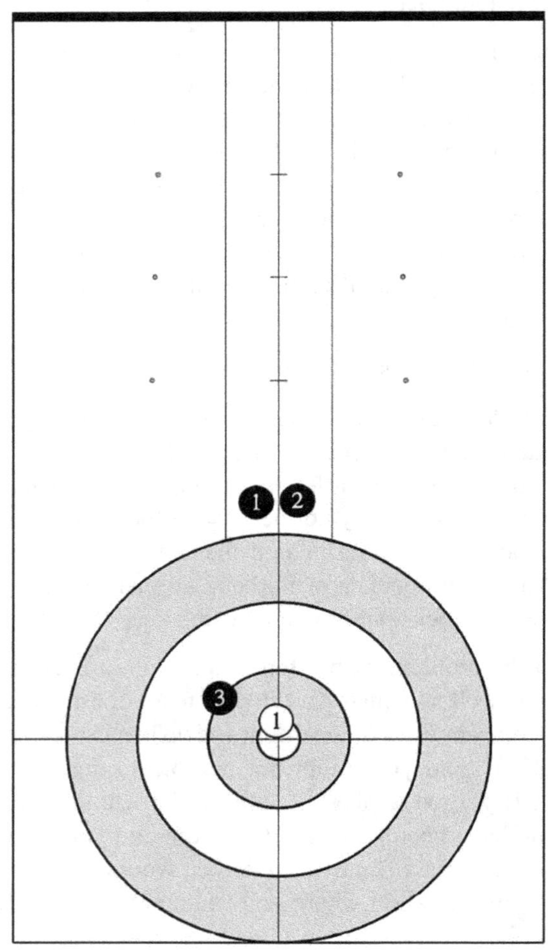

Shapes & Power Rocks & Timing

I look at this situation and I'm one-hundred percent gunning for Brad Jacobs to bump back that R3, lie 2 yellows and take a stranglehold on this game right here in the first end. End of puzzle, let's move on. Right?

"Wrong," says Mickey. "This is a great example of a Skip who knows exactly what he's doing. He understands the timing or phases of the end, knows his goals and most importantly, knows the shape of an end that increases the odds of achieving those goals. This end illustrates three fundamental principles: timing, shapes or structures that increase your probability of reaching your goals for the end, and rocks in the 'Control Zone'.

Phases? Shapes? Structures? Control Zone? What's the old guy on about?

"Let's deal with timing first," Mickey continues, ignoring my befuddlement. "It's early in the end. There are ten rocks to be played after this next shot, so we're just setting up. If you played your hit-and-roll to lie 2 now, what do you think the odds are of those rocks being there after ten more shots? Zero? Certainly at this level, it's zero. At the club level, that shot might be an irresistible choice to play now. Lie shot – lie two shots if you can – let the other guys try to clean it up, maybe get a miss and hopefully score another with your hammer. That's not a bad strategy at a recreational level.

"But depending on your standard of curling, angling for shot rock so early in the end is relatively unimportant. Timing matters. At this phase of the end, there are more important factors, as Brad Jacobs illustrates with his call."

I'm thinking that one of those important factors is the shape of the end. Am I in the right ballpark?

"Yes, for sure," replies Mickey. "People think curling is a precise game where Skips map out all their shots from any given point until the completion of the end. But there are eleven rocks still to be played. There is no way any Skip – Olympic gold medalist or otherwise – can plot out each of the next eleven shots. There's just too much variability and error, even in the pro game. With a half-miss here and a half-miss there, Jacobs' plan would be completely irrelevant after just four or five shots. So we can't play tic-tac-toe and plot each shot so early in an end.

"So what we do is try to set up situations that increase the likelihood of success, and I call those situations 'shapes' or 'structures'. You can call them rock positions or whatever you like, but the point is that some rock scenarios increase the likelihood of you achieving your ideal or acceptable outcomes, and some reduce the likelihood of you achieving those results and increase the chance of you achieving your unacceptable outcome."

Okay, I'm getting this. Early in the end we try to set up favourable situations, just like Brad has done here, right? Jacobs has hammer, so his aim is a deuce or a blank. A force would be a minor failure – but it's much better than giving up a steal. With one lying on the button and an easy bump-and-roll to lie 2 behind guards, that's a pretty nice shape in my book!

Mickey disagrees. "The type of end that often leads to a score of 2 or more is open and expansive with rocks scattered around the rings. You would perhaps have a couple of counters off to the sides under corner guards and lots of what I call 'breathing room' down the centre of the sheet to get at your opponent's rocks or create something with your Skip's stones. And if things don't quite go to plan, the four-foot would ideally be uncongested, and you'd have space to draw for a single and make sure you don't give up a steal. That's a great scenario when you're playing with hammer, and that's why we throw corner guards early in the end. We try to get rocks out around the edges and create breathing space. That's the shape we want to play this end."

Is that the shape Jacobs would get if he played the hit-and-roll on R3 and tried to get something going in the four-foot behind two tight enemy rocks, I ask, pretty much already knowing the answer?

"No. That would concentrate play in the middle, and Brad doesn't want that. Concentrations in the four-foot often lead to tippy-tappy, congested ends where you really need to outplay the other team to get two rocks inside theirs and score your deuce. Most often, someone scores 1 – and it might even be your opposition. So Brad doesn't want congestion that risks a steal. He'd rather open it up so he can score a 2, or blank it, or take a single if that's what it comes down to."

The video shows Jacobs' solution to his problems, a lovely little double and spin-up for a useful corner guard. The end was changed to a shape that favoured him reaching his goals – play moving out to the corners and creating breathing room down the centre.

"It also accomplishes a couple of other things with regards to shape or structure," continues Mickey. "R1 and R2 are hovering over that four-foot area and threaten Jacobs' chances of scoring a multiple – or even of scoring. We can call the area immediately above the four-foot the 'Control Zone', and rocks in this area can dictate play in the four-foot and determine who scores and who doesn't. Those rocks are certainly in it."

Personally, I'm not so crazy about 'rocks in the Control Zone'. Blah. We need some imagination in this game, something a bit snazzier. I'm going with 'Power Rocks'. Any rock hovering over that four-foot are hereby christened Power Rocks.

"Well, whatever," continues Mickey, slightly puzzled himself. "You are right that rocks that threaten that four-foot area have a lot of power. If Brad was to leave them there, they can be moved back by the Gunner at any time to cut the scoring area or eliminate any yellows that might look like scoring. Even at the club level, the risk lies in ignoring those two tight enemy rocks near the centre. So those – and I can't quite believe I'm saying this – Power Rocks sitting up there in that shape reduce Jacobs' likelihood of meeting his ideal or acceptable goals. He wants to change that shape if he can and does that with EJ Harnden's shot."

You said Jacobs' shot accomplishes a couple of other things. What else did Jacobs manage?

"Well that R3 is sitting on the edge of the four-foot and if it stays there, Jacobs would be facing a shape where he needs to get two stones inside it to score his deuce. Getting two in the four-foot is harder than getting two in the eight-foot, so he'd like to change that shape too, and set it up so he has more room to score. Harnden's hit-and-roll knocked it out in a drive-by sort of way, and the entire shape of the end was altered to increase the likelihood of Jacobs scoring at least 1 (acceptable) and maybe 2 (ideal). And by eliminating it, he keeps the blank alive, as well."

I'm thinking that my Second isn't (yet) at the standard of EJ Harnden. Is this a shot I should be calling at my 'Improvers' level?

"Northern Ontario plays a superb shot here and accomplishes a few things at once. But even if your team won't make the perfect double and roll to a corner, clearing up the middle or nosing one of those centre reds is more likely to allow you to create a favourable outcome and avoid the steal. If you're trying to score or blank, get rid of dangers in the middle and move play out to the wings. That will make life a lot easier for you."

As a Newbie Skip, what are the Universal Skipping Principles (USPs) I can take away from this puzzle? First, think about my ideal, acceptable and unacceptable outcomes, then consider what shape of an end encourages those results. Play for that shape as the end develops.

Secondly, timing matters. It's early in the end here. If I'm playing at a competitive level, lying shot now doesn't matter because it won't be there for long. Take time early to create the shape I want, and don't worry so much about shot rock so early in the end.

And finally, recognize that rocks hovering over the four-foot area have much power. Use them if they're mine. Lose them if they're not.

Mickey's Last Word: "Remember the three questions and identify what type of structure is likely or unlikely to result in your ideal or acceptable outcomes. Use the early phases of the end to create those conditions."

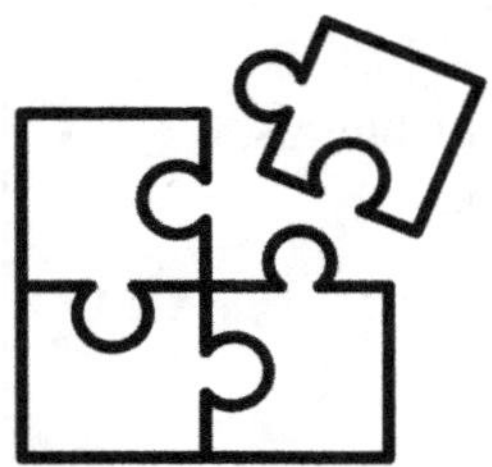

Think about your ideal, acceptable, and unacceptable outcomes, then consider what shape of an end encourages those results. Play for that shape as the end develops..

Puzzle #3

You've played this game to perfection, managing to steal in the 6th then keeping the hammer in the even ends all the way to the 10th. And this is your big reward: a wide-open house, very little shrapnel in the way and just two more rocks to go. Toss a couple down there, almost anywhere, and you've got the win. So easy – just like shootin' fish in a barrel. Or is it? Here's the situation:

- 10th end of 10
- You're yellow
- You're up by 1
- And you have hammer
- It's your Skip's first shot
- Five-foot swing on ice that's holding up well

C'mon Skip, give us a shot that lands a big one we'll be talking about for years. What's your call – and why?

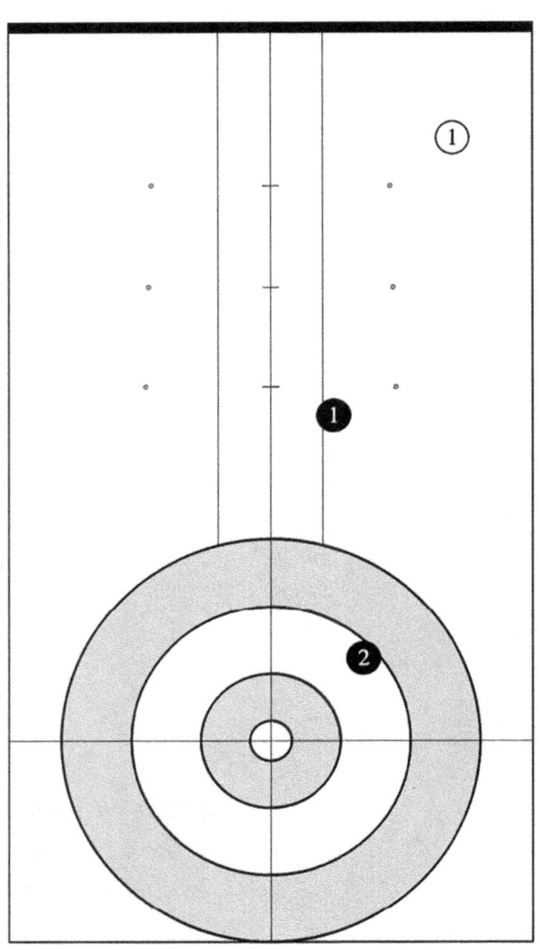

Twin Track Thinking & The Rolling Three Shot Window

"Many young Skips think curling is a game in which every move of the end is plotted out in advance," says Mickey. "But it isn't like that. In curling, anywhere from five to forty percent of the shots miss, and that error rate makes it impossible to plan more than a few shots ahead."

So true. I've often heard curling called 'chess on ice'. But in chess, pretty much every move lands on the square they're aiming at. At my level of curling, we are a long way away from that standard. For us, curling is like chess on ice but with the board 125 feet away, the rook or the knight or whatever rotating slowly as it travels over ridges and gullies, and two other blokes sweeping like demons oblivious to what I'm actually intending! Chess starts to look easy, to be honest.

Because of the error rate, I'm thinking I need to have a much shorter planning horizon than Garry Kasparov. Maybe view this game as a series of rolling three-shot windows. I throw A, he'll throw B, then I can throw C. If I don't like where that leads, maybe I think about a different option for A.

"Well, Skips have to think at several levels," Mickey replies, somewhat unhelpfully. "Before the end, we decide on our ideal, acceptable and unacceptable outcomes, and the type of end that we want to play – lots of well-positioned rocks in play for offence, a congested mess in the middle for forcing or stealing, or whatever type works towards our objective for this end.

"Then as the end kicks off, we're 'setting up', trying to create structures or conditions where we have an advantage – say corner guards or centre guards or good angles or catchers behind tee or whatever. We're setting up good conditions, but we're doing those in a rolling three or four-shot window. There's no way I can plot out the sequence between me throwing a corner guard and having a double for 2 with my last. But if they're trailing by a few with hammer and I call a rock in the house or a centre guard, I can predict that they're likely to throw something out to the corner. Then I can play to the centre and start building my preferred structure – congestion in the middle, ideally behind my guard. So I can try to see three or four shots ahead and try to build a better situation.

"In the middle of the end, we've done the set-up and now we're making decisions based on how things have gone – and trying to further create a shape or set up conditions that favour us meeting our ideal or acceptable goals. Bailing out and clearing the front of the house to make sure we can draw for 1 is an example of this. But we're doing all of this within three-shot windows."

Okay, but what does that have to do with this puzzle, I ask.

"Well, with three rocks to play, the abstract 'creating shapes and structures that are to our advantage' stuff is history. McEwen's into the short strokes and he's now thinking, 'If I play A, he plays B, which leaves me with C. But if I play a different A, he'll play a different B and that leaves me a new C.' So he's got to be very precise here and think through the combinations."

They look at splitting out the R2 shot rock. "You gotta think three shots ahead," says Mickey. "By hitting that, you're letting him put one back – only better. Dunstone will draw around to the edge of the four-foot fully buried, and now you have to pretty much draw the button to score. Looking ahead, you're actually making your last shot harder if you take out their rock in the rings now."

Well then how about the peel? "That's the shot they play, and it works out well. By peeling the guard, the best that Dunstone will be able to do is draw around his own rock and leave Mike a draw to a five- or six-foot target. For these guys, that's almost automatic.

"But at lower levels, peeling the guard at 1-up and letting the other team put two in the rings means you would be 'shooting against the game' with your last – a loss if you come up light or get heavy. Or you might opt to play a chicken shot if they're lying 2 – hitting one of theirs to at least tie the game and go to an extra end. Missing the draw would make for uncomfortable discussion in the bar later. Playing the chicken shot would be worse."

So if the peel could lead to the nightmare chicken shot, is it the best for us at club level?

"Being labelled a chicken is a bit of a problem. A bigger problem is that peeling guards at club level is not automatic. You might stuff it, leave a good centre guard and now the steal's really in play.

"There are other options though. First, you could play 'watch the birdie' and draw to lie shot in the four-foot on the open side. Because you're shot, he has to hit you. If he rolls out, you can chip his shot rock or draw the eight-foot to win.

"The risk here is that you are playing in the draw path that you've set up. What if you stop top-twelve and they plug the centre or nose hit you? Drawing the button suddenly gets complicated.

"But if you make the draw to the open side and he hits and doesn't roll buried, you might have an easy nose hit to score 1. If you roll out, at least you're going to an extra end with hammer."

That's a nice one. Sort of like a chicken shot – but not so obvious! But what about 'getting there first,' I ask? How about drawing around R1 and biting the four-foot to lie shot now?

"That would leave them a difficult freeze where they have to lie shot and maybe that's one-in-ten at club level. But you need to make sure you don't tick off the guard and roll to the centre, or slip behind tee and let him freeze for shot. Those would make your last shot harder.

"But at the club, I think it's OK," Mickey reassures me, "because if you make your shot, they might not make their next one perfectly and leave you something simple – or maybe you won't even have to throw. But at any competitive level, drawing the four-foot is Number One on a Skip's job description. You have to be prepared to play it, and the best actually love throwing it."

My takeaways that I can use in my game? I need to think along two tracks. The first is about the shapes and structures and the 'good conditions' I'm trying to set up to achieve my goals for the end.

And the second track is about the next three shots that lead to those good conditions and eventually the final result. I need to do this throughout the end, thinking about three shots to set up a favourable structure, then rolling it forward as the end progresses to probe or bail, then finally rolling it forward to cash in or cash out with my Skip's shots.

Mickey's Last Word: "Embrace being the Skip. Get draw weight and put it in your pocket. And then relish the opportunity to make that play. If that's not for you, think about playing another position. It takes several types of characters to make a good team."

Puzzle #4

Oh boy. So many options. Freeze to his shot rock, go around both centres, go around your corner, throw another corner on the same side, throw another corner on the other side? You're like a kid in a candy store! How do you keep track of all the ideas whizzing around your head? Somehow, you need to put all that aside and come up with one great shot. But which one? Here's the situation:

- 4th end of 10
- You're yellow
- You're down by 1
- You have hammer
- It's your Lead's second shot
- Five-foot swing on good ice

C'mon Skip, give 'em a shot that hits the sweet spot. What's your call – and why?

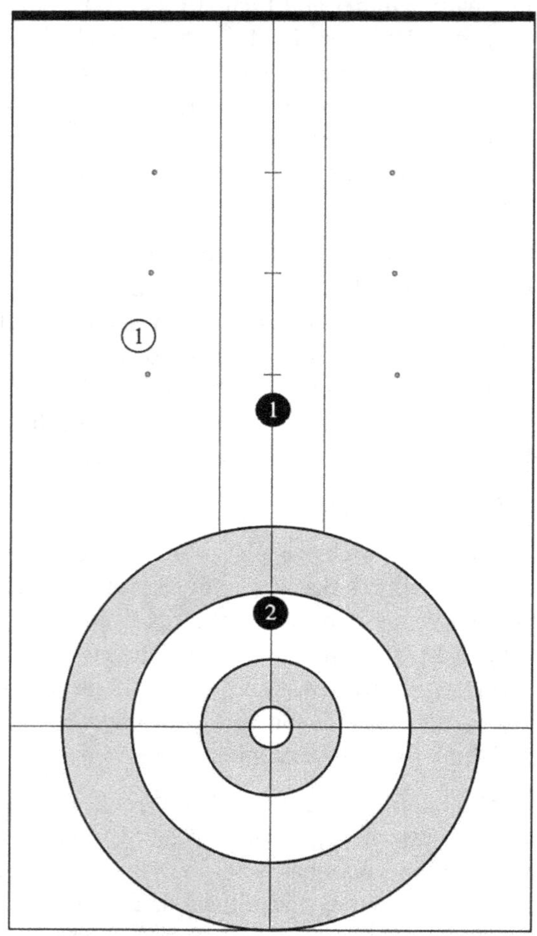

The Hierarchy of Offence

We're using this puzzle to discuss several offensive options and which of those is most appropriate given differing game situations.

Let's back up a bit from our puzzle shot and discuss Bruce Mouat's options with his Lead's two rocks just after Sweden throws their centre guard, R1. By my reckoning, he's got at least four different ways to create offence, each option with different risk/reward profiles. I've asked Mickey to outline them for us.

"When we talk about generating offence, what we really mean is creating opportunities. If we can make some shots and set a path in the set-up stage (the first two or three rocks) and keep that going through the decision stage (the next three or four rocks) where we go for it or bail out, then our Skip can step up, apply the finishing touches and close it out to reach the objective that we are going for. But early in the end, what we're trying to

do is set up a structure that *might* lead to offence as the end plays out."

Okay. I think I get that. We're just planting seeds here in the set-up portion of the end. And in my never-ending quest to make this game simple, I'm giving each set-up play a name, just like they do in chess. I have a very good memory but it's quite short, and tagging these plays is going to help me remember them. Mickey, what's the least risk but least reward play Bruce could have made?

"The least risk-reward option – the one Bruce could have played on his Lead's first shot – is to come around their centre guard, bury one top-four or in the eight-foot, and set up a nice big scoring area above the tee. They'll follow you, you'll follow them and you end up with rocks clustered in the middle and angles and taps and pockets.

"The way you score in this type of end is by gaining a superior position before someone blows it all up. When someone runs that centre guard back in or it gets moved off and there's a strike thrown into the bunch, you hope your rocks are protected through better angles with more backing, and a couple of yours will stay. As the end plays out, hopefully you can keep them far enough apart so they can't be doubled out and you can score your deuce.

"But looping around their centre guard with your first is a pretty cautious, low-risk type of end. You don't get much shrapnel built up out front, so you're usually going to have relatively good access to the four-foot. And because the rocks are grouped in the middle, you can likely clean up the centre with one or two hits. You can often blank the end or get forced to take 1, but you're not likely to give up a steal. And the stats show that avoiding giving up steals is critical, something the top teams all know but might be under-appreciated by the rest of us.

"But if the come-around on Lead's first is low-risk, it's also low-reward. There aren't many rocks out in front to cause them problems and so to get your deuce, you need to win the battle of the angles in the centre or get a miss or a bad call on their part. And unless that happens, it's rare to score 2 or more."

OK, I'm going to call coming around on Lead's first 'The Chicken Little Offence.' There's a little offence going on – but it's mostly chicken. What's next on the list?

"The second response to their opening centre guard is to throw up a corner. If you do that, they'll usually go around their centre, and now you freeze to that shot rock. Let's call it the Corner-N-Freeze. This is what you see Bruce Mouat do in our puzzle.

"Bruce isn't in real all-out chasing mode being 1-down with hammer in the middle of the game. What he's doing is creating a chance for some offence without going all-in for it. By throwing the corner and then the freeze, their next shot will be to freeze back on us to try to win the battle of the angles and control the centre. We might get a chance somewhere along the line to spring one over towards that corner and use it to score 2, or to clear up the middle entirely and use the corner guard later in the end. The other good thing that can happen when you're coming around is you rub their centre guard and roll across under your corner. And if things aren't going our way at any point, we've only let the other team throw up one guard, so hopefully, we can bail, clean up and score a single.

"But a key point of this puzzle is where to throw your freeze, and I agree with Bruce's approach. You want to freeze to their rock on the side of your corner guard so that play is taken in that direction, not the other open side. If you watch this end play out, Scotland's freeze comes up a little light and Sweden's is a bit heavy, and then Mouat gets a chance to tap-and-roll towards his corner. If they had frozen to the other side, their tap-and-roll would have been the mirror image and towards the open side, not the guarded one. So you want to get this right so you can take advantage of the guard you threw and get the best chance for offence."

I like that Corner-N-Freeze option. Mildly probing for mildly offensive situations. And at my level, it's a cagey play that sets me up to capitalize on a miss by the other guys. I like it. What's next?

"The next option is to throw the corner then go around it. This is a higher risk because you're giving them a head start in the centre while you throw and immediately use your corner. They could have three rocks down the middle after you've gone around your guard and come to throw your third shot. You're going to have to deal with those.

"But it could also generate a reward because you've now got one in the bank under the corner, and you're going to have more rocks in play and a more complicated end. The other team could throw three down the middle, or they might do something else like chase you and freeze or tap or something. So it's gonna get messy and it might work out for you if you execute – but it might not. But going behind your own corner on Lead's second rock is the more aggressive, messier 'We're definitely going to stick one in the bank now and go for it' type of shot."

Mickey suggests caution in using this at club or aspiring levels. "At lower levels, this is a higher risk play because if they throw another good centre guard, you have to start peeling and might never get a chance to count the one you buried. I'd only play it if my Second can throw big weight and clean up accurately."

I like this. My Second's pretty good and my guys can sweep for technical shots coming down the stretch. And who doesn't like messy! Anyway, let's call this one the 'One in the Bank' play. We use Lead's second to go around the corner and put one in the bank. Hopefully we can bring it in to score later.

And what's the final X-rated, definitely-just-for-adults call, Mickey?

"Well, this final one's for the truly desperate or the truly reckless. It's used when you're down by 3 or more especially late in the game and need to make up some ground fast. The conventional idea here is to use the five-rock free guard rule to put up two guards, then go around with your next shots. When the five-rock rule expires, you've got a few in the paint and hope to score a bundle."

That sounds perfect. Let's name this 'The Perfect Offence.' Is there a catch?

"The problem is that your opponents have thrown their first into the four-foot and, while you've been throwing your two corners, they've very likely put another in the rings, maybe frozen to their first, and a guard out front. Or perhaps they've thrown one top-button and then one to choke off your corners. (We'll cover choking corners later.)

"The point is that under five-rock, teams can't play defence by peeling every corner so they now put them in good positions down the middle or in the rings and make you come to them. Your opposition just keeps clogging the centre, protecting their shot rock and getting in the way of your draw paths behind the corners. If you're lucky and their rocks are pretty close together or slightly offline, you might get a chance to clear multiple stones with one peel or chip-and-roll the tight guard or even chip their shot rock.

"The risk is that under five-rock, if they see a chance to protect their shot rock, they might forget about your corners and just go all out for the steal. If you clear quickly or chip-and-roll-under, you might score a few. But if you don't execute, you might just lose the game right here. It gets really complicated really quickly."

Okay, not so perfect then. Let's call this the "Go Big or Go Home Offence." You might score a few. Or you might end up shaking and, well, going home.

But when to play which option, I wonder?

"And that's the key," replies Mickey. "You have to know when to play these options. You're not going to see Bruce throw double guards when he's down by just 1 in a tight game. And you won't see him loop around their centre when he's down by 3 late in the game. Different options carry different risks and different rewards. Think about when to play them."

Mickey makes one final and important point. "These options assumed we are in a fairly close game or trailing. But if we find ourselves up two or more with hammer, especially later in the game, we could just draw open side in the rings with Lead's first, knowing they're throwing guards. We may even do it again on our Lead's second to ensure less congestion out front. We would have some clean-up to do after they throw their centre guards, but at least we're not providing any building blocks by sticking rocks out front or in the centre of the rings."

Now I get it. Four or five good set-up options, but each having a different risk and reward profile and therefore moment to be played.

My general takeaway? Memorize the hierarchy of offensive options: the Chicken Little, the Corner-N-Freeze, the One-in-the-Bank, the Double Corner, and the Open Side Draw. Know them and decide when to play each.

Mickey's Last Word: "There are several recurring setups in five-rock, based on the scoreboard. Understand how the first few rocks dictate the balance of the end and have a plan that fits your team's skills and what your goals are for the end."

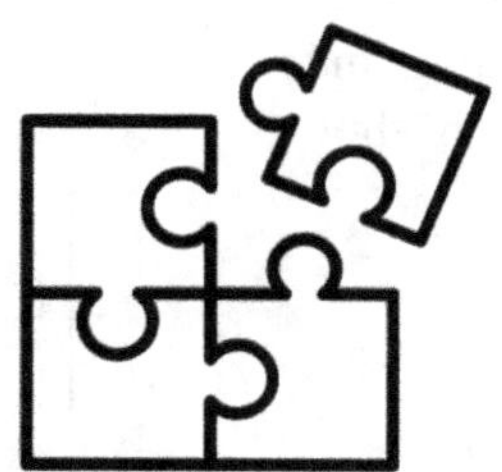

Memorize the hierarchy of offensive options:
the Chicken Little, the Corner-N- Freeze, the
One-in-the-Bank, the Double Corner, and the Open
Side Draw. Know them and decide when to play each..

Puzzle #5

Don't you love it when the commentators and the Coach are in complete disagreement! The broadcaster thinks you might be lucky to score but your Coach thinks you could lock up the game right here, right now. You don't know who to believe! Sure, the lady on the TV has an Olympic Gold around her neck, but your Coach has three world championships, three Briers, and eleven grand slams. Anyway, it's time you decide your own shot. Here's the situation:

- 8th end of 10
- You're yellow
- You're down by 1
- You have hammer
- It's your Third's first shot
- About four-feet of swing

C'mon Skip, give 'em a shot that shows you can think for yourself. What's your call – and why?

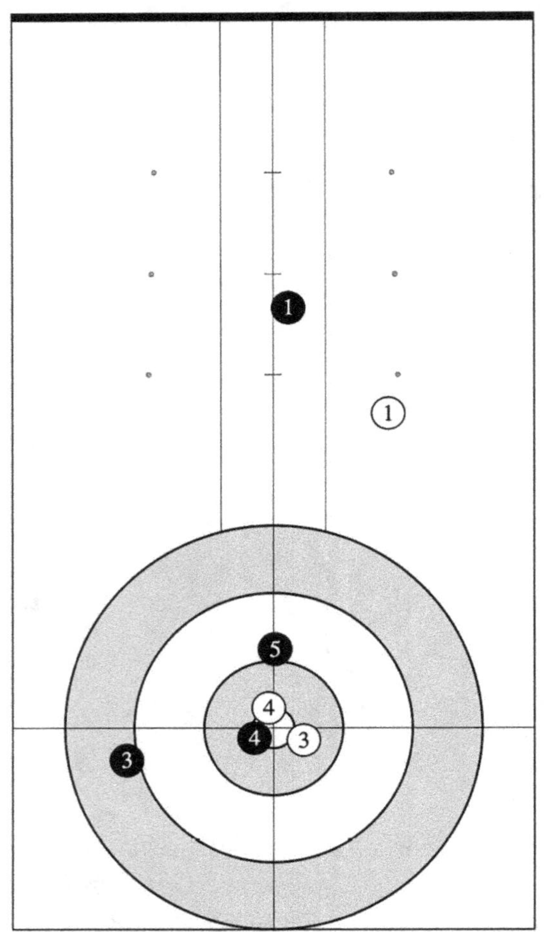

Death Rocks & Security

"They're in huge trouble here. They've got nothing. At any time, if the guard is gone and they just keep guarding, then you can pick the back one for two." – Wayne Middaugh, Team Sweden coach

"According to Wayne Middaugh, Scotland should be in huge trouble." – Sander Rolvag

"I don't think they are, to be honest. Scotland could quite easily force the 1 at this end." – Rhona Howie (2002 Olympic gold medal-winning Skip and General Legend), just a couple of shots before Scotland gave up a gulp-inducing 4.

Well, it's an amusing quote but Rhona wouldn't have thought that Scotland would miss their next three shots and open the door to a Swedish 4. I guess when you miss your last three shots against a world-class side, bad things happen.

Anyway, we're doing a bit of sleight-of-hand here and are using this puzzle to discuss a few shot calls, rather than just one. We've bookmarked the video early to show the lead-up and highlight a few missteps that led to Scotland being in 'huge trouble'. Then we'll get to Wayne Middaugh's call for the puzzle shot. First off, how did we get here?

"The key turning point is Scotland's fourth shot, when they tried to sit on top of Y3 with their R4, got heavy and rolled beside it. And we're highlighting one of our universal principles of front-end play at the club or pro level: you can't throw what we're going to call 'Death Rocks'. Can't be heavy on a freeze. Better to be light than heavy. That shot, just a foot heavy, set up a pocket and allowed Sweden's Y4 to get into a protected position where Scotland couldn't get them out in one shot.

"Keep in mind that if you're trying to score multiples with hammer, the whole objective is to get rocks into positions so they can't be removed, and then capitalize with your last couple of shots. You can get behind guards or you can freeze pockets or get backing, but the general aim as you're building the end is to get rocks into positions where your opponents can't remove them. Scotland's heavy R4 Death Rock lets Sweden do that."

After Sweden plays their immaculate Y4, it continues to go sideways for Scotland with their next. Eve takes a long look at whether Y4 or R4 are shot rock, then calls a freeze with R5. When it comes up a hair short and left R4 probably lying shot, Eve calls out that that's okay. As a somewhat curling-literate quasi-Newbie, I'm agreeing that this is a good position, lying shot with one hovering over the four-foot, ready to be used. Mickey thinks Eve and I are looking at the wrong issue.

"With half-an-end to play, the important question is not who's lying shot – none of those rocks will be in those positions when the end is over. The important question is 'Who's secure and who's insecure?' Right now, the team with hammer has Y4 wedged in there, the meat in the sandwich that's not going anywhere without a couple of plays on it. R5 and R4 are the two slices of bread which will always go with one shot. So the fact that R4 might be shot rock is unimportant with half-an-end to play. The fact that it's securing Y4 is very important.

"Eve needed to make Y4 insecure. Imagine if she calls for a nose tap on it with back-eight weight. Sure, yellow would now be sitting two. But Eve's R5 would be frozen on top and secure with several shots to go, while Y4 would be dangling there, ready to go out the back if it were ever hit. And Y3 is always available through the port if we need to cut them down."

Okay, so maybe R5 isn't as good as Eve and I thought it was. But did it leave them in as much trouble as Wayne thinks, or were they in good shape to score 1 as Rhona believes? Mickey comes down on Wayne's side.

"The situation at this timeout completely favours Sweden. As we look at the puzzle, any hit gets both of Scotland's reds going and one yellow stays. So if you ask who is in the more precarious situation here, it's Scotland, for sure.

"Wayne comes along and sees that his team has established that secure position and if they now open it up by peeling the guard, they'll have two ways to get their deuce. If Scotland put the guard back on over and over again, Anna could eventually use her hammer to pick out the back R4 and score 2. And if Scotland forgets about the guard and picks out Y3 instead – which they tried to do – then Anna could run back R5, keep the Y4 meat in the sandwich, and keep her shooter somewhere to lie 2 with hammer. Scotland would be chasing her around the rings trying to get a double."

What can I take away from this puzzle that I can apply at my 'improvers' level? First, my freezes need to be a little light, not heavy. Leads and seconds need to err on the short side and avoid 'Death Rocks'. Throw 'em light and let the sweepers drag 'em into position.

Secondly, I need to think about secure and insecure. When they're secure with hammer, that's a bad thing and could easily lead to a score of multiple points. With half-an-end to play, I still have time to do something about that. Getting rid of backing – regardless of whose rock it is – would put them in a more precarious position.

And finally, as Sweden here, I need to recognize when I achieve a good set-up and have my rocks in more secure positions than theirs. Then I need to have the courage to open things up and capitalize upon my good front-end play.

Mickey's Last Word: "This puzzle is really all about establishing a strong position where one or two of your rocks are secure and theirs are precarious, and then recognizing what that position could lead to. Wayne saw that they were secure and that Scotland was insecure, and that by opening things up now, Sweden would always have two ways to score their deuce."

Puzzle #6

Oh no. These guys are part of the golden generation of curlers from their country and seem to know their stuff. They've managed to clog up that four-foot and are making it hard for you to score. Fortunately, you're lying shot and you have hammer. Maybe, just maybe you can eke out a deuce. But how? Here's the situation:

- Second end of ten
- Score is tied
- You're yellow
- You have hammer
- It's your Second's second shot
- About four feet of swing on good ice

C'mon Skip, give 'em a shot that sends the Golden Boys back to the bronze age. What's your call – and why?

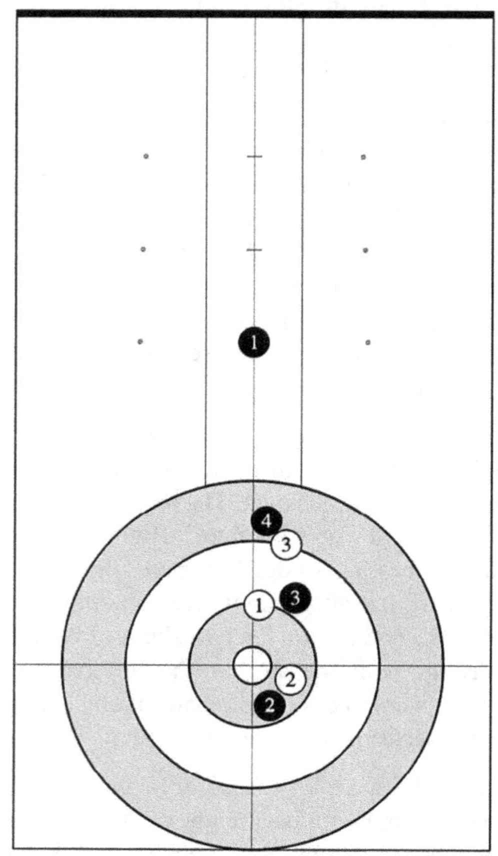

The Battle of the Angles

As a Newbie skip, I am befuddled by this 'battle of the angles' idea. What is it? Where is it played? When is it won? Fortunately, Mickey is here to explain.

"Simply put, the battle of the angles is about whose rocks sit in vulnerable positions and whose rocks are more secure," he says. "Here, we see Canada's front-end put their yellow rocks into positions where they are hard to remove while the Americans' red stones end up being easily knocked out. So, Canada wins the battle in this end."

We're starting the video early to watch how this end develops. The first thing we see is that instead of freezing on top of Canada's Y1 rock at top-four, the American Lead gets heavy and throws a Death Rock (R2) which slips behind tee.

"By doing that, he immediately hands Canada the advantage," says Mickey. "Karrick Martin freezes to it with Y2 and now Canada has a rock with some backing while the Americans' R2 is low man on the ladder. When the granite starts to fly, Y2 might go depending on the angle of attack – but R2 is definitely going no matter what."

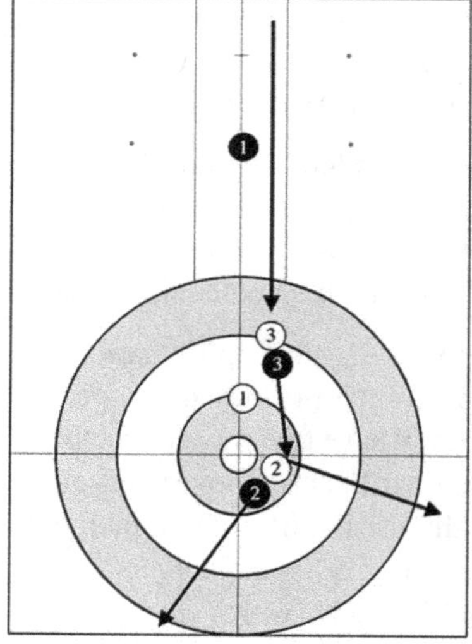

The American Second, Matt Hamilton, makes the same mistake on his first, R3. Trying to freeze to Y1, he gets a hair heavy, throws a Death Rock, bounces off and hangs out in the open. Brad Thiessen takes advantage and freezes Y3 to the inside of it (see above). Using Mickey's test – whose rocks are vulnerable and whose rocks are more secure when the Skips start calling for the hits – we see that Canada has a big advantage after only a few stones. Both reds would go. Two or three yellows would stay.

Mickey pauses to make an important point. "We see right here why front-ends can be light, but not heavy. Landsteiner slips deep and the Martin freezes into a more secure spot. Hamilton throws a hair heavy, bounces and rolls exposed. Had his rock stopped say a foot or two short and edge buried, can Canada get across nose to an angle that makes the red vulnerable? Probably not. The only way to miss if you're a front-end player is light, not heavy. Don't throw Death Rocks. Throw 'em light and let the sweepers do their job."

With his second rock (R4), John Shuster asks Hamilton to bump to change the angles a bit, but it over-curls a hair, gets to the inside of Y3 and brings us to our puzzle situation.

"So this is the Canadian's fourth shot," continues Mickey, "and around this point in the end, Brendan is asking himself whether he should keep going for his ideal outcome or cut bait and make sure he gets his acceptable outcome. As he looks at it (see diagram right), any future rock hitting R4 will likely spill all the American reds and leave at least two Canadian yellows in the house. Canada has won this 'battle of the angles' and Brendan has the advantage.

How does Bottcher capitalize upon his front-end's victory? "A lot of curlers would be tempted to throw a counter-clockwise draw to top-button to lie 2," Mickey says. "But with half an end to come and just like the last puzzle, it doesn't matter who's lying shot now. None of those rocks are going to be in the same position when the dust settles. And if you miss, the end gets more congested in the centre behind an opposition stone – not the shape of end you're looking for when you're tied with hammer. You want airy and access to the four-foot, not congested behind guards.

"Anyway, what Bottcher wants to do is make use of his good positions and their bad positions, so he decides that now's the time to make sure there's nowhere for Shuster to hide, peel off that guard, and ride out his good set-up play."

The Newbie (i.e. me) is troubled by this. Won't the Americans just start hitting yellows, I ask?

"Brendan's fine with Shuster starting to run into the pack now – because of the angles. When the hitting starts, Canada's rocks are more likely to remain while the Americans' are more likely to get knocked out. With hammer, Canada could score 2 or more.

"But even if it doesn't work out like that, Brendan knows they're playing in the rings with no guards out front so he's always likely to be able to get his single, which is acceptable here in the second end of a tied game. And if the Americans make a bunch of doubles, then maybe there's a blank, which is acceptable too.

"So the peel is the right play. Strip off junk in front, give them nowhere to hide, and ride out your secure positions. It's a situation in which you could score a bundle – because of your front-end play."

So what lessons can I take away for play at my level? First, an important way to protect my rocks and keep them in the paint is to freeze or almost-freeze at good angles. The aim is to make mine secure and theirs unsecure so that later on, mine stay and theirs go. The battle of the angles has to be won.

Secondly, front-end players need to miss light, not heavy. Don't slip behind tee where the opposition can freeze and be hard to remove. And don't bounce and leave your rocks exposed. Get my rocks into hard-to-remove spots.

And finally, I need to recognize when I've reached a good secure set-up position, then make sure they can't take it away from me by getting behind a centre guard. When I get to that go/no-go point and decide to go for it, clear up the front and don't let them wriggle out of it.

Mickey's Last Word: "The peel is the right shot for both pro and club curlers. Canada has established a good position where their rocks stay and the Americans' go. We've reached that point in the end where we make the decision to go hard and take advantage of that set-up and give Shuster nowhere to hide. Of course, if the set-up hadn't gone so well, we'd be hitting and clearing and making sure we can get our single.

"Finally, I can't emphasize enough the importance of good front-end play. When you're trying to establish your angles, setup shots are okay if they're a couple of feet light, but disaster if they're a couple of feet heavy. They should be thrown so that they need to be swept into position, not thrown to the spot with a prayer that they stop in the right spot."

Puzzle #7

Geez, these ladies on the other side can play – and now they've engineered you into the dreaded split-the-house conundrum. How the heck do you get out of this? Could you make the double? Can you throw it that hard? Have you had your Wheaties this morning? Still, you've got a guard to play with and there's half-an-end to go. Maybe you can coax them into a miss and survive this mess. But how? Here's the situation:

- First end of ten
- Score is tied
- You're yellow
- Red has hammer
- It's your Third's first
- About a four-foot swing

C'mon Skip, give us a shot that shows you've got the muscle to get out of this. What's your call – and why?

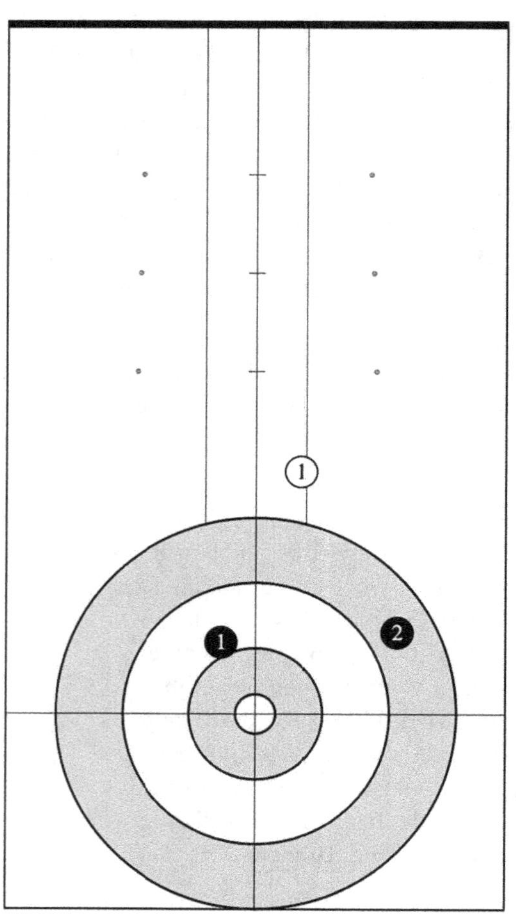

The Grouping of Stones

Mickey's unhappy. "This situation is one of my pet peeves and I even see some top teams get it wrong."

Really? It's a pretty basic set-up, I think. We're playing without hammer, trying to defend against a team splitting the rings to get their deuce. How exactly can you get this wrong? Hit and roll closer to theirs and try to get their rocks grouped so we can make a double, no?

"The instinct here is to hit shot rock. Because, you know, it's shot rock. You see Chelsea Carey, one of the world's best skips, play it here.

"But if you do that, the best outcome is the perfect roll under the guard – but that doesn't happen very often at any level. So let's look at the core principle here. We're going to simplify the situation by taking away that guard.

"Now red has two perfectly level rocks (Diagram A), R1 near the centre and R2 out in the twelve-foot. You are yellow, defending without hammer and throwing Y1. You hit shot rock R1 – because it's shot rock – and roll closer to the outside red R2, trying to get the rocks together and set up a double.

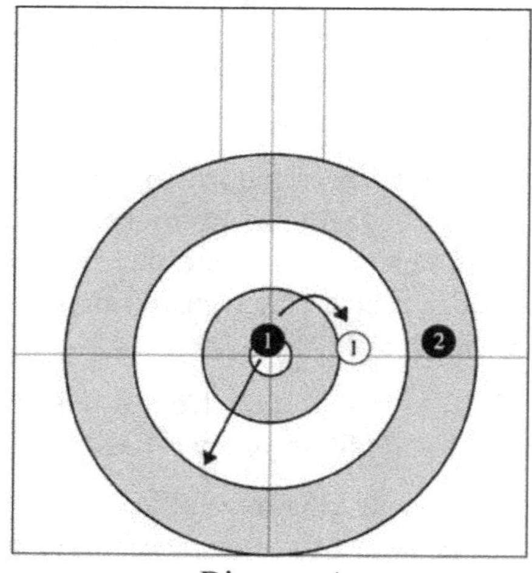

Diagram A

"

"But now red can hit your Y1 shooter, roll anywhere left and has almost the entire sheet to play with (Diagram B). They have all that space over on the other side of the house available to them. They could roll seven or eight feet across and get ten or eleven feet apart from their other rock. Even Mark Nichols and Oskar Eriksson don't make that ten-foot double very often.

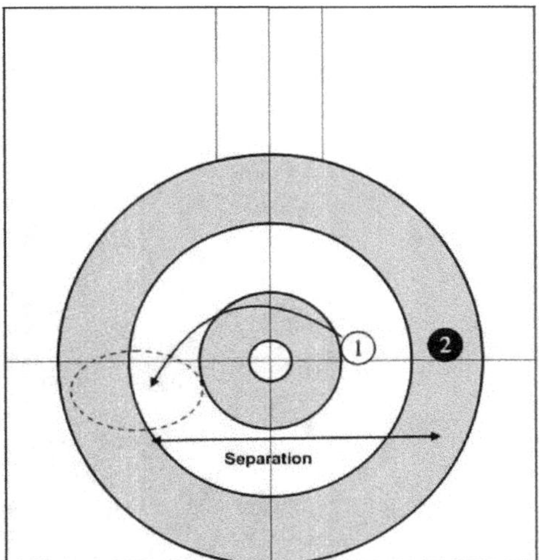

Diagram B

"So that's bad. But think about what happens if you roll out when playing the hit in the centre without hammer. Red can truly split the rings and put their next rock 10 feet away from R2. And even if it's a couple of feet heavy or light, the double is still tough. We see the Swiss do this in the video when Sarah Wilkes' second hit on the centre rock rolls out. Silvana Tirinzoni lobs her second out anywhere in the weeds on the far side and Chelsea pretty much has to concede the deuce right there.

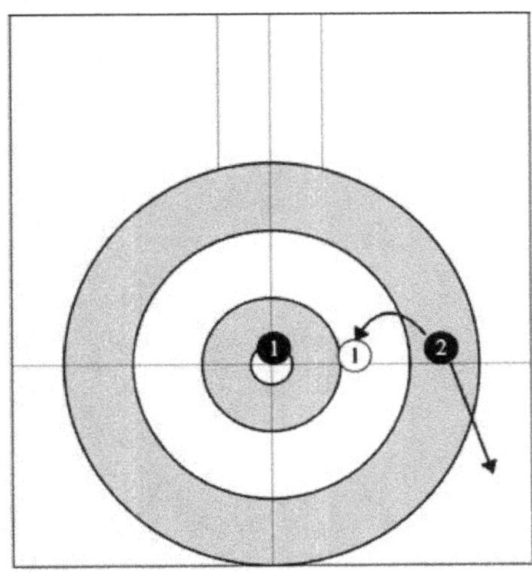

Diagram C

"To be clear, if you've got hammer and they're splitting the rings, hit the centre stone because you don't want them guarding it and putting you in trouble. But when you're defending against an opponent who's trying to get their deuce by splitting the rings, hitting the centre stone is the wrong play.

Now consider what happens if you hit the outside R2 instead. You might get lucky and flop in a foot or two inside (Diagram C). Now when red hits your Y1, they have to flop right and have only a couple of square feet to find any separation (Diagram D). They must be very precise with their roll, and as we all know, hit-and-rolls are very difficult shots to control.

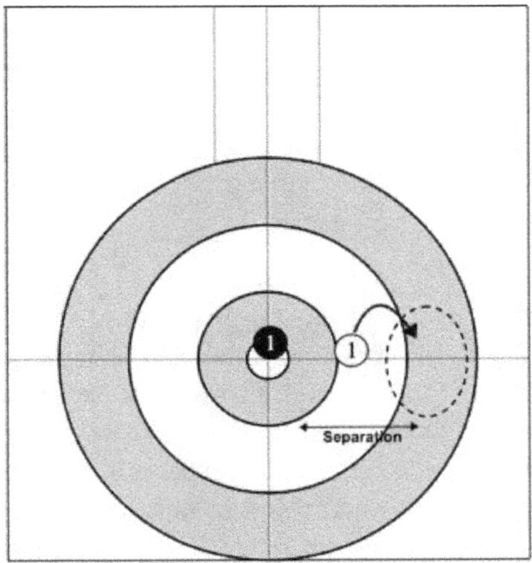

Diagram D

"But even if you just nosed R2 and don't get the roll inside, red is still in a jam. When they hit you back, they have nowhere to roll inside that won't leave a makeable double. And if they nose the one that you just nosed, they're now two rocks above where they started and there's a height differential building up that makes it a lot easier to find that double.

"And finally, what if you're really unlucky and roll out with your hit on the R2? They're still left with one in the centre and now they have to find a spot that leaves no double for you. But of course, they'll never be more than five feet from the one on the button and now they have to be pretty precise to avoid leaving you a double somewhere. If you had gone after the centre rock first and rolled out, they don't have to be precise at all. Just lob it somewhere over on the far side and it's job done – just like Tirinzoni did."

I'm starting to catch on. Any play I make on the side red in the twelve-foot leaves me in decent shape. If I roll in, they have to make a very precise roll back out. If I nose, they have to nose or roll in – but never out. Even if they make the nose or slight roll in, both of those outcomes might leave me a crack at a double.

Finally, if I roll out after hitting their side red, they'll be left with one in the centre and will have to place their next somewhere within six feet of it – yet leave no double. Trickier than placing one twelve feet away, that's for sure.

Mickey makes the general point. "The thing we're really talking about here is the 'grouping of stones' idea. One way to protect your rocks is to separate them as far apart as possible and make any double or triple very difficult. You see the Swiss do that here. If Chelsea can work to pin the Swiss on one side of the sheet and group their stones closer together, then those rocks are going to be at risk of being doubled out. So the core principle is that any time rocks are closer together, the more risk they are of being cleaned up. The farther apart they are, the safer they are. So always pay attention to that grouping of stones notion. It can win or lose you games."

What happens in our puzzle? Chelsea Carey goes to town on shot rock and noses, giving the Swiss acres of opportunity to hit-and-roll to their left. They fail to take advantage of it though and also nose to set up a height differential between their two rocks. Being only five feet apart, Canada has a very makeable double. Sadly for them, they miss and roll out and the Swiss draw to the acres of space on the left. Chelsea basically has to concede the deuce before she even throws her first shot.

So my takeaway on this puzzle? First, always keep the grouping of stones idea in mind. When mine get close together, they're at risk. Keep them further apart for safety.

Secondly, if I'm defending without hammer, hit the outside one first and cut their space. They'll have to make more precise shots, they might roll out or they might leave a makeable double. Even if they nose, the height differential might give me a crack at a double.

Mickey's Last Word: "Hitting the centre shot rock is the natural inclination, but it's the wrong play without hammer. Hit the outside one, play the rest of the end in half the house and group their stones closer together. They'll be forced to play much more precise shots and you have a better chance of finding the double."

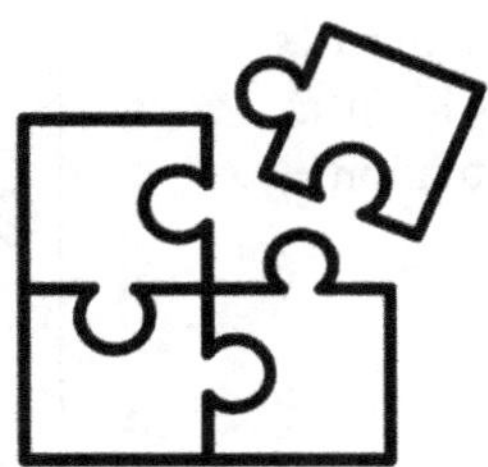

Always keep the grouping of stones idea in mind.
When mine get close together, they're at risk. Keep
mine further apart for safety. Keep theirs closer
together so they can be removed with fewer strikes.

Puzzle #8

You are playing like a god. Up by 1 late in the game, lying two rocks with hammer. This should be eaaaasy. Sure, the other guy's been around the block a few times, and he's made an unlikely comeback, but your team has the angels on its side today. Surely, it's just a matter of lying three now and using your hammer to rack up a game-winning big score. But how? Here's the situation:

- 8th end of 10
- You're red
- You're up by 1
- And you have hammer
- It's your Third's second shot
- About a five-foot swing on slightly fudgy ice

C'mon Skip, give us something divine to conjure up a big score. What's your call – and why?

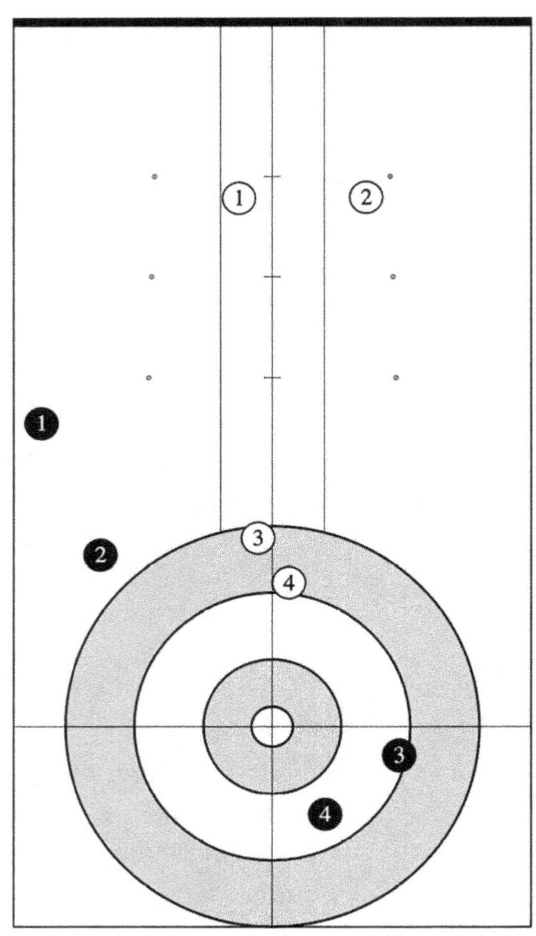

Use Them, Lose Them, Never Ignore Them!

This surprising call by John Epping is all about recognizing the dangers of well-separated double guards and overlapping 'staggered guards.' Coming down the stretch in a tight game, Wayne Middaugh has put together a threatening situation, and John recognizes it and then deals with it.

First, let's look at what's going on. Wayne Middaugh, yellow and the comeback kid at the 2021 Brier, is down by 1 without hammer in the 8th. He wouldn't mind forcing or blanking but doesn't want to give up a deuce or more. A steal would be ideal, but everyone says that going too hard for a steal can be risky. Why is that, I ask Mickey?

"The way for Wayne to set up a steal under the five-rock rule is to throw double centre guards. But the risk is that the other guys get under them first. If they get one buried, you might be spending a few rocks peeling off or chasing around your own guards, and they'll be using their shots to make life difficult for you. If they're successful and you can't dig them out, they'll have their last rock to draw in for two or more.

"That's why it's risky to go for it right off the bat. A more patient strategy is to wait for things to play out, encourage play to the middle and see if a stagger develops or maybe some long double guards appear that you can use to get underneath and perhaps poach a steal from there."

And that's what happens here – but Epping is alert to the danger.

"This is kind of a funny one," says Mickey. "Scott Howard was trying to throw a guard on their yellow Y4 and bring play back to the centre and away from the corners – where John would like it to be. But Scott sends his shot deep and sets up a pair of long, slightly overlapping guards with Y1 and Y3 and a pair of tight, slightly overlapping guards with Y3 and Y4. Both of those are dangerous to John."

But they're only ever-so-slightly overlapping guards, I say. Surely, they're not that dangerous.

"The problem is staggered guards set up dead zones behind them (see the examples below). We've drawn Y1/Y2 to show how a big overlap creates a big dead zone. But even a slight overlap – like we see in our puzzle with Y3/Y4 – creates problems. John can't get at the four-foot area running Y3, and he can't get to nose on the Y4-rock. If John leaves them and Wayne gets one into that dead zone behind, John will have to spend a rock clearing the guards before he can start addressing the one behind. In the meantime, Wayne will throw more guards, and John could end up in a real mess and give up a game-threatening steal.

"So there's a universal skipping principle about overlapping or 'staggered' guards: use them or lose them – but never ignore them! There are two staggers set up in our puzzle: the Y1/Y3 and Y3/Y4. Getting rid of the Y3 eliminates both."

The Newbie makes a note of the 'use or lose staggered guards' rule. But why doesn't John just use them, I ask? That could lead to an acceptable outcome for him – a score of 1.

"Well, you have to be aware of execution risk," warns Mickey. "Say John gets slightly offline and buries behind Y3. The fact that the stagger is made up of yellow rocks means Wayne could run Y4 in and sit behind the long Y1/Y3 stagger. Just to get at that situation, Epping would first have to clear the overlapping guards and then he's down to last rock.

"Or maybe he comes around and slips just behind tee, allowing Middaugh to freeze on the button – behind staggered guards.

"So going behind them would be very risky and, knowing that giving up a steal is his completely unacceptable outcome, John would never play that. He'll pick out Y3, remove both staggers with one shot and roll for another counter that might come into play later."

But these are pros. What about us aspiring curlers? Could we take a shot at using them?

"A key principle here is about scoreboard management and your ideal, acceptable, and unacceptable outcomes. You're up by 1 in the third to last end. Any blank or score is fine by you. Any steal is completely unacceptable. So that has to be your priority – keeping that steal off the table. And that principle applies even at club or competitive levels. Get rid of that steal threat by removing the stagger, take your 1 if you must, and then let the scoreboard take care of itself."

As you see in the video, the irony of the outcome is that John comes up short on his next draw – and sets up the stagger again! He gets a bit of execution luck when Wayne draws deep, and John can draw for his deuce.

But what are the Newbie's takeaways here? First, I really need to keep my ideal, acceptable, and unacceptable principles in mind – all the way through the end.

Second, I need to be constantly aware of execution risk. A great shot behind staggered guards would be, well, great. A poor one – always a threat at my level – could spell disaster.

And finally – **and it's Mickey's Last Word as well** – when it comes to staggered or overlapping guards, I can use them or lose them, but never ignore them!

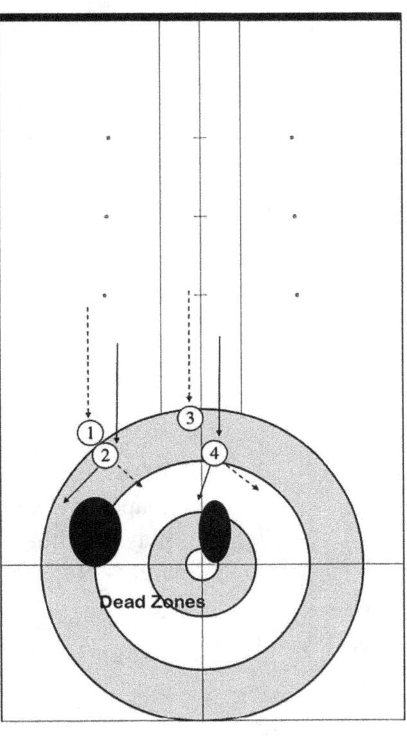

Puzzle #9

The other guys are one of these goofy teams where their Skip's not really their Skip and their Third isn't really their Third. They seem so confused. You've set up some nice centre guards here in the second – and the other guys have just slipped behind tee. "Not ideal" murmurs Russ disapprovingly up in the commentary booth. You could really turn the screws now. But how? Here's the situation:

- 2nd end of 10
- You're up by 2
- You're red
- Yellow has hammer
- It's your Third's last shot
- About six-feet of swing on fresh ice

C'mon Skip, give 'em a shot that shows that your screw isn't loose. What's your call – and why?

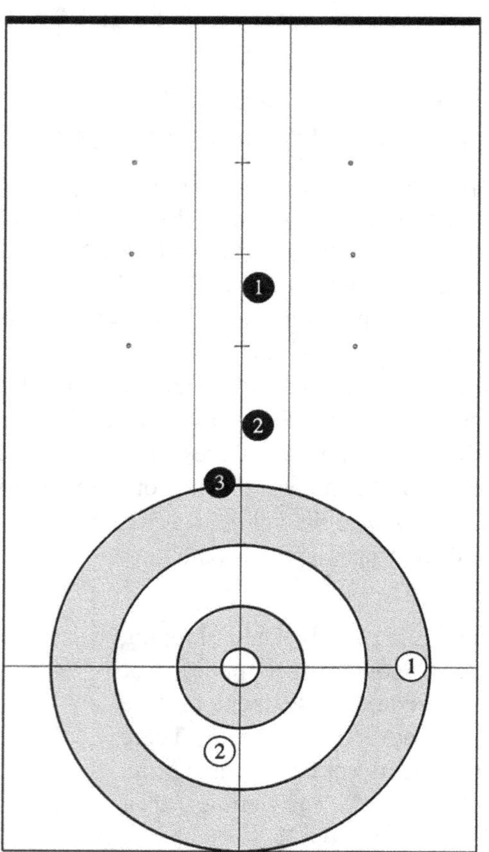

Ambition & Probabilities

"The draw looks so much easier. He could miss this in a heartbeat and then you're looking at two buried rocks." – Russ Howard

"Bit of a teaching point here." – Also Russ, after Reid Carruthers misses the hit-and-roll.

Let's put the moose on the table right now: was Mike McEwen as wrong as Russ thinks when he tried the six-foot hit-and-roll?

Mickey weighs in. "Up 2, Mike is playing defence. By killing that side yellow Y1, he's cutting down a potential big score. And by trying to roll to the middle, he's shrinking the scoring area and making it harder for Laycock to score a multiple. If he makes it, he's done two things at once.

"Keep in mind that without hammer, Mike wants a congested end in the four-foot where someone scores 1. What he doesn't want is a wide-open end with lots of yellow rocks sprinkled about and room for them to score

a few. Taking out Y1 and rolling to the centre builds that shape that he's looking for. It would be a nice two-for-one play – killing a counter while clogging up the scoring area – but only if it comes off.

The Newbie spots a problem. What are the odds of making a six-foot hit-and-roll, I ask?

"Well, you're right," Mickey concedes. "It's called a lot but rarely made. A lot of people will wax lyrical about how hard the perfect freeze is, and yes, freezing to one wide-open rock is nearly impossible. However, with great ice and superb sweepers, these guys make come-around corner freezes for fun. But a perfect hit-and-roll, well, that's another level of difficulty. When you're watching games, pay special attention whenever they call one. Keep track of how many they make. It's the lowest-probability shot, I think.

"Having said all that, that Y2 could act as a catcher in this case, and it increases the odds of a pretty good outcome for someone who throws big weight well. A club player often can't up their weight and make an accurate hit-and roll. They make that maybe one-in-ten or one-in-twenty, so they should be throwing a draw, trying to get one behind or even partly buried top ring. For a competitive or pro player, it's still only one-in-two or three so Mike knows there is a risk by playing this."

A fifty-fifty shot isn't something you see pros call unless there's a big payoff like a score of 2 or 3. Usually, they keep it simple and take the bird in hand. Why is he taking this chance, I wonder?

"Mike's holding two get-out-of-jail cards if Reid isn't dead on line. If the shot's a hair tight, they might get that flat Y1/Y2 double. And if they don't get a roll at all and Laycock has a 'free one' to draw around, Mike *should* be able to dig it out with a short runback using his R3. He'd expect to make that shot ninety percent of the time. Unfortunately for Mike, the video shows that this end was one of the ten percent."

But even knowing all those arguments for the hit-and-roll, Russ and Cheryl still wanted the come-around to top-four or even the freeze to Y2 in the back-8. We could almost hear the palm-to-forehead slaps when McEwen called his shot. Why didn't Magic Mike play the not-so-magic but very makeable draw?

"Mike looked at the downsides of the draw. First, Colin Hodgson, his Lead, just threw his second rock eight-feet short. In the second end with fresh ice, it's possible Mike didn't think the draw was as certain as Russ and Cheryl did.

"Second, a draw doesn't necessarily fix all Mike's problems. That R3 sitting at the top of the house is a 'power rock', and it's available to both teams. If Mike did play the draw, Laycock/Cotter can try that runback and dig him out. They could dig him out and sit their own at the top of the rings so McEwen would still have problems. If he's coming around, he'd be better to freeze right down to Y2 and give himself some backing. Laycock/Cotter would follow you down, and so Mike would still have problems even then."

Okay, that's Mike's argument against the come-around. But you're in agreement with Russ and Cheryl, aren't you Mickey?

"Well, yes, I am. The team has just spent five minutes in the warm-up practicing throwing draws to the button – which is essentially what the come-around is. It's makeable, even if Hodgson just came up light.

"And while the draw around would leave the runback with R3, it would be Laycock/Cotter playing it instead Mike. Generally, when you can play easier shots like draws and make them play harder shots like runbacks, things tend to work in your favour."

There's one more interesting factor which Mickey points out.

"There's an element of style or comfort in the different calls that Mike and Russ want to make. Russ was a guy who would often draw his way out of trouble, so he might prefer a clockwise come-around. Even if he's only top 8 and a little exposed, he'd leave himself a shot on both sides. He'd have a tap/run with his shooter on the clockwise side and the tap/run with R3 on the counterclockwise. He'd have them 'both ways'.

"But Mike's not Russ – and it's Reid Carruthers's shot. Reid's a world-class hitter and he has a 4-inch target area on Y1 to get either a roll or a double out of the shot. He'd expect to make that more often than not."

As you see in the video, Team McEwen misses their last three shots, allowing Mickey to make one final observation.

"You have to watch the ice in the second end," says Mickey. "Besides the track for draws to the button that you've played in the warm-up, you may not have a read on other lines, which seems to be the problem on Reid's hit-and-roll. Second, the path down the middle could be fresh pebble that grabs the rock so it curls more than you think it would and that might have been the problem with Mike's hits. In the end, his two-for-one play doesn't work out at all."

It's a funny old game for sure. McEwen makes a risky call, misses three shots and gives up 3, even though the end was played in the centre behind three rocks of his colour – just as Mike would've liked. As so often happens, even if you get the strategy right, it's the execution that lets you down.

Of course, if Mike had left the side Y1, called the come-around but rubbed a guard or just came up short, Laycock would then loop around to sit buried and it would be Mike throwing the runbacks. If he then went on to miss them all with Y1 still in play, Laycock scores 4 – and maybe the announcers would be saying he should have dealt with that open yellow when he had the chance!

So what are the general principles that this aspiring curler can apply to my game? First, the 'makeability' calculation has to be baked into each of my decisions. Before asking my fellow aspiring players to make a world-class shot, I'm going to see if there's not something more makeable. If we can play easy shots while they have to make tough shots, we should win more often than not.

Second, I'm going to watch the ice early in the game. It can be tracky and unpredictable. It might be best to leave the harder shots until the ice is broken in.

Mickey's Last Word: "Play the shot you're most likely to make. It doesn't always work out, but it's still your best chance."

Puzzle #10

Well, this is proving to be easier than you expected. Here you are in maybe the biggest game you've played in the last seven or eight years and you've leapt out to a 4-point lead. Sadly, you're up against your country's most dominant curler of the last decade and this guy never gives up. He'll be gunning for you the rest of the way home so you need to find a way to defend. You can't clear his guards under the five-rock rule. You could peel your own – the dreaded peel of shame – but is that your best call? Here's the situation:

- 4th end of 10
- You're yellow
- You're up by 4
- Red has hammer
- It's your Second's first shot
- Five-foot swing on good ice
- Five-rock free guard zone in effect

Come on Skip, give us a shot that doesn't leave us too red-faced. What's your call – and why?

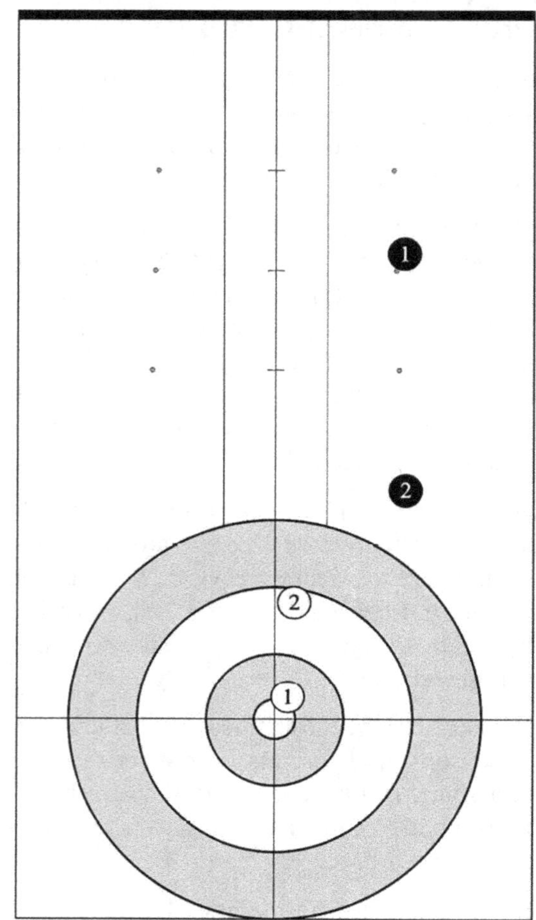

Defending Against a Hard-Charging Opponent

I think we can all agree that Brad Jacobs threw his two yellow rocks down the centre for a reason. He's not about to start down the peel of shame route just yet.

But at 4 down, Kevin Koe's in full aggression mode. He's thrown up two stacked corners and he's going hard for 2, if not 3. How can Jacobs defend? Mickey's here to outline his options.

"When you've built a good lead and your opponent is chasing hard, you've got a few different ways to try to hold them to 1 or 2. However, one of those ways is not throwing yours through then peeling. Back in the good ol' days of the four-rock free guard zone, Jacobs might have thrown two through, or maybe one top-four and the second one through, then started peeling on his Second's first rock. Using that "throw-through, keep it clean" strategy, Koe was pretty much limited to a score of 2 and often 1 or a blank.

"But if you're defending without hammer under five-rock, throwing through and then peeling guards is disaster. You can't peel until your fourth shot now, so that means your opponents get to throw three rocks before you can even think about taking off guards. By the time you get to start playing defence like you did in the good old days, they'll have two corners set up and one underneath. You'll be lucky to give up just 2.

"For instance, say you're up by a bundle and have played all three through while your opponents set up two corners on the same side and one underneath. With your fourth shot, you peel the top guard. They go around the remaining guard to sit two in the rings. You peel again. They could go open side to sit three in the rings – with hammer. Or perhaps they guard the two in the rings a couple times while you keep peeling, then throw a third in the rings later so you have fewer chances at a double. If they've done a good job spacing their two rocks on the same side, you're in trouble. If you can't make that double, you're giving up 3."

What if they put their guards either side? Would that make a difference, I ask.

"No," Mickey replies. "They'll have two corners and one underneath when you come to peel the first guard. You peel the guard in front of their sitting rock, they'll loop one around the remaining guard. You'll hit the open rock because you're going to take that bird-in-hand, they go around their remaining guard again. You peel that, and they draw the open side to sit three once again, or as in the previous example, guard their two in the rings a couple times before coming in. Throwing through and waiting to peel guards under five-rock is a recipe for giving up 3."

So if defence is no longer about throwing throw and then peeling, how are teams playing defence when the chasing team is coming after them, I ask?

"In today's game," replies Mickey, "defence is not simply about eliminating opposition stones. It's now about precise rock positioning, and teams approach it in a couple of different ways. One is by occupying the chasing team in the middle. Another is to choke off the corners and not letting the chasing team use them easily. And another is to tick their guards into the house and not let them set up an offensive position in the first place. We don't see that last option very often (although we might stumble across it in a later puzzle) so we'll just concentrate on choking the corners and occupying the centre for now.

"But you need to recognize that neither play is guaranteed to work. If the chasing team executes and the defending team misses one or two, the chasers are always going to have chances for a 3-ball. And that's the whole idea behind the five-rock rule: make it easier for teams who get behind to climb back in the game and thus make it exciting for the players and the fans. Now, very few leads are safe."

So what about the first defensive approach, choking the corners – the one that Brad Jacobs plays here?

"You'll see a few teams play this. It's an idea that balances the defensive notion of 'no junk short of the rings' with 'I can't peel their corners yet' with 'If I've got rocks in the house, they're going to have to deal with them sooner or later.'

"So the idea is to set up a couple on top-button / top-four then stick your third rock in the house not short of it; on the draw path that your opponents would use to get around their guards, neutralizing it instead of peeling it;

and somewhere where your opposition needs to remove you if they're going to score. So somewhere around the top-four or top-eight slightly off to the wing so that it cuts off the path behind the corners. Pretty much where EJ Harnden stuck his in the puzzle.

"The key thing is that the chasing team is going to need to get rocks secure in the rings, either by placing them behind guards or by putting them on top of some backing. So your rock to choke the corner can't be too deep and easily tapped for backing, and it can't be too narrow so that it can be tapped straight back into the four-foot while leaving their shooter on top of it. If the offensive team elects to tap it to back-four, their shooter must roll off to the side and open, not straight back and on top of backing. So your choking rock has to be high enough and wide enough so that it can't easily be repositioned to help them."

In my ongoing efforts to give memorable names to standard plays and thereby make them more memorable for the intellectually-challenged Skip with whom I so readily identify, I'm calling this the 'Choke the Corner' play. Block the draw path; don't leave it short where it can be used by the other guys; don't stick it close to tee where they can tap it back; get it wide so any tap back means their shooter rolls away. That's the defensive strategy number one. What's next, I ask?

"The second option is what we see Kelsey Roque play when defending against Kerri Einarson at the 2021 trials, and it's the stack'em down the middle approach. Scan the QR code to watch it play out.

"The idea here is to make them deal with you in the four-foot and keep them away from their guards. You'll see teams go top-button then either frozen or top-four /full-eight, then throw a medium tight guard. The aim of the rocks in the centre is that you want to occupy the four-foot so they have to come get you – and that's why frozen or somewhat split apart is best. Ideally, you want them to have to play two shots to get rid of these later.

"The guard placement should be fairly tight to the rings and directly on top of your rocks in the house. You want it tight so that they can't easily make a chip-and-roll on your rocks in the house, but not so tight that they can chip your guard off to the side and roll one on under their corner. And you want it stacked directly in line so that any runback attempt leaves their shooter right in the centre for you to use again – to draw them back to the middle."

But that's not exactly what happens between Roque and Einarson, I point out. Einarson tried to tick Roque's centre guard and stuffed it right back into the rings.

"That's right," answers Mickey. "Kerri could see that Kelsey was setting up down the centre so she tried to move their rock off to the side and roll her shooter for another corner. The fact that it stuffed and left another centre guard helped Kelsey. The fact that the ticked rock didn't make it all the way out probably hurt her. You don't want catchers in the back of the house that might help the chasing team protect their rocks in the rings. Kelsey should have made sure that was swept through.

"But watch where the rest of the end is played out: under those guards and in the middle, just where Roque wanted it played. It's the type of end where it's tippy tappy in the middle and usually someone scores just 1. Einarson's team made some great shots and they were still reduced to a circus shot to try to get their deuce. In this case, dragging them back to the middle worked out for the defending team."

My team adopted this strategy when we got ahead, setting up down the middle and making the chasing team come deal with us. We called it our 'Come to Momma' defence and it worked for us.

Mickey sums up the importance of positioning. "The key in playing a central defence in five-rock is to get your rocks in the right places. The chasing team will need to secure some rocks in the rings if they're going to generate their 2 or 3. One way they secure them is by getting under guards. The other way they do it is by moving you back and building pockets. If you're playing a central defence, don't slide behind tee and do their job for them. If you're choking the corners, don't slide deep and provide backing. These are precise shots – but that's five-rock for you."

As a Newbie Skip, I want to take away some general principles that I can apply to my game. The first lesson I'm taking away from this situation is that defending a lead under five-rock is no longer about throwing through then peeling and hitting as it was in yesteryear. Now, we can't avoid having rocks in play. I just need to put them in the spots where I want them.

Secondly, I now have two tactics to play when the other guys are chasing hard: Come to Momma and Choke the Corner. At my level, I'm thinking two rocks stacked in the four-foot and one semi-tight guard will be enough to keep the other guys occupied. Those are shots we throw all the time and seem to require less precision than choking off the guards. We're going to try that tactic first.

Mickey's Last Word: "Defence by rock positioning is a must in five-rock, but it requires precision on all eight shots. If you miss or make a couple of half-shots, the chasing team is going to have chances. And that's the whole intent of putting the five-rock free guard rule into play. It makes for pretty exciting curling."

Forty More Puzzles that
Build on the Fundamentals

Puzzle #11

What a start you've had. Scoring your deuce in the first end against a past World Champion, then forcing her in the second. If we're not being kind, we'd say you've been bossing her a bit. Maybe you should crank down the lid, turn up the heat and really get this pressure cooker a-boiling. But how? Here's the situation:

- 3rd end of 10
- You're red
- You're up by 1
- You have hammer
- It's your Lead's first
- About a 5-foot swing on good ice

C'mon Skip, give 'em a shot that puts this game on full steam. What's your call – and why?

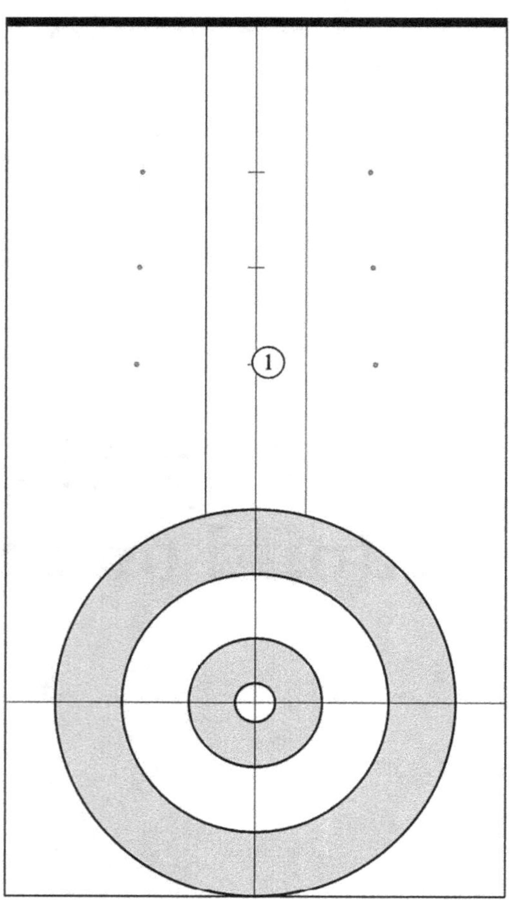

Neutral, Control & Dominant

This one is about team style or 'philosophy' and how you want to play certain game situations. At 1-up with hammer, Team Einarson has several choices. As we discussed in Puzzle #4 (The Hierarchy of Offence), each option sends them down a different road, creating a different style of end. And each of those styles of ends carry different degrees of risk and different opportunities for reward. Mickey sets it up for us.

"Before we get to their call, it's probably worthwhile thinking about the three general 'game states' in which you can find yourself. These 'game states' should dictate the type of end you want to play and therefore the first few shots you throw to set up the end.

"The first is Neutral. This game is in the balance. Of course, the odds of winning are never 50/50 once the coin is tossed, but these scores are as close as we get:

1-up without hammer, 1-down with hammer, and a tie game – unless it's the last few ends when tied with hammer is more of a 'control' situation for the team with last shot. See below.

"The second state is, well, Control. One team is in a decent position and are favoured to win. If you're 2-up without hammer or 1-up with, you have at least a seventy-percent chance of winning. This situation dictates that you don't want to do anything crazy if you're the team leading – throwing double corners or something. And if you're the team behind, you need to start taking some chances and junking it up to get some deuces or steals and get yourself back in the game.

"The final game state is Dominant, where one team has at least an eighty-five percent chance of winning. So this is the 2-up with hammer and 3-up without hammer. If you're dominating the other team, you're going to be playing serious defence to coax this game over the line. If you're the team being dominated, you're going all in with guards and pockets and whatever rocks you can leave in play to generate a score and give yourself a chance."

As a Newbie Skip, I'm thinking that Kerri Einarson is controlling the game at 1-up with hammer. And I'm guessing that she'll want to take some chances to generate some offence, but not throw the whole kit-and-caboodle at it. How does she do that and what opening shots does she call to play that way?

"At 1-up with, I think you'll see a lot of teams – Brad Jacobs, Rachel Homan – play the tick. It removes the defensive threats down the middle and moves play out to the sides where they want them. But you should only play the tick if you practice it and can make it 90% of the time or more. Otherwise, you're just wasting valuable shots.

"Other teams want to be a bit more aggressive by coming around – like Kerri does here. They keep the pressure on their opponent, try to get some misses in the four-foot and then jump on them to create offence. If it doesn't work out, the rocks are grouped in the middle, and they should be able to open it up with one or two shots and at least get their single point. This looks like Kerri's team philosophy. They're going to mix it up the first few rocks and see what happens.

"Most club teams would play this come-around because a one-point game is far from in the bag, so they'll be trying to generate some offence. If they don't want to play the tick because they don't practice it, coming around the centre guard is a good option to see if you can get something going.

"Another option to keep it simple in a close game is to throw it in the rings to one side. Your opposition will either hit it or ignore it, but you're not risking coming up light or heavy and complicating things in the centre."

Mickey recommends having a Team Playbook for how you want to set up ends given various situations. And that playbook should reflect your team's style, ability, and appetite for risk.

"It's good to know how you want to set up an end – your first two or three rocks – given the situation you're in. If you're 1-up with, do you tick here? Or do you play to the wing or come around like Kerri did? If you're 2-down with, do you throw a single corner then come around their centre guard? Or do you be aggressive and go around your corner, knowing that your Second and Third can make the shots to clear out the centre later? Map out these situations earlier so you set up the end that the way you want."

During the break before this end, the camera zooms in on Team Canada's discussion. They chat about the ice for a half-minute, then Kerri says 'OK ladies, let's see where they go and do you like going four-foot?' The team says 'Think so.' Their plan takes just five seconds. They have mapped this out before and have a set plan to be offensively cagey in this situation.

Team Einarson wants to probe but they're not going whole hog and risking a steal so they loop around to the four-foot like they discussed. Perhaps they'll get a miss that Kerri can jump on to set up some offence. But if the first few shots don't work out, they've been playing to centre and all the rocks will be grouped. With Second's last or Third's first, they'll make a decision and if it's not looking good, they can throw a few bullets at the grouped stones, clear them out and at least get their single, if not a blank. At 1-up in the third end, both of those are acceptable outcomes.

Mickey says: "Ticking, coming around, going open side – all those options are good calls....if you make your shots. Never forget that great execution with poor strategy probably beats poor execution with great strategy. You have to make your shots – so call shots that you can make.

What happens? Sofia Mabergs, Sweden's Lead, throws the Death Rock, a freeze that gets heavy instead of light. It bounces off, letting Canada hit and try to roll to the side to set up a chance at 2. (Worth reiterating: a light rock can be promoted later, a heavy rock bounces or slides deep and can be used by the other guys. Be light, not heavy. Don't throw Death Rocks.)

The end doesn't quite work out for the Canadians, but the play remains grouped, their misses are on the pro side and they're able to blank it with their last. They had a crack at offence, but they were cagey about it. It didn't work out. They got their blank. Job done.

So what lessons can I take away from this for play at my improvers/aspiring level? First, have a playbook agreeing on how you want to set up each end, given the game state. Know what type of end each set-up leads to and agree on your plan given your team's skills and appetite for risk.

And secondly, don't be heavy on freezes. Be light. Let the sweepers bring them home.

Mickey's Last Word: "Have a plan for the common setups that occur based on score, hammer, end, and skill set. And miss on the pro side."

Puzzle #12

You're up against a team with a distinct advantage over you: they must be six inches shorter on average than your own hulking squad. Everyone knows that shorter curlers have a massive edge over the taller, more Bambi-on-ice-like players. For one thing, the hog line's a lot further away for them. In fact, if there was any justice, you giants be starting with a 2-0 lead! Sadly, there is none. The curling supremos (also short) dictated that no matter what your stature, you have to start the game all-square – and now you're 1 behind. What to do, what to do? Here's the situation:

- 3rd end of 10
- You're red
- And you're 1-down
- You have hammer
- It's your Lead's first shot
- Normal 5-foot swing on championship ice

C'mon Skip, let's squeeze 'em till the pips squeak! What's your call – and why?

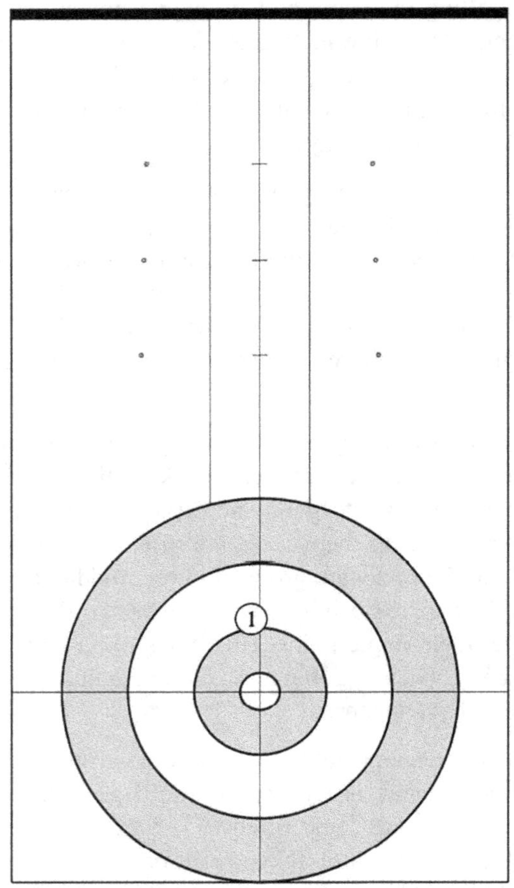

Another Route to Offence

Y'know, when Lead's first shots come up, I'm usually still slurping on my water bottle or stuffing my face with gummy bears, not fully engaged with the end yet. Knowing I have hammer, I just wave my broom in the general direction of the corner and ask my Lead to get on with it while I consider why I like green bears best. Mickey tells me I'm making a mistake.

"First of all, red bears are best. Secondly, when the other guy with the lead goes into the rings like Sweden did, the choice you make on your first shot sets the whole direction of the end," he explains. "In our puzzle, Scotland throws up the corner, Sweden clogs up the middle and the rest of the end gets played in the area they want it – right there in the centre making it hard for Scotland to score 2. In fact, in our puzzle video, Scotland needs to play a highlight reel shot on Duncan Menzies' first to open up the middle, and Scotland's Skip still ends up shooting against 3 with his last. Here, Sweden gets their ideal outcome, while Scotland has to settle for the force. Now they're tied-without going into the fourth end, so even this early in the game, they have ceded some control to Sweden."

But what other choice is there, I ask? If I hit Sweden's rock on the four-foot, they hit me and we're playing the blank. Sure, I'd rather be scoring in the even ends, but the third is a long way out to be worrying about who has hammer in the evens and odds. I'd rather take a stab at my deuce, I argue.

"Ya, for sure. As Kevin Koe says, you only get three or four hammers per game so you don't want to waste them. But throwing the corner here with your first rock isn't the only option to set up a scoring chance. You do have another choice – and that's the Delayed Corner."

I look suitably puzzled. Mickey starts to walk me through it. "The first key to this is knowing that you, with hammer and trying to score, would like to play a nice airy, uncongested end with rocks spread around the sides and an open four-foot that you can use to get your single if things don't go your way.

"On the other hand, your opponent – who is defending and wants to limit your scoring ability – would like to play a congested mess in the four-foot where it's hard for you to score a multiple unless you really out-execute them. So, you want to play in the wings and leave the centre open while he wants to play in the centre and create a congested mess.

"The second key to this is appreciating that under the five-rock free guard rule, you get two guards that he can't touch. So that means you don't have to use your first rock for a guard. You can do whatever you want with your first and still have your second to throw a guard that he can't remove. And we call that the Delayed Corner Guard."

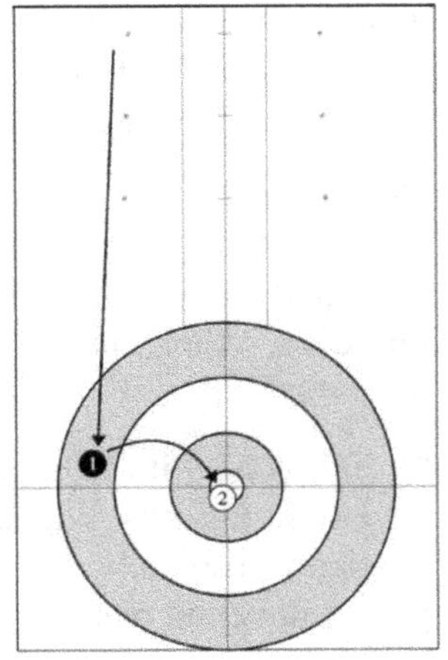

Hmmm, I'm not sure I've seen this played, to be honest.

"You don't see it much at the pro level, mostly because the team without hammer usually throws the centre guard with Lead's first – that's the only way they can control the four-foot. And you won't see it when teams are down – most competitive teams will take on more risk by throwing a corner, like Scotland does here. But you might see it in a tie game, and I definitely recommend it at the club level to avoid the massive clutter that so often develops.

"Here's how it works: if he comes in with his first (Y1), you hit it with your first and roll off to the side, preferably the twelve-foot (diagram above). If he's smart, he won't leave your R1 there because that could go on the scoreboard later. He'll probably hit it, and if he sits or rolls out, it's no worries – that's where you'd like him to be, out in the wings. If he's good, he'll get a roll back to the middle (Y2 at right) – where he wants the end to be played. But because you've already hit his first, he only has one stone out of the two he's thrown sitting down the centre line. It's already more open. Quite often, they don't

make the roll and their rock sits out in the wings, of no consequence.

"Anyway, on your second shot you leave Y2 wher- ever it is and throw the corner on the other side (R2 below). Because he's about to throw just the fifth rock of the

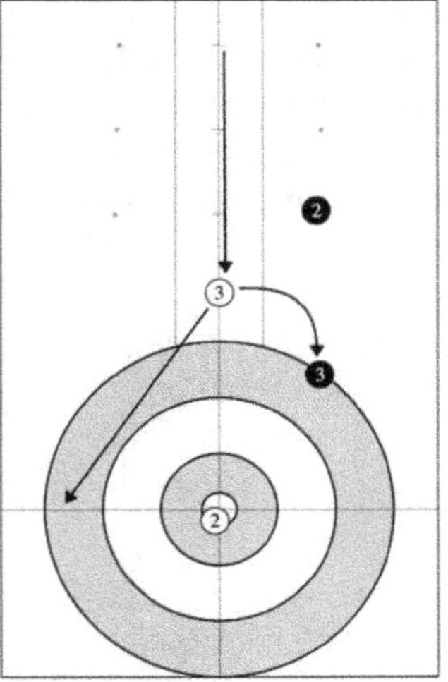

end, he can't remove your guard. He could go around it but going around corners without hammer this early in the end is always risky. (We cover this later.) If he got the roll back towards centre with Y2, he'll probably guard that.

"But it's hard to guard one rock with one rock. If he's too high, you might have a chance to chip his shot rock and roll under your guard. Or if he's too tight to the rings, you might be able to tick the guard and roll onto the rings under cover (R3 at left) or corner freeze to shot rock and start hitting on Second's stones.

"But who knows where the end goes from here. The point is that playing the Delayed Corner sees you remove one of his down the centre so that after the five-rock rule expires, you'll have a corner to work with and he'll only have two in the middle, not three. And that leads to a more open centre of the rings, which is more conducive to the type of end you want to play with hammer. If you execute, it gives you a good chance at scoring a deuce."

What are the takeaways I can use at my level? First, don't be chewing gummy bears on the ice. How I played delicate draw shots for years while being completely stoned on all that raw sugar, I'll never know.

Secondly, the Delayed Corner play seems to give me a chance at some offence without going 'all in'. It's cagey offence. I like that.

Mickey's Last Word: "Y'know, the bigger point here is that you need a playbook about how you want to open each end given the game situation. You need to nail down what shots lead to what type of ends and have a mental playbook for the most likely situations – up with, up without, down with, down without. In this case, the Delayed Corner Guard gives you a cautious way to go for offence without going 'all in'. It's a good option for a situation like early in a tight game. If you're down 2 or more, you might want to be more aggressive."

Puzzle #13

Ah man, it must be so much fun being the GOAT. What a record you've collected! And here you are, working your way towards putting another notch on your belt. But still, it's a blank slate in the first end, and you've got to make your shots just like the rest of the mere mortals you're playing. Fortunately, your team (maybe also the GOAT Team) has put you in a great position for your 3. You just need to call a good shot, then cash in your chips for a well-earned lead. But how? Here's the situation:

- 1st end of 10
- Score is tied
- You're red
- You have hammer
- It's your Third's first shot
- Five feet of curl

C'mon GOAT, don't be a sheep. What's your call – and why?

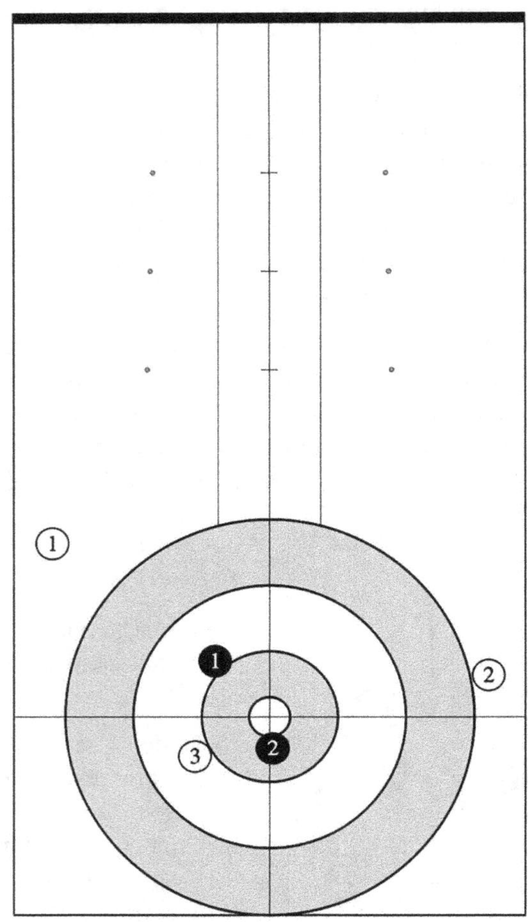

Three Shot Window & Grouping of Stones

We're going bookmark the video a few shots before our puzzle shot – on Scotland's Lead's second shot. Mickey wants to make two points about how Scotland ended up on the wrong end of the stick here in the first end of the 2019 European Semi-Finals. What caught your eye, Mickey?

"Well, I don't want to be too hard on Scotland since it's the first end and picking up the weight is, as we all know, a bit tricky. But I just want to use this as an example of erring on the wrong side. Watch the set-up in the video and you'll see their Lead's second rock and their Second's first stone both make the cardinal front-end sin of being heavy rather than light.

"Take a look at both those rocks. If they had stopped in, say, the eight-foot edge-buried, they have what we call 'power.' Scotland can always tap them into a better position or use them to remove the reds that are exposed behind them. If Nik Edin wants to remove them, then he very likely has to sacrifice his own reds. Even then, they likely jam and might not get cleared out of the four-foot area because they're edge-buried.

"So, once again, the key rule for front-ends is to miss light rather than heavy. These guys throwing the rocks obviously know that, and it's always easier said than done – especially in the first end. I'm just using this circumstance to make a point for our Puzzlers, in a drive-by sort of way. Sorry Scotland."

Unfortunately, one of those throwers is my friend and former teammate, but we'll try to gloss over that tricky issue and file away Mickey's drive-by point for future reference. What's the second lesson we can take away from this?

"It has to do with controlling your shooter. As the end develops, Rasmus Wrana leaves a rock top-four that Scotland absolutely has to remove. It has too much power, hovering over the scoring area.

"But the Scottish Skip asks for strike weight rather than 'just enough' weight. Duncan Menzies, your former teammate – and now, after my comments, perhaps your former friend – is a very precise hitter and is asked to throw something like seven-and-a-half seconds hog-to-hog. First of all, that weight reduces the effects of sweeping, so the thrower has to be very precise. And secondly, bigger weights mean much less chance of controlling your shooter. Duncan's rock spins off to the side of the eight-foot, where it's not really doing anything.

"Think about how much better the outcome would be if he'd thrown less weight and left his shooter around the top-four area. Instead of Rasmus Wrana getting a freebie shot on his next to freeze another one into the four-foot area, he'd have to deal with Scotland's rock and make a terrific shot if he's to leave it somewhere even half as good as what he does.

"The point I'm making is that it's easy to get sucked into focusing on their rocks when you're chasing. But you need to use that shooter as a way to put pressure on the other team, not just ease the pressure on you. Throw 'just enough' weight and have the shooter do two jobs: remove their rocks and make them respond to you. Don't give them free passes by not controlling your shooter."

OK, Mickey, I'm glad you got those off your chest – and I am definitely filing those away. But what about the flippin' puzzle?

"OK, good point. In Nik Edin, we've got maybe the best to ever play the game, and he makes a beauty of a call here. Most of us – especially less experienced skips – would be tempted to deal with Y3 now and try to set up a really big end.

"But Nik shows a great ability to peer a few shots ahead and map things out. If he were to play that short R1/Y3 run now, he'd be leaving his three stones grouped, and Scotland would have almost half-an-end to make a couple of doubles – something they're very good at – and get out of this mess.

"And Nik sees that the R1/R2 double in the puzzle would see Scotland lose their shooter, leaving Y3 wide open for him to hit it. So by playing over to the wing as he does, he's kind of splitting the rings in advance. If he puts one over on the side about tee line, the next three shots will see him lie 2 well split apart and set up for an easy deuce.

"To me, it's a great illustration of a Skip playing in a three-shot window. Nik sees that:

- Playing the short run to eliminate Y3 would group his stones, making it more likely to leave doubles and triples and let Scotland clean up
- Sees that Scotland will make the R1/R2 double but knows they'll lose their shooter in the process
- Sees what that leaves him – a wide-open nose hit on Scotland's Y3
- So he places a rock now where a double is not makeable after he noses Y3. It's kind of brilliant, actually.

"I like this call at the club level as well," Mickey continues. "Be patient, no need to kill Y2 yet-it's actually making it harder for them to remove R1. As long as you hit the rings drawing to the open side, you're in control of the end. They'll be playing riskier shots and you'll have three in the rings to their one."

As a relative non-GOAT, I would have been so tempted to thrash away at Scotland's Y3 and sit three in the rings. Edin shows us that a little foresight goes a long way.

But what are the essential lessons I can take away and apply to my level of curling? First, I need to operate in a three-shot window, peering into the future and asking myself, 'What are they throwing next?' Anticipating their next moves might point me in the right direction for mine.

Secondly, I need to be aware of that 'grouping of rocks' principle. Keep my rocks spread apart and hard to remove if I'm trying to score. Get their rocks clumped together if I'm trying to defend.

Third, my front-end are going to be thrashed day and night with the 'throw light, not heavy' mantra.

Fourth, I'm calling for 'just enough' weight and using that shooter for two purposes: to remove their rocks and put pressure back on them. Most every hit can be both defensive and offensive at the same time.

And finally, I'm taking away the fact that there's no shame in getting a bit bossed by maybe the best Skip and best team to have ever played the game.

Mickey's Last Word: "Don't worry too much about who is shot rock, second shot, or even third shot early in the end. Focus instead on how the end is shaping up and what is likely to happen over the next three or four shots, then plan accordingly to achieve your end goals."

Puzzle #14

OK, this is nice. You've got one of the world's most accomplished curlers on the run here with two perfect centre rocks. You could be on for the steal, but you'll certainly get the force. Of course, that assumes that your guys come through for you on the next few shots. And you know what happens when you ASSUME things, don't you? What to do, what to do? Here's the situation:

- 6th end of 10
- Score is tied
- You're yellow
- Red has hammer
- It's your Second's first shot
- About a five-foot swing on good ice

Come on Skip, give 'em a shot that doesn't make an ASS out of U and ME. What's your call – and why?

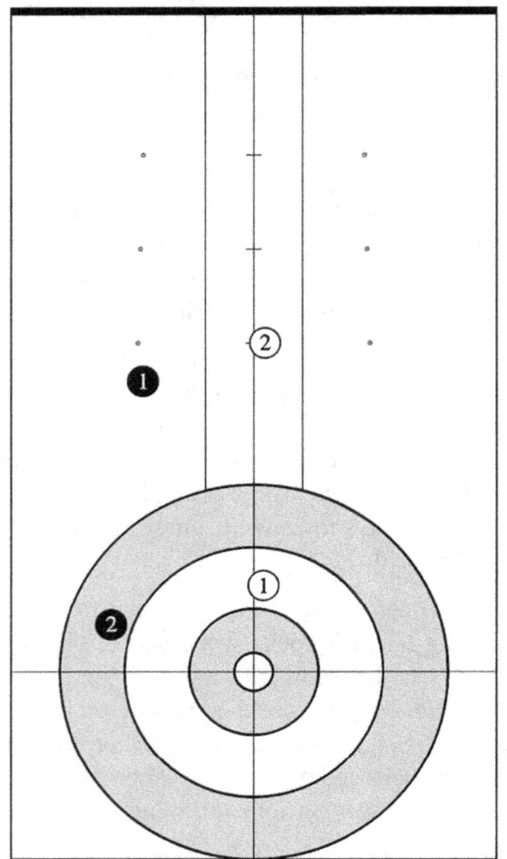

The Wing Nullifier

We talked earlier about curling being compared to chess on ice, and how that's not quite right. But in chess, they have done a useful thing by naming certain moves. Geller's Rook and Pawn Endgame. Vladimirov's Thunderbolt. And the dastardly Shirov's Jaw-Dropping Bishop Sacrifice.

I think we need a bit of this in our game, so we can remember the great tactical plays. I'm naming today's play the 'The Wing Nullifier'. Let see how it goes.

So where do we find ourselves at this puzzle? Tied in the sixth end with hammer, Koe (red) is probing for a 2 while Bottcher (yellow) is trying to find a way to force a single. Bottcher draws to the eight-foot with his first, Koe throws a corner, and Bottcher then throws a centre guard. Let's take a minute to consider Kevin's offensive options here.

His first is to freeze to Bottcher's Y1 shot rock, the Corner-n-Freeze play we spoke about in Puzzle #4. That's pretty safe – about 6/10 in aggression. Kevin gets a rock into the central scoring area and if things work out, he might get a chance to roll one under his corner later. A relatively short runback using R1 or Y2 means he can always deal with shot rock when he needs to later.

The second option is to loop around his own corner. He puts 'One in the Bank', but he lets Bottcher throw three rocks before he can start clearing. Bottcher could have two great centre guards and one on the button. If Koe can dig him out, he might score 2 with that rock now buried, but he's got to execute some good plays. Let's rate this play about a 7.5/10 in aggression.

Finally, he could throw a double corner guard, the Go Big or Go Home tactic. Like a good horror flick, this one is not for the squeamish. Kevin is letting his opponent throw three rocks before he even thinks about going into the rings. Sure, it might pay off if he gets one or two under his corners, but he might get a stake through his heart along the way. About 10/10 in aggression and unnecessary when you're tied with hammer.

In our case, Koe takes Door #2, goes around his corner right away and puts one on the bank. Not too hot, not too cold – he's hoping it's just right.

Mickey explains his former Third's thinking. "Kevin says he's only going to get three or four hammers a game, so he doesn't want to waste them. He's going to be fairly aggressive and try to generate some offence when he can. He's not at the double corner stage yet, but he's happy to take some risk to try to score a multiple."

So Kevin, true to form, goes around his corner and we come to our puzzle shot. I was thinking the best call I can make now is to throw up another centre guard and really take a position down the middle. Perhaps we could entice Kevin to loop around and get into a guddle with us in the four-foot.

"The best option is to deal with their rock behind the guard if possible," suggest Mickey. "If you can get to that R2, or find a way to neutralize it, it won't come back to haunt you later."

"And besides, Kevin is unlikely to take the bait and go around in a tie game, knowing you would follow him in and create a mess in the middle. He'd be in mixed doubles territory and it's possible that you execute better and generate a steal – and Kevin doesn't want to risk a steal. He wants to make sure that if things go wrong, he has a draw for his single. He's not going around – he's much more likely to try a double peel on your two guards. He's got his rock buried under his corner, so he'll be thinking he can clean up the centre now and maybe get a chance to use it to generate a safer deuce later."

Okay, but if I'm Bottcher, I'm not willing to give up on setting up my double guards. If I set them up directly in line and he peels, he might leave some shrapnel in the middle. We could get underneath and work towards our force perhaps.

"The problem is where that first guard is," Mickey replies. "It's close to halfway. If it was deeper or higher, you could get some separation from it with your second. But if you throw a second guard, it's going to be fairly close to your first. Colton Flasch and BJ Neufeld, Koe's Second and Third at the time, are likely to clear them and roll over to the wing or even out. That leaves an empty centre, a corner guard or two and one in the bank underneath them. They would be on their way to their deuce. Because of the position of Y2, the double guard is really not the play at the competitive level.

"At club level, the second guard would be a good call because double peels are rare. Of course, at the club, your opposition probably wouldn't have gone around the corner. It's too risky at club level to let your opponents dominate the centre, so they would probably have followed you in on their second shot and we'd have a completely different end."

Okay, but we are where we are. Kevin's no club player and he's gone around his corner. What's a good play for us now?

"Well, we see Bottcher play what you want to call the Wing Nullifier, so let's go with that. Brendan sends one out to the wings that sits and hovers over Kevin's R2, kinda like a choking corner but with backing. The key is to get it edge-buried and ideally lying second shot. If it's edge-buried, Kevin can't use it for an in-off to kill shot rock– he'd kill his R2. And if Bottcher's lying 2, Kevin will need to take care of both of them to start building his multiple.

"So the net effect is that Brendan has dealt with Kevin's R2 about as effectively as picking it out or running back the corner guard into it. It's lying third shot where it's doing no damage, is likely to be killed if Kevin makes a play on the wing nullifier, and Brendan's lying 2 with shot rock above tee and behind a guard. The end is now favouring him and Kevin has some work to do to get his deuce.

"Even if Brad Thiessen's shot doesn't get second shot, as long as it's edge-buried above Koe's stone, it's always a threat to that R2 sitting behind the corner guard.

"But – and I can't believe I'm calling it this – the Wing Nullifier is not without risk. It's a precise shot. If it's thrown heavy and bounces, then Kevin has a play on it to get two in the rings with hammer. That's not good.

It gets worse. "If it rubs the guard, Kevin might be able to double it out along with shot rock, perhaps get his shooter in the rings and sit one or maybe two buried with hammer. Now he's starting to see how he can score his deuce, or even more."

In our game, Thiessen makes it though, and Koe then needs to play tough runbacks while Bottcher throws straightforward draws the rest of the end. Koe gets forced to 1.

My takeaway from this puzzle? When my opposition throws a corner guard and loops around, I'm going to look to chip it out first. If it's too good and I can't take a good crack at it, I'm going to consider the Wing Nullifier – especially if my second centre guard wouldn't be well spaced.

Mickey's Last Word: "This is a common setup in five-rock. If you can deal with the one behind the corner by removing it with quiet weight, that will position you well for the rest of the end. If you can't get at it, putting one in front just edge-buried and out-counting it is just as good as getting rid of it."

Puzzle #15

Well this is nice. Looks like the other guys aren't so much focused on the job and are here just to enjoy the good Canadian beer. Maybe they're resting on their laurels, putting their feet up, and basking in the warm glow that comes with success at the highest level. Down 4-0 here, they already have one foot in the bar. You just need whet their whistle and encourage them towards the exit. But how? Here's the situation:

- 4th end of 10
- You're yellow
- You're up by 4
- Red has hammer
- It's your Second's first shot
- Good, controllable five-foot swing

C'mon Skip, let's make a shot that makes the other guys thinking their glass is half-empty. What's your call – and why?

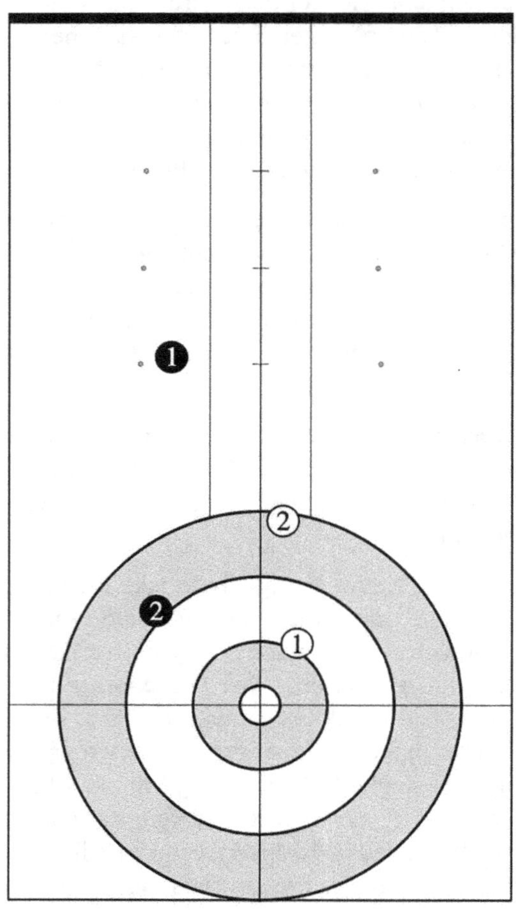

Keywords. And Pretty Good versus Perfect.

I can't think five shots ahead when skipping. Maybe it's not enough clean living or maybe I'm not that bright. And maybe it doesn't matter that much since my teammates miss most of their shots most of the time anyway. There's no way to anticipate that Steve at Second is going to bounce his freeze, and that Ian at Third is going to chuck his guard a foot wide. Playing tic-tac-toe curling at my level is not going to be that productive. I can look three shots ahead at most. I do this, they do that, we respond with that other thing. That's about as far as I'm peering into the future.

But what is useful to me is to rely on some keywords that keep me straight during the end. I think about my ideal and acceptable outcomes and come up with some words that illustrate in my mind what I'm trying to achieve. For instance, up by 4 in this situation, my keywords would likely be *'simple'*, *'clean'*, *'in the rings'*, and *'congested four-foot'*. If I was down by 4 like John Shuster, my keywords would be *'in front of the house'*, *'cluttered, 'rocks in play'*, and *'breathing room'*. If I keep these ideas in my head as I play out the end, I find they help guide me towards the situations – and outcomes – that I want.

In this puzzle, we're Bottcher and yellow, and we want to play simple this early in the end. My first inclination would be to throw a guard, protect my Y1 shot rock and cut the scoring area to the four-foot. Mickey isn't so sure.

"Up 4-0, a guard doesn't sound right," he says. "You throw another guard, then there's more junk out there, he's got R2 under his corner – and he's throwing. Those things start to add up. It's a shape that doesn't sound like your keywords: clean, simple, in the rings."

But I'm lying shot and could be well-buried, I argue.

"It's just a bit risky, certainly too risky at the top levels", Mickey replies. "Say you set up staggered guards but leave your shot rock a bit open. They might be able to tap it out and roll the opposite wing. You're playing defence so you would have to hit that, and if you roll out, they'll loop under the stagger, sit two well-buried with hammer and you're looking at giving up 3.

I never thought of that. Three-shot window, three-shot window, I repeat to myself.

"And besides", he continues, "you have a very powerful Y2 in the twelve-foot right now. It's controlling that four-foot area. Putting a guard in front of it takes all its power away.

"Having said all that, you're not playing at the top level and I could live with a tight guard in a club game. Stick it a couple feet short on the centre line. If they try double it off with Y2, it could kill R2, so they might leave it there, giving you a chance to get something behind it later, shrink the scoring area, and draw play to the middle. And a nice, tight centre is always good to run back if we get in trouble."

But this isn't a club game and Mickey, Kevin Martin in the commentary booth, and Brendan Bottcher have conspired to overrule my guard call. What's the solution?

"We've seen Bottcher call the Wing Nullifier in the previous puzzle, getting one edge-buried in front of R2. In this case, it's not quite as powerful. R2 is a little higher and so it's tough to sit second shot.

"But you would be playing in the rings and keeping the clutter down. And that rock will be hard to remove, always sitting there and cutting the scoring area even if it's not second shot. It's probably what I would play in this situation."

You wouldn't call what Bottcher called here, I ask, slightly surprised. The tick on the R1 corner opened up that R2 and brought play back to the centre.

Mickey explains his choice. "Only a handful of teams in the world would play that shot. It's super-difficult and it's maybe one-in-ten for good club or even competitive teams. Most pro teams wouldn't throw it.

"Brendan's call has a lot to do with the score. Up 4-0, you can afford to be a little brave and throw the Hail Mary here. If it doesn't work out (and it kinda doesn't, leaving staggered guards at the front of the house that Shuster tries to get under), Bottcher's got the firepower to play some doubles to get out of trouble and keep them to a deuce at most. For the rest of us, it's not a shot that we're going to be successful with on a regular basis. I would play a more makeable shot that plays to those keywords of ours."

I think Mickey's basically recommending that I 'Keep It Simple Stupid'. I'm going to take that in the best possible way.

So the lessons that I can take away as an aspiring Skip? First, know the type of end I want to play to increase the odds of me achieving my ideal and acceptable outcomes. Use my keywords to create a mental picture of that end, and let the picture guide my shot selection as the end plays out.

Secondly, favour shots that are makeable and have good outcomes over shots that have fantastic outcomes but are rarely made. One-hundred percent of pretty good is a lot better than zero percent of perfect.

Mickey's Last Word: "Keep your end goal in mind. Play early shots that favour your desired outcome, or at least avoid your unacceptable."

Puzzle #16

Come on, come on. This is your big chance to apply pressure and take control of this game. Your Lead has set up a nice guard and got one buried behind it, while their Lead chased, crashed your corner guard and has been removed. Now you've got a free one to really make life difficult for them. But how? Here's the situation:

- 3rd end of 10
- You're yellow
- You're down by 1
- You have hammer
- It's your Second's first shot
- About a five-foot swing on good ice

C'mon Skip, let's use this mulligan to take control. What's your club call and pro call – and why?

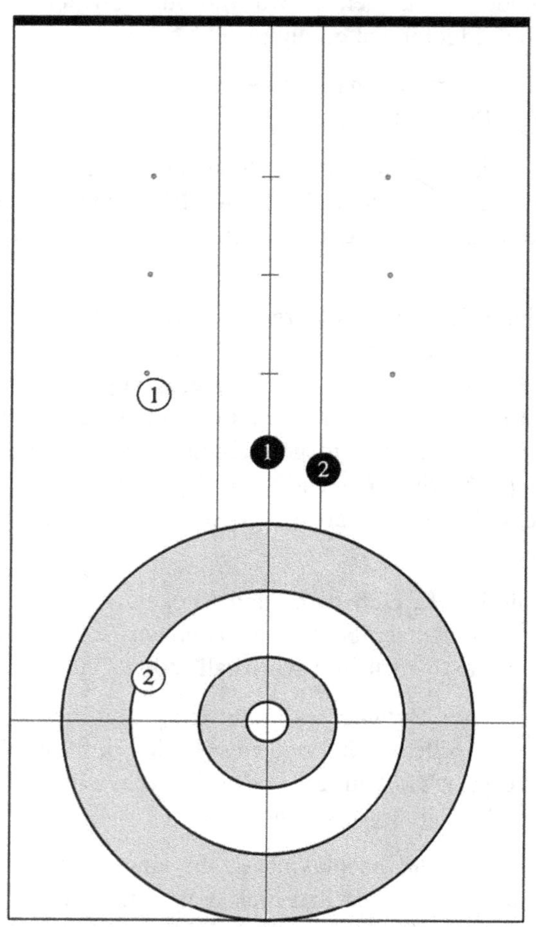

A Time & A Place

As they say, nothing is certain except for death and taxes – and that's especially true in our sport. No matter how well you set up an end, all your hard work can be undone by a flash of brilliance from your opposition – or ineptitude from your own team.

However, it is possible to say that some setups – or structures – in curling are more likely to lead to certain outcomes. And we see that here in the end between Laura Walker and Jennifer Jones at the 2021 Scotties. Walker leaves the double red guards and gets into a whole heap o' trouble and eventually coughs up a steal of 2. How did this happen, Mickey?

"It's the third end and Laura's down by 1 with hammer. A deuce would be good here, a blank OK, a force is not the end of the world, but a steal is unacceptable. Manitoba has just crashed a guard and so Laura's trying to generate her deuce here. She has a 'free one', and she's probably thinking something like 'Let's get two in the house and make them sweat.'"

I kinda like that strategy, I say. One of my yellows lying under a guard at the side, one lying in the four-foot under cover. They're gonna be chasing me until we count the rocks. What's the problem?

"Well, the problem is those two red tight centre guards," Mickey replies. "They're going to be a thorn in your side the whole end. You named them 'power rocks' in an earlier puzzle, and these are them. They're in a very powerful position – tight to the top of the rings, hovering over the four-foot area, not staggered. Manitoba is going to threaten that centre area as long as they are there."

He continues. "We know that if you decide to go around any centre guards, it's fairly predictable that it's going to be a messy end played in the centre. If those guards are tight and they're the opposition's, and if you don't have some backing for protection, they can be used to dig you out or tap you back or whatever. Holding those cards in that 'Control Zone' at the top of the rings, the other team has a better chance of creating pressure or escaping trouble than you do. They're powerful assets for them, not you."

Okay, those rocks sound like they are the beasts of the curling world – truly power rocks. If they're mine, then I have the power. If they're not, then I don't.

So coming around their power rocks without backing is not a good idea, I concede. What's the alternative?

"It's really important to think about timing, or where you are in the end. It's early here – we're only throwing Second's rocks – so structure matters a lot more than lying shot. It's not like we're into the final few shots of the end and trying to cash in our chips for a score. We don't need to be lying shot rock yet. We do need to set up a situation that favours us and puts them in a worse spot.

"For me, the shot to play is to double off the guards, hitting the back R2 first, removing it and pushing R1 to the side, right out or perhaps for an- other corner (right).

"Think about the structure you'd have then. Your shooter would stay in the centre, but it's your rock and now it's in a powerful position to control what's in the four-foot. And you'd have a corner guard, maybe two, and a rock partly buried behind them above tee.

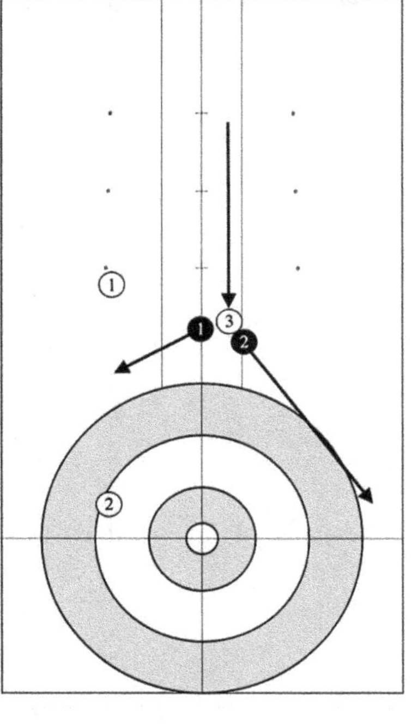

"Now we're starting to see a structure that can lead to offence down the line. Buried rocks, lots of breathing room, control over the four-foot. And all that's done by making one easy shot."

What happens after Walker leaves the red guards? Well, neither team covers themselves in glory and there are several missed shots. But that's curling – it's is not a game of perfect.

However, true to Mickey's prediction, it does end up in a messy, complicated end where Team Alberta is throwing difficult shots. Laura Walker is reduced to asking for tricky hit-and-rolls and even though things are going her way for a while, one miss creates a mess, and she ends up without an easy escape to get her single with her last.

Would this be the same at club level, I wonder?

"Even if your opponents are incapable of running back short guards, leaving them there means play is always coming to the middle and setting up congestion in the four-foot. That shape doesn't sound like your keywords of open, uncluttered, room to score – the type of words you want to be thinking about when trying to score with hammer. It does sound like complicated, cluttered, tricky – words that your competition would like to hear if they're trying to keep you to 1 or perhaps steal. So even though club curlers won't have a high rate of success on runbacks, those rocks sitting in the control zone are still a problem. Clearing them out and hopefully rolling to set up another corner guard is still a good idea."

This is a pro game, but there are still lessons that I can apply to my level. First of all, that keyword idea is really useful as I play an end. Knowing my goals, I need to create a mental picture of the shape I'm trying to achieve. Keywords can help me do that.

Secondly, timing matters. This is not the decision phase when I decide to go for my ideal or settle for my acceptable, or the finale when I looking to lock in a result. This is the set-up phase, and I need to focus on creating good conditions that favour me and not them.

Third, rocks tight to the rings in the centre have much power. We leave opposition power rocks there at our peril.

Finally, coming around tight opposition power rocks without freezing to something for protection is likely to lead to a difficult end for me. The other team will hold those cards until they need them and will have a better chance of creating pressure or escaping it than I will.

Mickey's Last Word: "During the set-up phase, focus upon creating a structure that will lead to your desired outcomes. Respect opposition rocks in the Control Zone."

Puzzle #17

This is an end where you'll be falling all over yourself to get a deuce. But your opponents have brought play into the house and you've decided to hit with your Lead's second rock. Of course, taking rocks out of play is never going to score you a bundle. And you're behind. You need to come up with something creative – but what? Here's the situation:

- 6th end of 10
- You're red
- You're down by 1
- You have hammer
- It's your Second's first
- About 4.5 feet of swing

C'mon Skip, give us a shot that keeps you upstanding in this game. What's your call – and why?

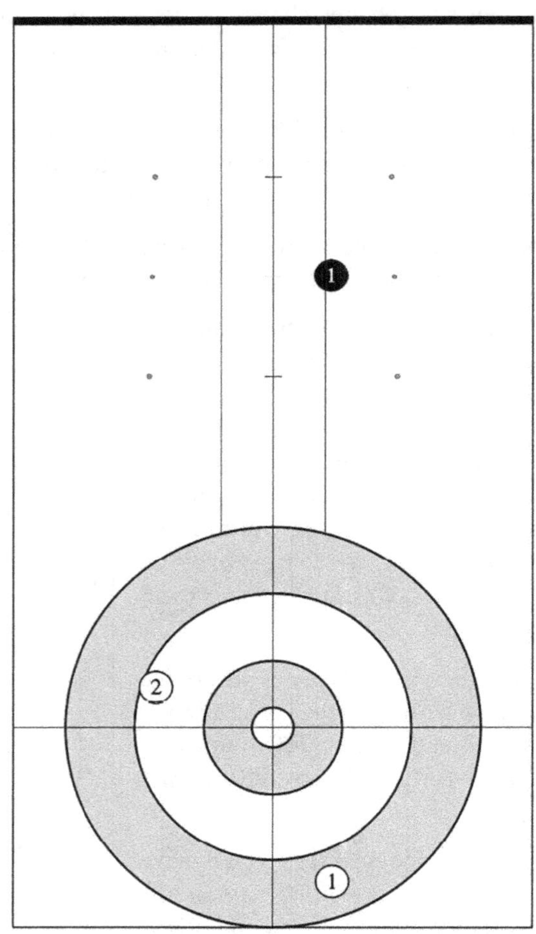

The Eve of Destruction

The sharpest amongst you will have no doubt spotted the reference in the puzzle to Eve's small tumble and are quietly chuckling to yourselves. It's a good one, eh? Well, I thought it was. My kids would laugh.

Of course, we've all been there and kicked a rock or toppled over one we forgot about. I suspect that where many of us haven't been is drawing to a rock well behind tee line, in a position that won't even give us shot rock. Isn't it an age-old rule to not be playing behind tee line? Does Eve (four-time World Junior Champion, four-time European Champion, two-time World Champion, and Olympic Gold Medallist) actually know what she's doing? Maybe it's just luck that got her to where she is.

"Eve knows exactly what she's doing," replies Mickey. "This is a great example of a Skip on top of their game and dictating play against a very competent opponent. It's a really patient call that sets up a low-risk, low-complexity chance for a deuce – and it pays off."

How can I get these so wrong, over and over again, I wonder? And what the heck is going on in this one?

"Think about timing," Mickey advises. "We're in that set-up phase, so Eve's simply creating conditions and building the shape of an end that favours her. What she's doing here is putting a rock in a safe place that can't easily be removed and is starting to work towards some offence. You need rocks in play to generate offensive opportunities. This one's frozen under a guard, so it's going to stay for a while and help build up some play.

"Look at what Sweden has if Eve freezes. Anna could peel the guard but that would let Scotland hit to lie 2 and then Anna's got to find a double or give up an easy deuce. So Sweden's almost certainly going to follow them down and freeze back to negate Scotland's rock, especially since Anna's freeze would leave her sitting two."

But how are a bunch of freezes behind tee helping Eve, I ask?

"Well, if you're the team behind, getting the team that's in front to throw draw shots, especially behind a corner guard, is usually a very good thing at pro or club level. Get some complication going, set up some building blocks and generate a chance at some offence. Get a pocket going or get something to freeze to. Keep your rocks in play and see what happens as the end develops."

Okay, I get that principle. Rocks in play and complication mean offensive opportunities. But Eve's asking her teammate to play behind the tee. Isn't that a cardinal sin?

"Well here's the thing: it's not a risky play. The last thing Eve can do here is give up a steal to go 2 down. Remember the three questions we discussed in Puzzle #1. At 1-down with hammer in the 6th, Eve's ideal outcome is 2+, her acceptable is a force or a blank, and her unacceptable is a steal. Now imagine if you went tee-line buried under the guard. Sweden comes down and freezes, then you freeze, and all of the sudden there are rocks building up in the four-foot in front of tee line and things could get tricky for you.

"But freezing to the back secures one of Eve's rocks in the rings and encourages Sweden to start playing draw shots and leave rocks in play. And it keeps the front clear to avoid getting into any complication that might set up a steal. The rock about to be thrown will never score, but it draws play to the area Eve wants to play in. Early in the end, don't think about who has shot rock. Think about how the house is shaping up. By looping one around, she's creating conditions that favour her here in the set-up phase."

What develops here is a cluster of rocks behind the tee line– with the front wide open. As we discussed in Puzzle #2, the early part of an end is about building shapes that point towards your ideal or acceptable outcomes. This shape points towards Eve's. If her team executes and gets one or two misses, then they're going to get a crack at scoring 2, with an open front-of-house and very little risk of giving up a steal.

"Timing matters," adds Mickey. "If this is Third's second or Eve's first, then she's not going to freeze deep where it's easy for Sweden to freeze back and basically eliminate it. If there were fewer rocks left to play and not much chance of creating a mess that could lead to a steal, Eve would try to wrap one around and put it top-four where she might get a Swedish miss and pick up an easy deuce.

"But this is Second's first and there are still eleven rocks to come. She can't afford a mess in front of the tee so she simply puts one back rings where it's secure for the time being, and she gets a building block that might lead to a score as the end develops."

I guess 'Don't play behind the tee' isn't the hard and fast rule it used to be. I'll take that one off my list.

"Well, there are very few hard-and-fast rules when it comes to skipping," Mickey advises. "You need to think of them as suggestions. In general, you'd rather have a rock in front of tee so it's still available to promote back into scoring position and they can't freeze to it for shot.

"But Eve is focused on the type of end she wants: rocks in play, a sniff at some offence, no drama. So by ignoring that 'golden rule' and freezing to the back, Eve is securing a rock in there and building a low-risk situation – a building block – where good things might happen while maintaining all that breathing room out front. I like it a lot. It's a shot that I play all the time."

What are the takeaways I can use at any level of curling? First of all, during the set-up phase of the end, keep in mind the key factors or keywords that point in the direction of my desired outcome. Here, it's 'rocks in play', 'soft weight shots', 'open front'. Use these terms to guide the type of end I want to play.

Secondly, this tactic of freezing to a rock deep in the rings under cover is a low-risk way to generate a chance at some offence. It encourages the other team to start playing soft-weight shots rather than hitting, complicates things and gives me a sniff at offence while keeping the front open for my last shot if things don't go my way. It's pretty sweet.

Mickey's Last Word: "Think about the general type of end you want to play. Here, 1-down in the 6th, Eve wants to score so she wants rocks in play. But she doesn't want to take any chances. She sees that if she draws, Anna has to follow her down. Now Eve will have one in the rings, some rocks as catchers at the back but the front is still open for her single if she needs it. By playing this shot early in the end, she's building the shape of an end that could lead to a low-risk score, maybe even a deuce."

Puzzle #18

Oh man, you've got half of that medal between your teeth already, biting down and smiling for the cameras. Sure, the young whippersnappers took a 2 off you in the first end, but that won't last. They're young and likely very nervous, here in the biggest game of their lives. Your squad is vastly more experienced with Brier and world championship golds in your bag. All you have to do is apply pressure and watch them break apart like a cheap piñata. But how? Here's the situation:

- 2nd end of 10
- You're red
- You're down by 2
- But you have hammer
- It's your Second's first shot
- About four feet of swing on arena ice

C'mon Skip, take out the big stick, give them a good whack and watch them spill points all over the place. What's your call – and why?

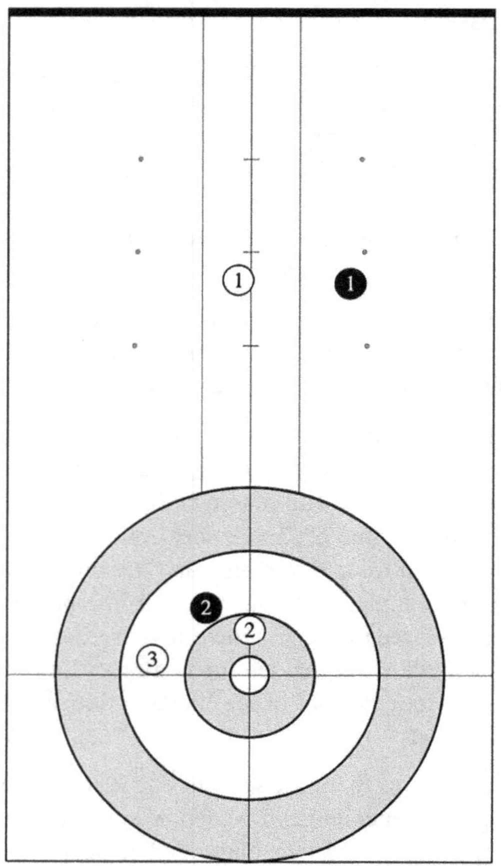

Strategy & Tactics, Order & Junk

Before we dive into this epic contest between Jeff Stoughton and Brad Gushue at the 2005 Olympic Trials, we need to define some terms.

Most of the situations in this book deal with tactical considerations – what's the best shot to throw in this end.

This puzzle, in contrast, deals with Jeff Stoughton's strategy – how he sets out to play this entire game. It's about knowing your team and your competitors, and about picking an approach that plays to your strengths and their weaknesses. Are you going to keep it clean, wait for some half-shots and seize your opportunities? Or are you going to junk it up, force the other guys to play technical shots and create opportunities for yourself? Perhaps you'll probe here and there, applying pressure where you can, but not become reckless.

In this game, Jeff Stoughton must think he has experience on his side, with two Briers and a World gold medal around his neck. The team from Newfoundland – except for the highly-decorated Russ Howard – were largely unknown and were just setting off on their careers. Mickey says that was a crucial factor in this call.

"If you think your team can outplay the other team, why wouldn't you throw a freeze, junk it up, get lots of rocks in play and make them play tough shots?" he asks. "I don't know Jeff well, but I bet he was thinking that Gushue and Nichols – at that time, very young guys in the biggest game of their lives – would buckle under the pressure. He was probably thinking that if he keeps piling it on, sooner or later he would get a couple of big ends.

"And that suits his style anyway. He always played an aggressive game with rocks in play. Play the angles, try to develop offensive situations, and generate some points."

But didn't Russ Howard play that style too?

"Yes, he liked to play an aggressive game. But in 2005, Gushue and Nichols were unknown. Stoughton probably thought his team could outplay them on the more complicated and precise, technical shots. That turned out to be wrong."

So what are the technical shots?

"Taps and freezes and hack-weighters and runbacks all need high levels of precision. And of course, hit-and-rolls are the toughest. They're the types of shots that are played when teams leave lots of rocks in play. You don't see them a lot on wide open, simple ends."

We know from the video that Stoughton played the freeze into the pocket so that neither of his rocks could be easily removed, complicating things and trying to win the angles. He kept lots of rocks in play and forced Howard to call delicate shots. What would Stoughton call if he was keeping it simple?

"To simplify the situation, Jeff would hit Y2 and a roll over to lie 3rd shot," replies Mickey. "Russ would chase their shot rock (R2) on top of the four-foot and maybe leave his stones grouped. Stoughton might then have a double to sit two with hammer.

"So, the hit-and-roll across would be a safe, patient call where you avoid a technical, tippy tappy situation in the centre and play to make sure you have the four-foot to draw to get your single if necessary. You might get a deuce, but you'd be unlikely to give up a steal.

"In contrast, the draw to centre is more aggressive, you'll get into some technical shots, and you might set up a situation to score a bundle. But you risk creating a situation you can't get out of – if you don't execute."

Stoughton goes all-in, creates a guddle in the centre and tries to win the angles. When the dust settles in this end, his team has out-executed the whippersnappers, and he scores 2.

"I think at the club level, the freeze or quiet tap is a good call because it has options," says Mickey. "Anywhere from top-eight to back-twelve is likely to leave you in a decent position. The alternative – chasing a half-buried rock with hack to board weight – could result in a roll-out or rub the guard and you've lost the advantage of this nice pocket."

Jeff Stoughton's strategy – his approach to the game – worked in this end. Unfortunately for him, it didn't pay off over the entire game. The team from 'The Rock' were equal to the technical challenge that Stoughton posed, beat him down the stretch and went on to get their choppers on gold for Canada in 2006.

As a Newbie, aspiring Skip, what can I take away from this puzzle? First, strategy is different from tactics. Strategy is the overall approach to the game, given the strengths and weaknesses of you and your opponents. Tactics are really about your plan for a specific end or situation.

Secondly, if you think you can outplay your opponents and are better technical curlers, perhaps an aggressive strategy with lots of rocks in play and lots of offensive shots like freezes and taps and draws might be the best approach. If you think you're a weaker squad, perhaps a defensive approach with lots of hits and a simplified house might be better. If you're not sure, a balanced, probing approach might be best where you get aggressive when you can and defensive when you need to.

Mickey's Last Word: "First, look for pockets when you need offence and it's early in the end. Secondly, play to your team's strengths and the other guys' weaknesses. If you're a good technical team, look to play a complicated game and put the pressure on."

Puzzle #19

Not the Curling Smurfs! Up by 2, lying 1 top button – these little guys know how to make life difficult for you. Everyone knows that the closer to the ice you are, the greater the advantage in this game, and you guys tower over them by at least six-inches. Anyway, you are where you are – fighting for your lives against one of the best teams ever. What to do, what to do? Here's the situation:

- Second end of 10
- You're yellow
- You're down by 2
- You have hammer
- It's your Second's first shot
- Five feet of swing

C'mon Skip, give us a shot that turns the Curling Smurfs blue. What's your call – and why?

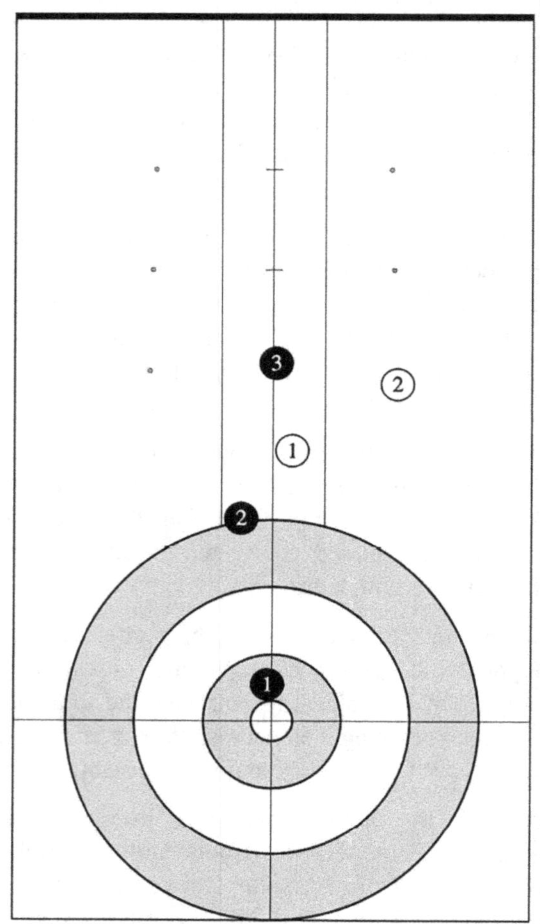

The Pivot to Acceptable

After hundreds of hours of discussions with Mickey, this Newbie has come to appreciate that early in an end, a Skip needs to see the abstract shapes or conditions that can help or hinder in meeting his goals for the end. The threats and opportunities start off kinda blurry in the distance – a set of rocks down the centre or stones out to the side – and gradually, they come into sharper focus as the end progresses. This puzzle is all about seeing how an end is shaping up and deciding when to do something about it. We're not setting up anymore. We're making a decision to pivot.

"We've discussed the importance of knowing your ideal, acceptable and unacceptable outcomes," Mickey reminds me. "It's just as important to be aware of how an end is shaping up – and when to switch from going for your ideal outcome to making sure you at least get something acceptable."

"Here, we're just getting going, and Ross Patterson is trying to set up a shape that could lead to his ideal outcome, a deuce. So he wants some rocks in play but preferably out to the side so he can use them to hide one or two and bring those in to score with his Skip stones later. That's typically the shape of an end that points towards a deuce or more.

"What he doesn't want is a cluster in the four-foot, shrinking down the scoring area and leading to a force of 1. And he definitely can't let his opponent get buried in there and give up a steal.

"So what he sees in our puzzle isn't very good. The shape – a set of staggered centre guards, a Swedish rock (R2) at the top of the twelve-foot and another one biting top button – definitely favours Niklas Edin. Scotland can't squeeze two in behind Edin's rock on the button to get a deuce – and even getting shot rock would be tough – so they need to do something about that. And they can't do something about that until they get rid of some of the junk down the centre. He needs to bail."

Aha, the proverbial bail point, I exclaim!

"That's right. Ross must decide whether to continue attacking to try to score 2 – his ideal outcome – or switch to defence to make sure he takes his unacceptable outcome off the table – a steal. So, the choice is to give up on 2 for now, keep the blank alive, but make sure you get your 1. It won't be ideal, but at least it's acceptable."

I struggle with this part now and then. 'Attacking' in other sports usually means moves with lots of power and force, but not so much in curling. Attacking shots in our game are often low-weight, delicate plays that position rocks under cover or in other hard-to-remove places. Defensive shots are usually big-weight takeouts and runbacks that remove stones from play and keep the score down. It's kinda confusing. Sometimes I wish this game were a little less contrarian.

Anyway, Ross is switching to defence here. Sweden's rocks are too well-positioned to ignore by playing delicate shots around his corner guards, so he decides to clear out some granite from in front of that four-foot scoring area to make sure he at least gets his single. But what to play?

"The aim is to clear up the middle, dig out as many rocks as you can and make sure you get 1 at the end. Duncan Menzies played a pistol of a shot, cleared out the stagger and shot rock, and rolled to the corner. Not only did they remove the threatening reds in the centre, they now have three yellow guards to perhaps still find a way to score a deuce. An elite player can do that. But at club level, maybe it takes a few goes. Even if it does, you need to hammer away and open it up. You can't let them steal and go 3-up."

I can't see many of my teammates making the shot that Duncan played. I think I might start by addressing R2.

"I suppose a club or aspiring team could play a quiet weight hit on R2, hang around the rings and see if the opposition might hit you. That could give you a chance to chase the R1 shot rock a little later. But you're giving them the chance to get around the stagger. I think that's another reason they played to kill 2 or 3 reds instead of the ones in the rings"

Back to our pro game and to be a little contrarian myself, I point out that Sweden stole 1. Maybe clearing out the centre wasn't so effective after all?

"You have to understand that there's a monumental difference between tactics and execution," Mickey explains. "Curling is a game where most shots don't work out perfectly, and some don't work out at all. We try to develop good conditions and situations and shapes that increase the chances of us meeting our goals, and then cash in on those shapes with our last couple of shots.

"But one or two missed shots or one or two pistols from the other guys can scupper all our plans and put us on the wrong end of the stick. When that happens, we just have to bail out and salvage the end. Of course, the bailout shots have to be made as well. The Scottish Third flashed a hack-weight hit so you'd expect to have trouble securing a positive outcome. Good execution trumps great tactics all the time. If Scotland had made a few more good ones down the stretch, and if Sweden would be kind enough to miss the occasional half-shot, then Ross's switch to defence would have at least allowed him to score."

So what are this Newbie's takeaways? First, I'm thinking more about 'shapes' and 'conditions.' Offensive shapes include corner guards and backing rocks and pockets and rocks spread about in hard-to-remove positions. Defensive shapes include centre guards and guddles in the four-foot with small scoring areas, fewer rocks in play and no backing or pockets. Those are the shapes I will try to spot as the end develops.

And secondly, I'm going to start asking myself – even after just a few shots – whether the shapes are building in my favour. If they're not, I'm switching from pursuing my 'ideal outcome' and concentrating on taking my 'unacceptable outcome' off the table. Sometimes acceptable is good enough.

Mickey's Last Word: "Recognize when the shape of an end tells you it's time to bail out. If you bail early enough, you might just get a chance to create a little offence later on."

Puzzle #20

It's showtime here in the main ring, and you're punching for victory. Sadly, the other guy has landed five blows to your three, and you're feeling a little beat up. But the bout is not yet decided, and you could throw a mean hook here, maybe catch him a little off-balance and plot your way to victory. But how? Here's the situation:

- 6th end of 10
- You're red
- You're down by 2
- You have hammer
- It's your Skip's last shot
- About five feet of swing

C'mon Skip, give 'em a shot that floats like butterfly and stings like bee. What's your call – and why?

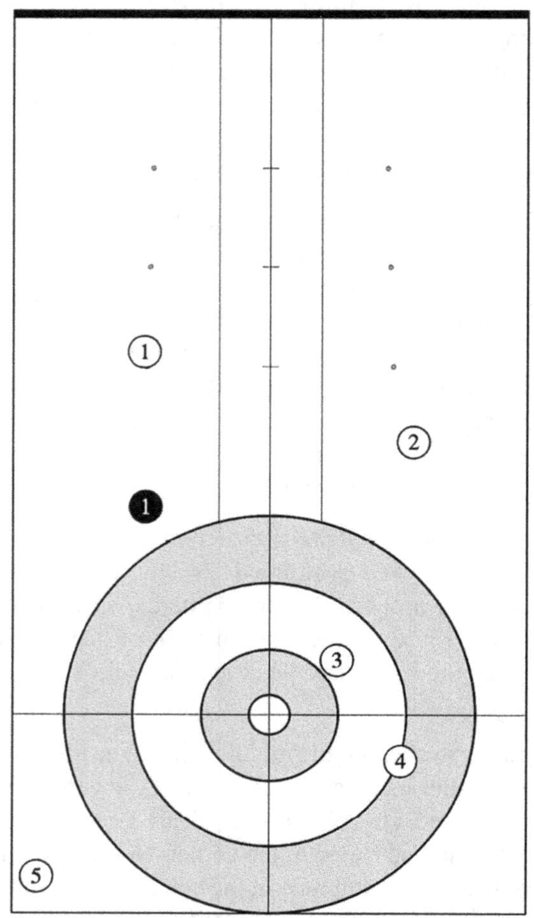

Risk and Reward and Acceptable Outcomes

"So it's decision time," says Mickey. "Dunstone (red) is down by 2 in the 6th and set out in this end to score his deuce. But that goal is long gone now, and he's facing a decision about an easy force or a risky blank.

"Normally, you'd just go for the blank. A blank is almost always better than a force, right. But the double he's facing is no gimme. He's got to hit two-thirds of the top rock and roll out. A hair less and he stuffs Y3 and gives up a steal. A hair thicker and he leaves Gushue's back yellow, maybe rolls out of the eight-foot and gives up a steal. So there's a degree of risk involved in going for a blank. What's the best thing to do?"

If I apply Mickey's three questions about ideal, acceptable, and unacceptable outcomes, it seems to me that it's acceptable to take a single and stay alive, and unacceptable to give up a steal and go 3-down to a team like Gushue's. That suggests the better play is the easier nose hit for the force. But of course, getting forced is never good and I bet it leads to a lower likelihood of winning than blanking and keeping hammer.

But does it? The good folks at CurlingZone.com track worldwide ranking events and compile statistics about the likelihood of winning from various situations. In this puzzle, Dunstone faces three potential outcomes: a blank, a force, or a steal. CurlingZone says the probabilities of winning given each result are:

- Make the double and blank to stay 2-down with hammer with four ends to play: 21.8% chance of victory
- Nose hit to get forced and be 1-down without: 19.6%
- Or, give up a steal by missing the double and go 3-down with hammer: 9.4%

Clearly, Team Dunstone is up against it here. Make either shot and they have only a 1-in-5 chance of winning. But go for the double, miss it and give up a steal? That cuts their chances of winning in half. In this situation, the third rail is giving up a steal. Touch that thing and you've got a ninety percent chance of getting fried. I'm sure we can all agree that if we were Dunstone in this situation, we would rather be Gushue.

"For a big-weight hitter like Matt, making the double and rolling out is more likely than it is for you and me," says Mickey. "Matt probably makes that double three-out-of-four times. You and I make it a lot less often. But if it is the one time he stuffs it, Matt likely loses the game right here. Going 3-down with four ends to play against a team with clean-up hitters like Brett Gallant and Mark Nichols, well, that's just too much to ask."

I think it's surprising that the statistics show virtually no difference between being 2-down with hammer and being 1-down without. Both hover around the 20% mark. And perhaps that tilts the decision in favour of going for the easy force versus the risky blank.

"Matt's coach at the time was an analytics guy," Mickey explains. "I'd be surprised if the players didn't know that their odds are pretty much the same regardless of the force or blank. When the hit-and-stick is virtually assured vs the double-and-roll-out blank being a little iffy, they make the right call.

"The guys do show an excellent feel for where they are in the game. You hear them map it out, saying, 'Force in the seventh and a deuce in the eighth.' That would get them level, and then it's a two-end game and force-deuce from there gives them the win."

Sadly for Saskatchewan, it doesn't work out that way. Dunstone takes the single here, but Gushue manages to blank in the seventh and take a single in the eighth to get back to 2-up. Dunstone scores his deuce in the ninth to level the score, and Gushue draws for his single point in the tenth to win. It turns out the odds were correct.

What about at club or improver level, Mickey? Do the same stats apply?

"No, at that level I'd say it's even more important to take your one and stay close. Of course, there are no stats on club play, but miss your double and go down 3 with hammer with three ends to play is definitely worse than making your nose hit to be down 1 without. At the club level, steals occur fairly often so keeping the gap small is important."

What is my takeaway as wannabe competitive curler? The big lesson for me is that 1-down without hammer leaves me pretty much in the same position as 2-down with going into the last part of the game – both suck! I'm only winning one-in-every-five games from that position. Better to be Gushue than Dunstone here. Get the lead, keep the lead, win games. That's my takeaway!

Mickey's Last Word: "Having a plan about how you're going to win beats not having a plan," says Mickey. "But the one universal truth in curling is that execution beats tactics all the time. Whether you're going for the double-and-blank or the nose-for-1, if you don't execute, your stats and tactics and plans don't count for very much."

Puzzle #21

Well, it's your unique privilege to play as World Champions for the whole year, but maybe reputation counts for nothing in this game. These upstarts have had you on the run since the first end, building a lead and playing you like a fiddle. But thankfully, we've seen the last of that pesky four-rock rule that lets front runners sail off into the distance. Now, with the new improved five-rock free guard zone, anything is possible – and this could be your game to win. But how? Here's the situation:

- 8th end of 10
- You're yellow
- You're down by 2
- You have hammer
- It's your Second's first shot
- About a 5-foot swing

C'mon Skip, give us a shot that makes you thank the Almighty (i.e. the World Curling Federation) for creating the five-rock rule. What's your call – and why?

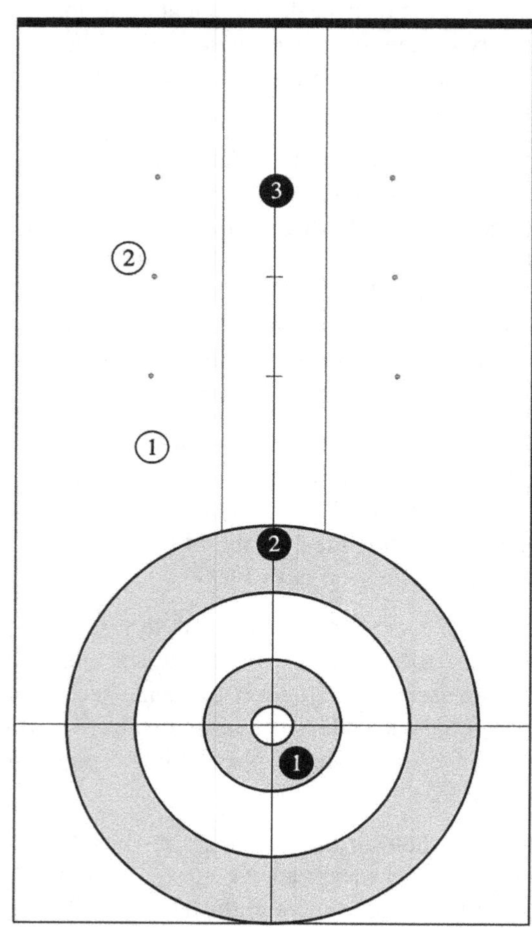

Changing Gears

Canada Link

Rest of World

This puzzle is about pivoting to a different type of offence under the five-rock rule. What's going on?

Silvana Tirinzoni (yellow) is down by 2 late in the game and needs points. She's thrown the very aggressive double corners and would like to use them.

On the other hand, Kerri Einarson of Canada (red) is ahead by 2. She'd love a steal, is happy enough with a force, could live with giving up a 2, but might self-combust if they gave up more than that. Her aim here is to play defence and make sure they don't give up a bundle.

To me, it seems like Kerri is playing the 'Come to Momma' defence we spoke about in the Fundamentals section. I think she's got them stacked up down the middle pretty well and the Swiss are going to have to start clearing them out. Mickey's not so sure.

"At first glance, you might look at the Canadian set-up and think it's pretty good. You see that while Switzerland was setting up their guards, Canada has taken up position in the four-foot scoring zone, setting up three down the middle and dragging the Swiss away from their corner guards. Einarson wants to force Tirinzoni to deal with her rocks in the centre area, hopefully creating a congested, tippy tappy end where someone scores 1. That's what Russ means when he talks about the Swiss wanting to use their guards, but Canada isn't going to let them.

"But look at R1. It's slipped a couple of feet deep and that provides an opening for the Swiss. That two-foot overthrow proves to be the decisive factor in the whole end.

"We see that after five rocks have been played, we get to our puzzle shot and Switzerland has a decision to make. Normally, they'd want to clear R3 and R2 and maybe even get R1 too. That way, they put Canada back to square one, develop some breathing room in the middle and maybe bring their corner guards into play later. That's the type of end they'd prefer to play.

"The alternative is to switch gears, abandon the corner guards for the foreseeable future, draw to the four-foot and try to win the battle of the angles to score their multiple. And that's what Tirinzoni does here."

So why chase to the middle instead of clearing out, I ask? Surely Tirinzoni has the firepower to clean the centre up.

"The slight misplacement of Canada's first three rocks opens the door for the Swiss pivot," Mickey says. "Lead's first is 2-3 feet heavy and behind the tee, providing backing for the Swiss and actually hurting Canada. You have to recognize that to score a 3-ball, the Swiss need to set-up a couple of rocks protected in the rings. One way to get that is to use their guards. The other way to get that is to find some backing or a pocket-take advantage of opposition stones if it's advantageous. By slipping deep with their first, Canada is setting up a potential catcher and loses the chance to own the top of the rings."

"The other set-up problem is that R2 is a bit light, serving more as a guard than anything. You want that to be a little deeper to shrink the scoring area and be either frozen to your shot on button or sitting in around the eight-foot, so the opposition can't deal with both rocks with one shot.

"And finally, although it's good for R3 to be long and in line with R2 so the Swiss can't play a double without leaving the shooter in the centre, it's so long that Canada can't use it for a runback either. The Swiss give up on taking it away and start to see it as a potential asset, providing cover for anything they get into good position in the centre.

"Ideally, you want this guard three or four feet outside the rings, depending on how swingy the ice is. Swingy ice, tighter guard. But anyway, the aim is to be tight enough to make chasing the central rocks hard, but not so tight that the chasers could chip the guard and roll in behind cover or make the runback easier."

In our puzzle shot, Tirinzoni decides to give up on her corners and on clearing up the centre, and comes around the red guards and secure a rock for later. She uses the counter-clockwise turn because the too-deep R1 provides a potential catcher as long as she gets it edge-buried. And if Canada chases a rock on that side of the sheet, it might create some action on the side of the Swiss guards. The Swiss want to be playing on that side of the house.

"This would be the right call for most club teams as well," says Mickey. "Even though we'd prefer not to play around centre guards, we are getting desperate down 2 late in the game. And there is no chance to clean things up in the middle, so we need to use what we have."

Canada could then hit something on Second's last but commits to their plan to congest things in the four-foot and plays the draw. Unfortunately, they compound their error, coming deep again. Tirinzoni pounces, cleverly tapping the reds to make them vulnerable, Canada scrambles, Switzerland outplays them and scores 3.

What can I take away as an aspiring Skip who hasn't (yet) reached the professional ranks? First of all, rock placement is key if I'm going to play Come to Momma defence. To shrink the scoring area, my first rock needs to be tight to the button – but never behind it. My second needs to be in the rings, either frozen or in the eight-foot, but not leaving an easy double with my first; those two rocks shouldn't be able to be removed with one stone. And finally, my guard has to be tight enough to make the chase on my rocks in the rings difficult, but not so tight that they can chip it and roll into the rings behind their guard. Now I see what Mickey means about defence being about precise rock placement!

Secondly, I need to be mindful that I can always 'cut bait' and fish in the middle if the situation dictates. Here, the Canadians have offered the Swiss building blocks in the form of the rock that slipped back-tee and in the form of the long guard that's too long. If my main tactic isn't shaping up, maybe I shouldn't overlook a gift horse in the mouth (or something like that).

Mickey's Last Word: "This is a good example of why Lead rocks are so important, and how a top team is constantly reassessing the situation and changing gears towards something more promising. It's often an option to pivot to the middle, but you just have to recognize that you'll need to outplay your opponents in that four-foot if you're going to avoid the force or steal. In this case, the Swiss did."

Puzzle #22

Well, some days you're the dog and some days you're the hydrant. Here, you are definitely not the dog! How you managed to get all your rocks behind tee and all theirs above it is a bit of a mystery. You might want to have a quiet word with your team about being light and not heavy. In any event, you've got to figure out some way to clean up this mess. A little magic is required to avoid the steal – but what? Here's the situation:

- 6th end of 10
- Score is tied
- You're red
- You have hammer
- It's your Skip's first shot
- About four feet of swing on good ice

C'mon Skip, give us a shot to restore your status as Top Dog. What's your call – and why?

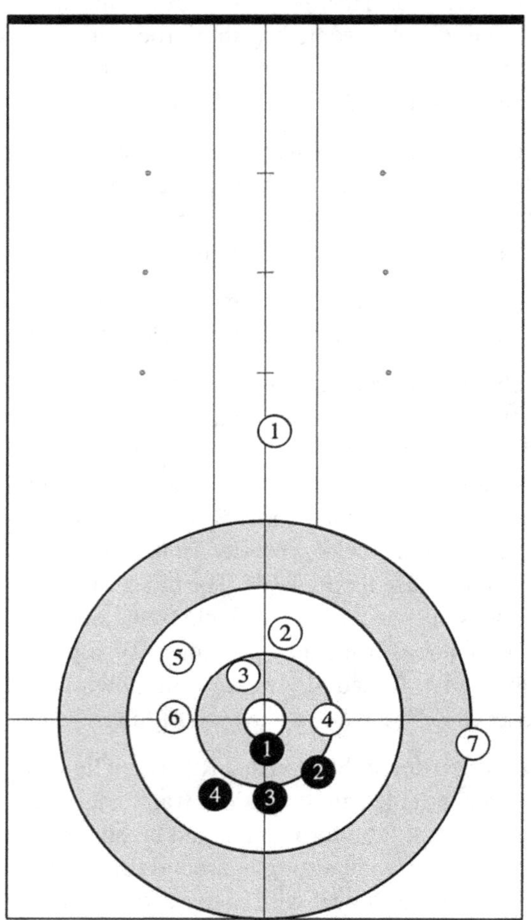

If You Play With Fire…

We've bookmarked the video right at the beginning of this end so you can watch how Canada's misfortune develops. Of course, we've all been there. Going from lying five to giving up a steal just a couple of shots later. It's an awful game sometimes.

Halfway through this end, Jennifer Jones and her team seemed to be in a great position, sitting a bundle within the four-foot and seemingly cruising to a big score. Just one hit and a couple of taps from Korea turned the entire situation around. What's going on?

"There are a few things to recognize here," says Mickey. "The first is about the shape of the end. Jones chooses to play a technical end with hammer in the four-foot behind the Korean's lone centre guard. So we get that congested, tippy tappy situation where the odds are that someone will score 1. That might not be the team with last shot.

"On Jill Officer's first stone – when Canada was sitting two – Jennifer could've peeled the tight guard and brought play into the rings. Chances are there would've been a blank, or things may have worked out for a deuce. She certainly wouldn't have been conceding one as it turns out here. But that's no fun! And in the sixth end, sitting two buried and throwing, most of us would be stepping on the gas. Certainly Jones would. That's her style that's worked so well for her over the years.

"The point I'm making is that choosing to play this type of end – congested and in the centre – can make for a complicated, technical situation, and your team needs to execute at a high level if you are to score a multiple. It's easy to get burned, as Canada did here.

Even the Newbie can spot the next key aspect to this end. The Koreans have managed to keep their yellow rocks in front of Canada's reds, giving them a substantial advantage. You can see through the whole end that they've been tapping red rocks back, keeping their shooters in play, and leaving the Canadian stones just behind the tee line to help protect their own stones from being removed.

"That's right," confirms Mickey. "The Koreans don't worry about who's shot rock and play a patient end, moving the reds back and leaving their shooters on top. By the time we get to the puzzle shot, the yellows are stacked on top of reds, and the reds are behind the tee line. Now, the yellows can only get better, and the reds can only get worse.

"Remember the fundamental principle. Generally, it's better to be light and leave your rocks in positions that can get better or can be used later than it is to be heavy and leave your rocks in positions that are only going to get worse – or provide backing for the other team. I'm not saying Canada got heavy here, other than on Kaitlyn's last. The Koreans just did a great job of moving them back. But generally speaking, it's much better to miss light rather than heavy."

Another thing Mickey notes is how Korea threw only enough weight to move the reds back and keep their shooters in play. "I think it was Wayne Middaugh's statement about you only need two skills to be World Champion: hit-and-stick and draw the eight-foot. There are probably a few more than that, but he makes a good point about throwing weights to keep your shooters in play. So many players run their hits down the ice at thermo-nuclear weight, and the shooters always go. Maybe it's to control the swing on the ice or because they don't trust their sweepers to hold it if it starts to go, I dunno.

"But generally, it's a good idea to throw only enough weight to do the job and no more, especially at the club or improvers level. It's much easier to be accurate with quieter hit weights. So when you're trying to generate offence or perhaps clog up the four-foot without hammer, keep your shooters in play where you can use them. You always hear Russ say 'Control the cue-ball,' and Korea does a good job of doing that in this end."

And that brings us to our puzzle shot – the attempted guard by Jones that turned into a small bump. Mickey didn't like the guard idea.

"There's an old saying about never guarding an opponent's stone. If they make something good in behind to get shot and you've guarded their rock, then it's hard to dig them out and you feel a little foolish. You see what Kim EunJung, the Korean Skip, played on her last – that nice slash to lie 2. If Jones had been successful on her guard and Korea plays that shot, Jennifer would have no way to clear out at least one of the yellow rocks, and she might have given up a steal of 2.

"But Jen has a problem – well, lots of problems because of how the Koreans got their rocks in front of the Canadians'. The Koreans have a shot 'both ways' – from either side – to lie a couple on the button. There's the little tap back on Y3 that Jennifer tries to guard. And there's the in-off on off using their side Y4. You hear Jennifer say 'Make them play that' when she discusses it with her front-end.

"Generally, it's a good idea to play easy shots like guards while making your opponent play hard shots like hit-and-rolls. I like that idea. I think what caught Jennifer here is that she doesn't appear to spot that slash/in-off that Kim EunJung played with her last. It was very makeable, as we see in the video.

"But Jennifer's in a tough position when it's her turn to throw. And the damage was done by Korea moving Canada back behind the tee line and keeping their shooters in front of them. They held all the cards."

What are my takeaways for my level of curling? First, playing in the centre with hammer often leads to congested, tippy tappy ends where someone scores 1. You have to execute at a high level if you're choosing to score your points in the four-foot.

Second, rocks above tee can get better and have power. Rocks behind tee can only move further from the button.

And finally, don't throw big weights unless you need to. Control your shooters, keep them in play and keep them useful.

Mickey's Last Word: "Be patient, keep your rocks in front of theirs, and don't miss heavy. If you do and it's not setting up well, look for the bail point before it becomes too late."

Puzzle #23

Well this is just like a walk in the park. Your team has been executing flawlessly while the other team can hardly hit the broad side of a barn. But those ladies have accomplished an awful lot – much more than you had at their young age – so maybe they could claw themselves back into the game. You just need to slam the door and wrap this thing up. But how? Here's the situation:

- 6th end of 10
- You're red
- You're up by 5
- Yellow has hammer
- It's your Second's first shot
- Four feet of swing

C'mon Skip, slam that barn door before the horse bolts. What's your call – and why?

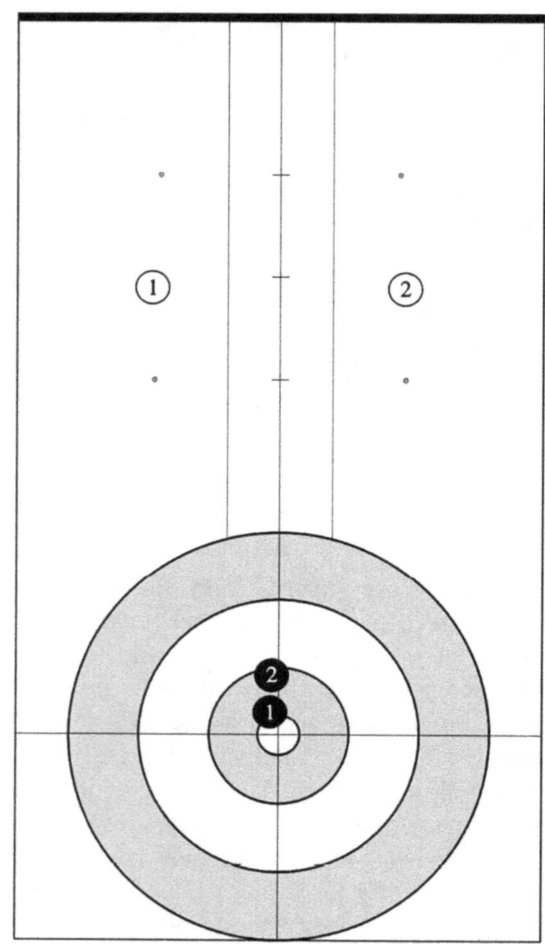

Five-Rock Defence

Ah, remember the good ole days of holding a lead under the 4-rock rule. Throw our first through, they throw a corner, throw our second through, they throw another corner, and we start peeling. The most they score is 2. And if we're RCF with a 5-point lead here in the 6th, that's just fine with us. Even if they score 2 every time they have hammer and we score just 1 when we do, we still win in the 10th. Count 'em up. It's true.

But with the five-rock free guard rule, those days are well and truly behind us. If we persisted with the same throw-through tactics from the 6th end all the way home, we'd lose by a bundle – even with a 5-point lead. So we need to do something else – but what?

"Russia's not alone in trying to figure these tactics out," says Mickey. "Even after several years of playing five-rock, nobody knows for certain how to play this situation. Some teams are throwing centre guards, others are trying to choke off the draws behind the corners, and some are even trying to tick the corner guards into the rings so they can hit them. It's going to take a while to agree on the best tactics here, and it has a lot to do with what your team can make."

Mike Harris in the commentary booth wants to throw another in the rings. Mickey isn't so sure.

"Bringing it in is better than a long guard that just creates another hiding spot for more rocks. But another stone in the rings might leave a quiet hit-and-roll to dislodge R2/R1, set up a pocket, and roll behind a corner. Or maybe the Swedes will just start moving your rocks back behind tee and now they've got a couple of good corner guards and their rocks are starting to build up in the house. Those are not ideal situations."

So how do we decide the best approach, I ask?

"An important factor for Russia in this end is how good those centre rocks are. They are as close to perfect as you're going to get. The scoring area has been shut down to nothing, there's no double and stick, and it's going to take Sweden two shots to deal with them. For the team without hammer, you want to drag play back to centre and away from those corners, close down that scoring area, and make your rocks hard to remove. These two Lead stones do all of that.

"Now if you go into the rings as Mike suggests, you're letting Sweden get after those stones, and I'm not sure I'd want to do that just yet. The Swedes could rattle them around a bit or start moving them behind tee and into a pocket. Keeping those two centre rocks intact where they are for as long as possible is to your advantage. Sweden is going to have to deal with them sometime. Making it so that they have to get through a guard to do that makes it a lot harder."

But what about Mike's point about leaving rocks in play and making your opponent happy? We don't want to make Anna Hasselborg happy. She plays pretty well when she's happy. (Of course, she also plays pretty well when she's unhappy, but maybe not in the first half of this game.)

"This is where we get into this debate about five-rock tactics," Mickey explains. "Mike's right that more rocks in play favour the team trying to score – especially rocks out in front of the house that they can get under quite easily.

"But in five-rock, you're going to have rocks in play whether you like it or not. That's the genius about the rule change. The defending team can no longer just clear things off, especially if they don't have hammer. Sweden will have three good rocks placed before you get a chance to clear. So unless your Second and Third can consistently make a lot of long doubles and clean things up, you're going to face rocks in play. And the way to defend against that is by putting your rocks into good positions and outplaying the other team. RCF has a chance to do that with those two perfect Lead stones."

As you see in the video, RCF throws a guard, trying to protect those two Lead rocks in a terrific position. Sadly, they throw a half-way guard on swingy ice. Now my Russian is only a bit better than my Swedish so I'm not certain that they meant to leave it sitting so high. Mickey thinks it's worse than useless where it ends up.

"Basically that's a shot for Mike's point about rocks out in front just helping your opponent," shrugs Mickey. "It's not in good position."

Mickey explains further. "Sweden has to deal with R1 and R2 at some point. And they want to get rocks in the house in protected positions so they might go on the score sheet later. By leaving that guard so long, Sweden can do both of those things. They can get around it with a bit of weight, start moving those two perfect rocks back and lie

frozen underneath – which is exactly what they did. That guard is not helping you at all. It's helping them."

"I think the tight guard is what I would play here, whether we're an elite or a club team. Sweden wouldn't be able to hit-and-roll on R1 or R2, and they wouldn't be able to get around it with any weight to tap back and lie frozen. They'd have to deal with the guard first."

Mickey throws a spanner in the works here. He might be trying to mess with my head, and if he is, it's working. "I think there's also an argument for throwing this rock through at the competitive level. Sweden probably then goes around a corner – let's say Y1 – trying to get something in the rings. We'd peel Y1. Now they go around Y2, and we'd peel that. They'd play something on our R2/R1 combo and now we'd have three cracks at a double or hit-and-roll to hold them to a deuce. I still like the tight guard, but throwing it through could be an option if you don't want rocks in play and don't mind taking on some doubles."

So what are the Newbie's takeaways for defending a big lead? First of all, get one! Playing with a big lead looks like more fun than being 5 down.

Secondly, I'm going to get my Lead to throw two perfect rocks, the first top button and the second frozen to it perfectly in line. Getting our first on top button leaves them a scoring area the size of a postage stamp. Welding the second one to its nose means it will take my opponent two shots to get rid of them – even if they're wide open.

Third, think about playing into the house and choking off their draw around their corners. But do not, do not, do not get heavy and give them backing around a corner guard.

And finally, if I'm throwing a guard to protect stuff in the four-foot, make sure it's tight to the house and accomplishes my objective of protecting my shot rocks while not letting them tap back and get buried underneath.

Mickey's Last Word: "Five-rock means you often need to defend by getting your rocks into good positions. But leaving your guard so high on swingy ice means it's not in a good position to protect those two gems in the four-foot. In fact, it's bad. If you're going to defend the four-foot, throw rocks that do that: tighter guards. RCF would have been better to err on the side of being too deep and in the rings instead of too high and helping Sweden."

Puzzle #24

Your opponents look like they're about to crack wide apart at any moment. Sure, they're leading, but their Third is shooting daggers at their Skip, and their front-end can hardly make eye contact with either of them. Still, they've managed to put you in a bit of a pickle and you need to respond. Maybe you can be the wedge that drives this team apart. But how? Here's the situation:

- Last end
- You're red
- You're down by 2
- You have hammer
- It's your Second's second shot
- Five-foot swing on ice that's holding up

C'mon Skip, give us a shot that splits this team apart like an episode of Divorce Court. What's your call – and why?

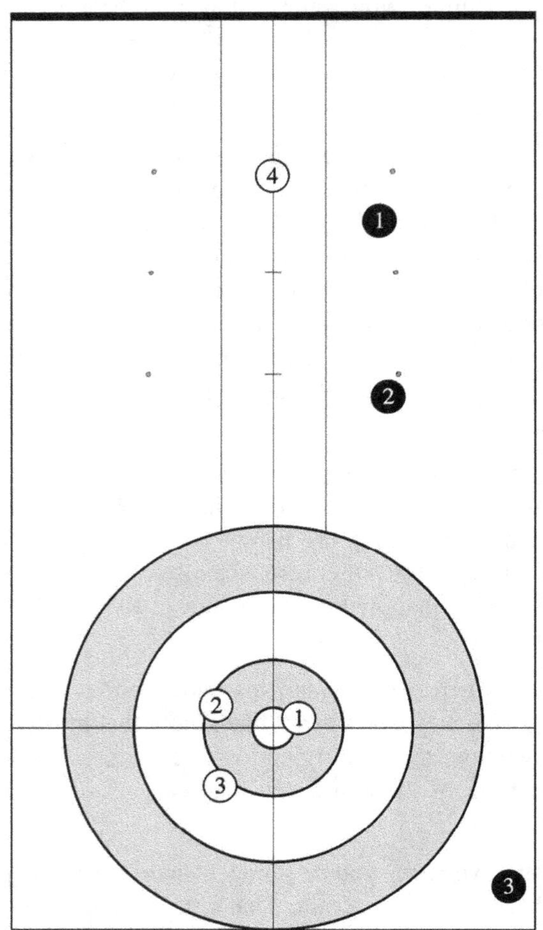

Offensive Weapons

"It gives us a fighting chance, eh." – John Morris, trying to keep one more rock in play so it might go on the scoresheet.

I never played the game before the free-guard zones came into effect. Imagine trying to generate a deuce without guards in play. How about trying to find a 3 – Kevin Koe's task in this puzzle – without anything out front? Sure, he's up against a team that was beginning to sputter and was just a few months away from a spectacular separation but scoring a 3 is always a challenge. This puzzle is all about ways to generate offence when you really need to put a bunch on the board.

In this situation, Kevin's down by 2 so that's his minimum score to keep the game alive. But ideally, he wants more than that. Scoring 2 and then stealing in the extra at club level is one thing. Stealing against a team with Brad Thiessen and Darren Moulding lobbing bombs from Second and Third is quite another. So what's the secret to scoring 2 or 3, Mickey?

"The whole aim when you're trying to score is to put rocks in hard-to-remove places during the end, then make them count with your last two or three shots. And the ways you make rocks hard to remove are placing them under guards, sitting them on top of backing, leaving other rocks as catchers so your rocks jam when the other team is trying to remove them, and splitting your rocks far apart or at good angles so there are no doubles. Those are the weapons at your disposal.

"The standard play when you're trying to score a few is to get your corners established, get one or two buried underneath as the end develops, and bring those in to score later in the end. But of course, while you're throwing corners, the other team is sticking them in the centre, just the way you see Bottcher do if you watch the set-up of this end. So after you set up a corner or two, you'll have to address what's going on in the middle of the sheet and hope to eventually use your guards later.

Okay, so is that what's happening in this end?

"Yes, pretty much. Kevin would like to go around those guards and sink one in, but he can't leave all those rocks in the middle. If Kevin goes around the corner here and Bottcher sticks a fourth in the rings, then Kevin's got to make three doubles just to score his deuce. He's running out of rocks to throw so he needs to address the middle now. You hear Johnny Morris say 'This is the only way we open up our corners, boys', meaning this is the only way to bring those corners into play – by cleaning up a few in the house and giving them the freedom to get underneath on their next. Scoring multiples usually requires us to eventually remove some of their counters, reduce congestion, or put rocks in places where they will eliminate one or more of their rocks while getting rid of ours.

"What Kevin comes up with – and I don't know whether this was a Plan A or Plan B – is to have Johnny play the triple and try to spring one of Bottcher's rocks (Y1) under the corner to be used as backing later on. He calls for Benny to sweep it over so it was definitely one of the options. Anyway, you'll see on BJ's next that he gets buried under the corners, and that Y1 that Johnny bumped over provides a potential catcher.

"So, Kevin's done a couple of things with one throw, which is always good. He's cleared out the problem in the middle of the house and he's established a pending threat – a rock under cover that that can be used to protect his next. To keep building this end, he needs a little bit of magic or luck or opportunity to make that set-up count. BJ Neufeld's first very nearly does that but rolls just a hair too far."

I think I'm starting to catch on to the ideal rhythm of an offensive end – throw guards, clear centre, try to use guards. Even at the club or aspiring level, although doubles and triples are less common, that general rhythm still holds-put some guards in play, put a couple more where they can't be removed or at least leave no doubles, then use your last two or three rocks to capitalize. We just need our opposition to play along.

"But if they don't," Mickey explains, "I think this end is a good illustration of the other offensive weapons available to us, and the aim of those weapons. On his first, BJ Neufeld tries to use that Y1 as backing under the corners to make his rock hard to remove and keep it in play so it might go on the score sheet later. His second uses a central opposition stone for backing under a long guard to make that rock hard to remove and keep it in play where it might go on the score sheet later. And Kevin's first uses a bunch of rocks in the centre for backing under a long guard to make his rock hard to remove and in play where it might go on the score sheet later. Bottcher can't

figure out a way to clear them out, ends up throwing a guard, and Kevin has a shot – a circus shot, but still an opportunity – to win the game with his last. I suspect he would have bitten your hand off for this chance before the end started."

My takeaway that I can use at my aspirational level? It seems to me that an all-out offensive end under five-rock moves in three stages. First, I set up good conditions for offence – the corner guards. Then I clear out the centre and move any rocks in the four-foot back out of the scoring zone. While I'm doing that, I try to keep my shooters in play by springing them towards my guards or finding backing or spacing them out. Then I clean things up and bring it home with my Third's last and Skip's stones. If I execute well and the other team cooperates, I hope to score my deuce or more.

Mickey's Last Word: "Remember that guards are one way to generate offence. Don't forget about setting up backing and catchers and spacing your rocks out so they're hard to remove. Each of those tactics can help you keep rocks in play and hope to get them on the score sheet when the end is over."

Puzzle #25

Your Second's a pretty nice guy, but nice doesn't go on the scoresheet. What's he doing flashing wide with his first attempt at R3, letting them build up a few rocks out in the wing? You really needed that pick to take control of this end and now you're scrambling. They've got a nice one underneath and two nice guards. Nice, nice, nice. It's all too nice – for them! What are you gonna do? Here's the situation:

- 5th end of 10
- You're yellow
- You're up by 2
- Red has hammer
- It's your Second's second shot
- About five feet of swing on good ice

C'mon Skip, no more Mr. Nice Guy. Give 'em a shot that makes them positively grumpy. What's your call – and why?

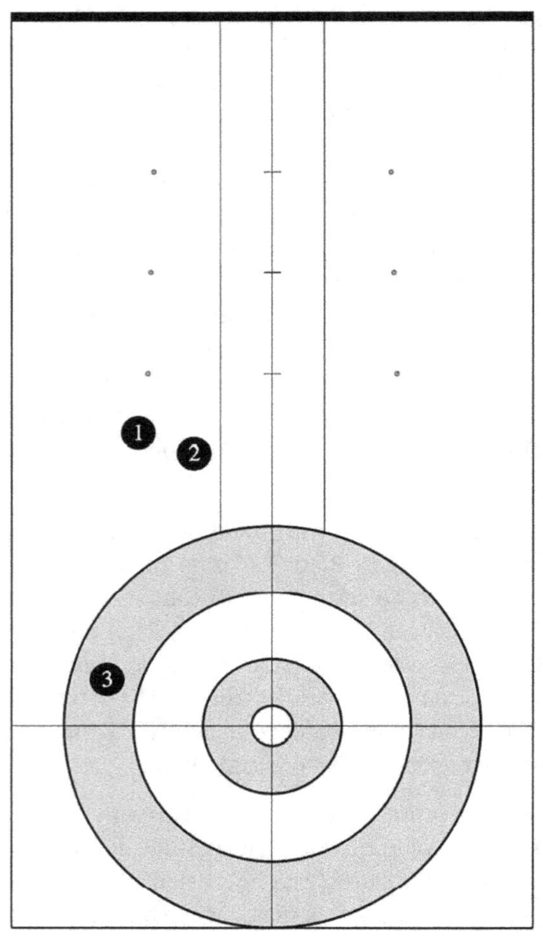

Finally, A Good Reason to Lie Down on the Job

"If I was your coach and you wanted to draw behind those guards, I'd call a time out – and tell the Lead to lie down across the hogline." – Mickey Pendergast, gobsmacked by my call to go around the opposition's corner guard.

What is this thing about drawing around corners without hammer, anyway? I'm looking at this puzzle and thinking that's about the only good place to bury one and get the force going. Get it to tee line underneath all those reds out front – what could be wrong with that? Mickey is about to set me straight.

"It's a pretty firm rule in skipping that you just don't do that too early in the end. Too many bad things can happen.

"Take a look at that set-up. All the stuff over on the side is good for red. They've got two good, usable guards and a shot lying fully buried above the tee. Sticking your yellow in behind their tight guard doesn't make it any less good for them. They'll just have a catcher for their runback to get another rock in the rings fully buried."

Okay, but runbacks at my level aren't automatic. Is it still that bad to sink one around there?

"The runback isn't the only risk. Let's say you draw down to tee line, maybe edge of the eight-foot to be one lonely yellow under all those reds. They'll follow you down and try to get close to a freeze. You'll follow them down – but now they're the meat in the sandwich. There are now three rocks in there providing a pretty decent target for a pretty short runback by players of even your modest calibre. If they make contact, your sandwich goes, and their meat stays, and now they're lying 2 or maybe even 3 if they can keep their raised rock in play."

Mickey's on a roll. "I get that it's tempting to lie shot rock now. But think about timing. You're so far from the end of this end – they still have five rocks to throw.

You'll never be there at the end, so lying shot now might be comforting, but it is of no consequence to who scores what in this end.

"Again, timing matters. Maybe if this scenario was Skip's first, I might go around and try to get a force somehow. I'd be hoping that they don't end up shot with their next rock and that I can split the rings with my last to lie 2 and force them. Maybe I'd do that. But at this point, I have five rocks and a lot of other good things I can try to bail myself out of trouble."

Okay, so we're not going to use the one shred of cover that we have. What are we going to do instead?

"Often, you face just one guard hanging out there, so it's a pretty straight peel. They might replace it or split the rings, but they'd have to make that work for the next four shots. One double and you'd be out of this mess. And worst-case scenario, you hold them to a deuce and go into the 6th tied with hammer."

But Saskatchewan has two guards up. What now?

"Gushue (yellow) is in damage control after Brett Gallant missed picking out R3. With three opposition rocks in play, he needs two doubles to clear off the guards, deal with any rocks in the house and get out of the end without giving up 2. He's got five rocks to do that."

(Note: The number of doubles needed equals the number of rocks in play, minus 1. So, if Saskatchewan has three stones in play, that's two doubles. Gushue would make Double #1 to leave one rock. Sask adds another to make two rocks. Gushue then makes Double #2 to clean up. Try the sequence with four rocks in play. I bet you'll find it's three doubles.)

Mickey carries on, undeterred. "Brad calls for the quarter-rock double hitting R1 into R2, but only the elite teams would take that on. Gallant almost clears them both. If you watch to the last shot of the end, you'll see Gushue get his second double on his last shot. He's a pretty good player."

But would you go for the sliver double, I ask?

"No, it's too tough for most regular players, and certainly at club level, I wouldn't be calling it. I think what I'd do here is play a centre guard and change the focus of the end. Let's get them playing in the middle. They can peel our guard if they want, and I would replace it a few times. We might get a stuffed peel and a chance to go around into the four-foot ourselves. Or if they go around our guard, we follow them down and close down that scoring area, taking their rock in the twelve-foot off the scoresheet. And I'd be sitting behind one of our guards – not their

red corners over on the side of the sheet. Any runbacks will be putting our yellows into the house."

I think I get it. There won't be a need for a coach's timeout. **My takeaway from this puzzle:** don't play around corners too early in the end without hammer. Nothing good comes of it. Peel the guards if I can or change the focus by playing a centre guard and bringing them back to the middle.

Mickey's Last Word: "Remember your Three Guiding Questions. Brad's absolutely unacceptable outcome for this end was to give up a 3-ball, so he made sure he cleared off the corner guards and held Saskatchewan to 2. Going around an opposition corner guard on your Second's stones when they have hammer lets them get more rocks in play in areas that they want them – off to the side – and it's a recipe for that 3-ball."

Puzzle #26

This is like an Ali-Frazier rematch, two heavyweights of the curling world going toe-to-toe, each waiting for the other to blink. Sure, you're the favourite, but the other guys have been ducking and diving, landing jabs and keeping the contest tight. You need to land some big blows and put these folks on the proverbial canvas. But how? Here's the situation:

- 6th end of 10
- You're yellow
- You're up by 1
- You have hammer
- It's your Third's last shot
- Five-foot swing

C'mon Skip, give 'em a call that makes the other guys see stars. What's your call – and why?

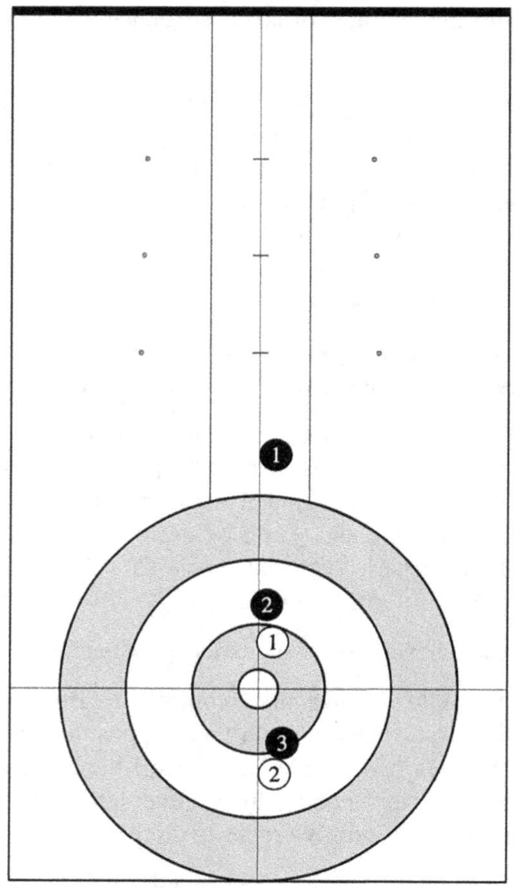

Keep Your Eyes on the Prize

This game features the high-flying US women's team against the stratospheric Swiss squad in the 2020 women's world semi-final, a competition Silvana Tirinzoni goes on to win. It's Third's second, and the Swiss (yellow and us in the puzzle) are up 1 with hammer. We're lying 1, and I reckon it's time to loop another into the four-foot, score a deuce and wrap up our place in the final right here. Mickey disagrees and sets me straight.

"The important thing here for the Swiss is the score and the end – and what they think is acceptable and unacceptable. At 1-up with hammer in the even-numbered 6th end, a score of 1 would be just fine. Going 2-up with four ends to play, they'd be in a good position to win the game.

"But the big factor here is that they definitely do not want to give up a steal to go level. Things would become a lot dicier and they will have sacrificed a commanding position.

"So keeping their objectives in mind, they've played a patient end, cleared the centre guards and have not let any nightmare scenario develop in which the USA might get a commanding position in the four-foot and generate a steal.

"Instead, it's the Swiss who have the strong position, and we know that by whose rocks are secure and whose are vulnerable. Remember The Battle of the Angles in the Fundamentals section? Imagine for a second that the top guard R1 wasn't there and the Americans threw a bullet at R2 to deal with shot rock. The only rock that stays in the four-foot/eight-foot area is the Swiss Y1 and the shooter. Everything else rolls out to at least the edge of the eight-foot or into the twelve-foot. Now the Swiss would have an easy hit on the shooter to lie 2, spaced reasonably well apart, with hammer.

"So the Swiss know that the US team can't deal with shot rock by hitting. The Swiss Y1 shot rock is secure."

I'm troubled and point out that the US team has to deal with Y1 eventually. If they don't, Alina Paetz would eventually draw down to button with her last shot and score 2.

"That's right. The Swiss know the Americans will eventually have to draw in – they can't hit their way out of trouble. So if Silvana just stays patient, peels the guards and leaves no junk out front, the Americans will eventually come around. And then Tirinzoni will have what she wants. There will be no guards out front and no steal in sight. And that's her prime objective: no steals."

I'm starting to get the picture. If the Swiss jump the gun, draw around now to lie 2, they leave the guard. The Americans follow, guddle things up and a steal is a possibility.

But if Silvana stays patient, keeps peeling the guards and waits for the Americans to make their draw, she'll be left with a clean, wide-open front-of-the-house and should be able to tap her Y1 back, avoid the steal, take a single, maybe get a lucky deuce somewhere along the line, and nurse this game over the line.

We see in the video that the peel is what they play. The last American shot (R1) came a little tight to the rings and the Swiss see an opportunity to do a two-in-one shot: get rid of the centre guard and its complication and roll on for a biter. It adds a little drama to Team USA's life, and they have to be really careful. Now there are two yellows in play and a big score could develop.

So the peel-and roll-in is a clever defensive / offensive shot. Simplify the end, make sure you avoid the steal. Roll one on and set up a potentially big score if things go your way. It doesn't really bear fruit – but that doesn't mean it's not worth doing.

"It might have worked depending on what the other team does and how well things come off for you," says Mickey. "In the end, there are one or two shots missed by both teams – there always will be since this is curling.

"But the Swiss have been patient, kept it open, and even though Paetz over-curled on her first and the Americans made a beauty with their last, the Swiss have a fairly straightforward shot for their 1. Which is not a steal – their whole objective."

So the general lessons this aspiring curler can take away for my level of curling? First of all, I need to keep my eyes on the prize. Here in the even-numbered 6th and with a 1-point lead, the prize is 'no steals'. Keep that as my overriding goal and choose shots to match. The peel keeps the end simple and keeps that steal off the table.

Secondly, I need to always, always, always be watching what my opponent is facing and use that to help guide my decision-making. If I put myself in the American's shoes, I see pretty quickly that they can't hit. Sooner or later, they'll give up on the guard and draw in to prevent

my deuce. That will leave me with my desired situation: a nice clear front for me to avoid the steal. So, put myself in my opponent's shoes. Do it over and over and over again.

Mickey's Last Word: "The Swiss keep a very clear-eyed view of what they're trying to accomplish. Club curlers always seem to try to score a multiple with hammer. Sometimes anything but a steal is the right objective. Silvana saw that by going for 2 and drawing around here, she'd be creating a mess and letting a potential steal creep into the end, which would be a shame when the angles are so good for her. The peel avoids that unacceptable outcome; rolling in just gave them a chance for the bonus point. Anyway, be clear-eyed about your objective. That's the lesson here."

Puzzle #27

This is a two-part puzzle covering two shots in sequence as this end plays out. We'll discuss what John Epping plays here, and then consider Kevin Koe's response in the next. We'll save the QR code until that second puzzle so we don't spoil the surprise.

Squeaky bum time here at the Brier. You've done well against the defending champion, and now you're heading into the final three ends with hammer and a good chance to take a famous scalp. But those other guys are good, and even when they're not at their best, they've got a Skip that can pull rabbits out of hats. You just need to find a way to bury them. But how? Here's the situation:

- 8th end of 10
- Game is tied
- You're red
- And you have hammer
- It's your Skip's first shot
- Good five-foot swing on good ice

C'mon Skip, give 'em a shot that shows a little magic of your own. What's your call – and why?

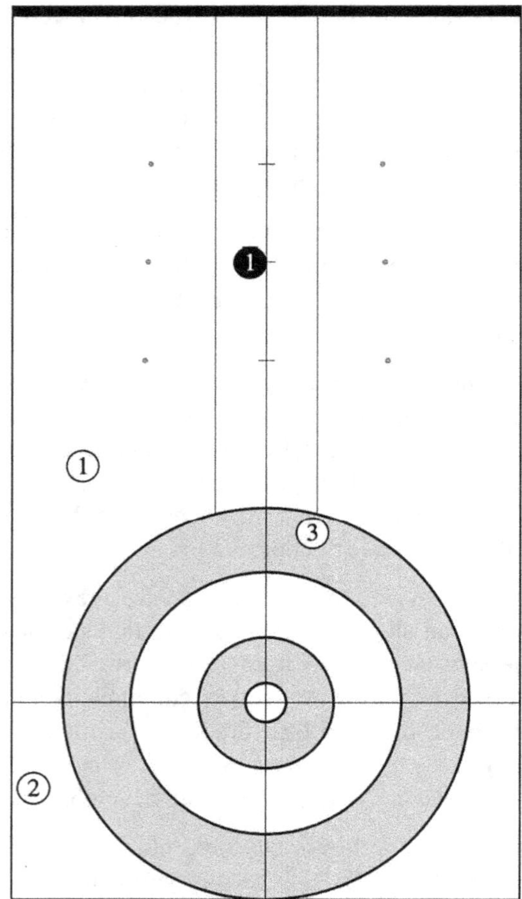

Anything But the Unacceptable

As a Newbie Skip, I'm constantly amazed by the calculations behind even the simplest of calls. Here, we pretty much have just two rocks in play. In the 8th end, tied, holding hammer and with almost no prospects of scoring 2, my gut reaction is to hit the yellow in the rings, make it go away and get the blank. But listening to John Epping and Ryan Fry think it through is an education. What's going on here?

"It's kind of a funny situation," says Mickey. "Both teams have an overlap of acceptable outcomes – a blank or a force. John could live with scoring 1 to get that even-end hammer situation going, but would be happier with the blank to keep hammer in the ninth. Kevin would be happier forcing John to his single to get hammer back with two ends to play, but he could live with a blank too, force in the 9th and win in the 10th. Anyway, you can see how both outcomes are reasonably acceptable to both teams going into the 9th.

"The most important concern for both Skips is not to lose the advantage right here – and that means avoiding their unacceptable outcomes. John wants to avoid anything that would lead to a Koe steal, and Kevin wants to avoid anything that would lead to an Epping deuce. So they're going to play a little cagey here, probing a bit to see if they can get their ideal result, happy to settle for their acceptable score but not risking anything that would lead to their unacceptable outcome."

In this puzzle, we're Epping, and we're red. John's route to a deuce (his ideal score) might be to hide a rock, hope for a Koe miss, then make his last to score 2. There are two places he could hide one away: under the centre guard or under the corner guards.

Brett Laing calls for the come-around on the centre guard to lie top-four. "That's my first thought," he calls down the ice. The aim here is to goad Koe into a miss – a missed chip or runback using his Y3 – leaving your top-four rock in play so you can score 2 with a draw on your last.

But there are a couple of problems with this call, says Mickey. "First of all, Kevin would make that hack-weighter nine times out of ten. On this swingy ice behind a longish guard and with his sweepers, that would be a pretty makeable shot. He probably keeps his shooter in play, splits the rings and Epping gets forced to 1.

"Or maybe Epping's counter-clockwise come-around over-curls, and Kevin makes a short run to sit two to get the force. Now that's still an acceptable outcome for John if he forces Koe back in the 9th or 10th and wins in the next end.

"But the key point is that any play into the centre adds complexity to the situation, and a mistake in that area could create a steal situation. What if you get a little heavy, go back button and Koe freezes? Or maybe you stop top-eight staggered, and Koe wraps one around the pack? Now you're bringing the steal into play. John's keeping his unacceptable outcome in the forefront of his mind and just isn't willing to flirt with something in the centre that could lead to a steal."

Okay, so if not the top-four draw, how about hitting Koe's Y3 and rolling under the centre guard? Now you've got one buried that can't be easily removed, and you're halfway to your deuce.

"They would never consider that," says Mickey. "It essentially sets up double centre guards. Kevin would loop around those, and now that steal is a distinct possibility."

I'm grasping at straws now. How about a nose hit on Koe's rock at the top of the rings, lying a biter and giving yourself a powerful rock to use on your last?

Mickey swats this away. "If you make it and sit right there, it's in a good spot. If Kevin wraps around, it will keep the blank or force options alive – assuming you make the runback.

"But what if you ever flop under that centre guard or even half-under? Then you've have those double centres again, maybe a little staggered. Now Koe's wrapping around and once again, the steal is in play."

Finally, we come to the option that Epping selects: the hit-and-seven-foot-roll to sit under the Y1 corner guard. Here's how Epping describes it to his guys.

"I try to roll buried (over in the corner). If he comes around top-four, then I chase for 2 (i.e. chip him out and keep his shooter in play). If he comes around buried top-eight (where Epping can't chip him), then I draw for 1."

Mickey likes this call. "This call – even though a seven-foot hit-and-roll isn't that probable – takes that unacceptable steal off the table. If John makes the shot, he's got a good chance at a deuce. But the odds are that he rolls right out or sits in the open. If he rolls out, Kevin draws to four-foot where John could chase him, or Kevin goes top-eight where John can draw into the centre for his single. If John sits open around the top-eight, Kevin would hit it and try to roll under, but John would always have the four-foot with his last.

"So it's a fairly risk-free shot with a chance for 2, as long as he doesn't roll under or get it half-buried. But by aiming for a big roll, he's unlikely to do that."

So is this a shot we should play at the club? "Probably not," thinks Mickey. "I think we'd just play the hit, they probably hit back, and you likely have a blank. But you still have to be careful not to roll behind and leave a staggered double centre guard. That would leave them no choice but to come around and maybe steal. You'd rather leave them the easy option of hitting you, and then you'd get your blank."

So what happens? Well, as you'll see in the video after the next puzzle, execution matters. John noses Kevin's Y3 and rolls just a hair towards the centre, but not enough to get edge-buried and overlapped.

My takeaway from this puzzle? Always, always, always keep my ideal, acceptable and especially unacceptable outcomes at the forefront of my mind. What am I trying to achieve, and what do I have to avoid?

Mickey's Last Word: "The key thing to take away is that the Skip needs to be one-hundred-percent aware about what they're trying to achieve and what they're trying to avoid. Weigh up your options against those three questions, and you won't go far wrong."

On to the next puzzle to work through the next shot and see the outcome!

Puzzle #28

In this second part of the two-parter, you're now Kevin Koe and about to throw your last yellow stone.

"It's terrible." – "It's not great." – "It's Horrible."

It's fair to say that John Epping's team is not thrilled after he noses Y3 in Puzzle #41 and sits half-biting the top-twelve. But why are they so glum? You seemingly have nothing and you're running out of ends. But wait – your Second has an idea! What's the joke about the last thing a Second says before he goes to look for another team? Answer: 'Hey guys, I have an idea.' But what the heck, let's see what he comes up with. Maybe, just maybe, he might have something good. Here's the situation:

- 8th end of 10
- Score is tied
- You're yellow
- Red has hammer
- It's your Skip's last shot
- Five-foot swing on good ice

C'mon Skip, let the Second have his moment in the sun. What's his call – and why?

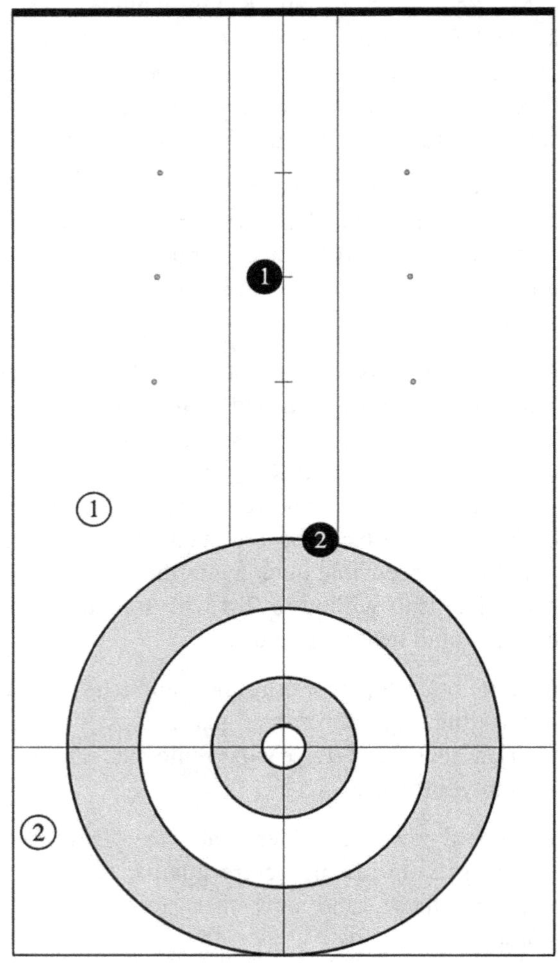

Take a Second Look

If I were Kevin Koe (and my teammates will tell you I'm not, I'm really, really not) I'd be in the hack ready to launch a bomb at Epping's R2 biter at the top-twelve, get the blank, move on and try my luck in the 9th. But Colton Flasch, Koe's Second – and Mickey – have other ideas.

"I don't think hitting is wrong," says Mickey. "At any level, giving up the deuce is the big risk here. The hit on the biter makes the deuce impossible, so I don't think it's a bad call. But if you do that, Epping throws it through and it's a blank. As you see in the video, Kevin would rather force and get hammer back in the 9th if he can."

Coming around the centre guard and sitting top-button or top-four could get a force, and maybe even a steal if Epping misfires. Why not that call, I wonder?

"Kevin would never throw that. First of all, with a long guard on swingy ice and with his sweepers, John would make that quiet hit to score 2 say eight out-of-ten times. And that would be Kevin's unacceptable outcome – the deuce. Kevin won't take that risk.

"Even at club level on club ice, you might be tempted to try that, but I don't think it's a good call. It's a reasonably high guard, so if you don't make the come-around perfectly, you give up 2 and probably the game.

"You might be tempted to go top-eight and see if you can get a miss on the chip. But if you don't get fully buried, he chases and scores 2. Or he plays an angle raise on his tight R2, removes yours and perhaps rolls his shooter in. Anything on that line gives him that chance, and that's why you see Koe reject that call."

OK, how about hitting the biter and rolling under the centre guard? That could give me the force.

"Well, you could try that and it could work out. Of course, hit-and-rolls are about the most difficult shot in curling. You've got about a one-inch-wide target on the object rock, and you have to throw the perfect weight to get the right roll. In the video, you see John try a hit-and-roll on his first and he doesn't even come close. They're difficult, low-percentage shots.

"And keep in mind that that shot never brings a steal into play. It leaves a pretty big scoring area – basically the entire twelve-foot. Epping makes that draw every single time. Even at club level, any decent Skip will make that nine-out-of-ten. So yes, if you make the roll, you get your force, but that's all you get-never a steal. And Colton's idea was much better.

"If Kevin can place his rock anywhere on a straight line behind Epping's biter, it does a couple of things. First, it takes away any chance of Epping scoring 2. There's no quiet tap around such a tight guard that would let Epping score 2. And there's no way Epping can run R2 straight back into Kevin's rock and get his shooter into the rings. He pretty much has to nose it and that means his shooter never rolls in.

"Secondly, this rock gives Kevin a shot at a steal. You see in the video how it bites the button. If John tries to draw to button, he might miss. And if he plays the runback, he might miss. Ya, he probably makes contact on the runback nine-times-out-of-ten, but this could be the one.

"So it's a crafty shot that leaves no possibility of Kevin ending up with his unacceptable outcome – a deuce – while keeping his ideal outcome – a steal – in play. As long as Kevin gets it on a direct line behind that biter, it's kind of a two-for-one risk free shot. And he'll put it on that line around the four-foot area eighty or ninety percent of the time, so it's a good choice."

My takeaways from the situation? First, listen to your Second. He just might be the smartest guy on the team. On my last team, he certainly was.

Second, I need to be clear about what's truly unacceptable to me, and make sure that I do everything I can to keep that out of play.

Third, a nose hit on a rock half outside the rings stays outside the rings. Stick one on a line behind it and their shooter can't score.

And finally, the essence of this call is Kevin evaluating what it leaves John. Every option is weighed up with 'What will John have?' I put it there, he plays this. I put here, he plays that. That's the mental thought loop I need to perfect.

Mickey's Last Word: "The key to Kevin's shot was knowing what his unacceptable outcome is, and never playing something that would put that on the table. Lining up perfectly under a biter means that John can never get his shooter into the rings, and that means he can't score 2."

Puzzle #29

Oh boy, oh boy. You gotta do something about that scoreline. We're into squeaky bum time here in this crucial match and you're trailing these guys. Sure, they're neighbours of yours, but they're not nice neighbours. They're bossing you about here, flooding the middle and making you play in the four-foot. That's definitely not nice. Time to get angry and take a few points back! But how? Here's the situation:

- 8th end of 10
- You're yellow
- You're down by 1
- You have hammer
- It's your Third's first
- About a five-foot swing on good ice

C'mon Skip. Give us a shot that's more Incredible Hulk than Snow White. What's your pro call and club call – and why?

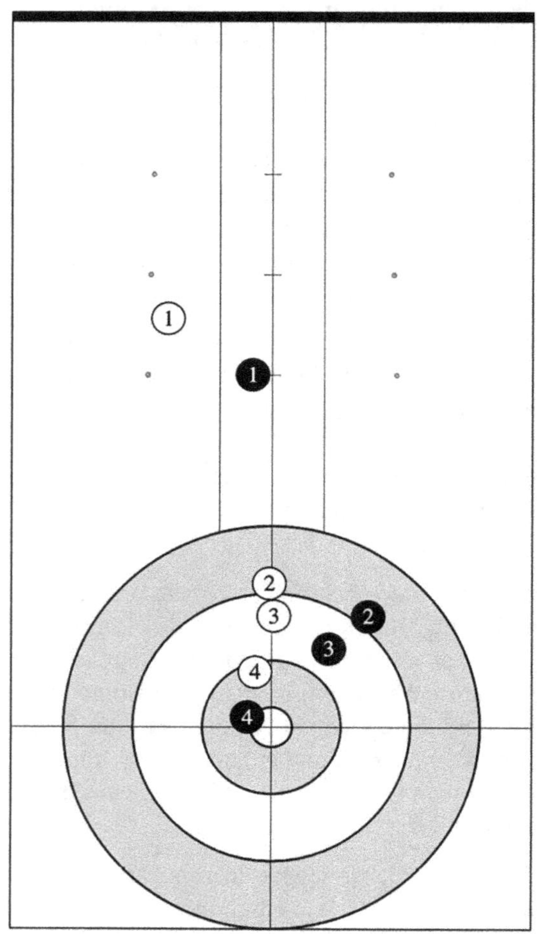

Enough is Enough

"It's one thing to decide your three outcomes before each end," Mickey suggests. "but you need to remind yourself of them when things get messy or go sideways. Keep 'em in mind as the end plays out and you won't go far wrong." They'll guide your decisions and help you achieve the results you're looking for."

He continues, not sure I'm really making the link between his guidance and this puzzle. (He's right to be suspicious.) "At 1-down in the 8th, Alberta (yellow) has to score or blank here. Ideally, they'd get 2 or 3 to go up in the game, but a force to level the score is not the end of the world. And a blank to keep hammer is okay too.

"The real unacceptable outcome is giving up a steal to go 2-down with just two ends to play. That would just be bad and leaves them with about a fifteen-percent chance of winning. That's what Brendan is playing to avoid here."

Okay, I get that. To go 2-down into the last two ends, even if you keep hammer, well, that puts you at low odds to win. They force or even give you two in the 9th and now you're playing the last all-square without hammer. You're gonna lose at the pro level.

But what about the puzzle? What's the link?

"The link is this," Mickey explains. "It's knowing when to stop 'setting up' and pressing for a score, and when to settle for the situation as it is, 'cash out' and make sure you at least get your minimum acceptable result.

"When you're the team with hammer, the set-up is about putting rocks in good positions that can turn into points. It's about winning angles and getting stones behind guards and building pockets for backing.

"Cashing out is about deciding that the set-up is good enough and making a move to turn that set-up into your desired outcomes. It's about addressing shot rock if you don't have it and about digging out theirs and lying a couple of your own."

But when do we make the switch from setting up to cashing out?

"It's not a hard and fast rule – there are too many scenarios and possibilities. But it's often somewhere around Third's first or Third's second shot that you might want to start thinking about getting shot rock – or rocks. If you're down a couple and scoring 2 or more is critical, you might go a little longer and risk a steal. If avoiding a steal is the main thing, then you switch earlier and make sure you take that off the table."

So Bottcher, knowing he has to score or blank, decides he needs to 'make the move' now and address shot rock here on Third's first shot, right?

"That's right. That's exactly what's going on here. Bottcher's thinking better safe than sorry. If he played that other set-up shot he was looking at – doubling out their R2/R3 reds but still not addressing shot rock – BC might just throw a guard on it or something and Alberta could be scrambling get that shot rock out.

"So Brendan decides he'd rather be too early here, and perhaps get forced, than make his move too late and perhaps give up a steal. He makes a play that pushes shot rock back and gets his shooter into a position where they have a good chance to score a multiple."

How did things work out?

"It's a great example of the drag effect," says Mickey. "Even though Y2/Y3 are lined up to get only a piece of Y4, contact on the right-hand side of Y2 will drag Y3 directly at Y4, leaving it buried.

"I would have liked to see them play it with a little more weight to move the R4 shot rock further back and spill Y2 further across the rings so there's no double for BC. But Darren Moulding (Bottcher's Third) was more concerned about spilling it right out of the house and losing a potential point when the rocks are counted. I'd rather be sure of taking the steal off the table than be worried about scoring a deuce here.

"For aspirational or club curlers, this is the right time to take advantage of these angles, hit Y2 hoping to also kill R2 and R4. You'd be sitting two buried with at least one kicker in the rings. Chances are good you'll get a positive outcome."

Execution issues take over from this point forward. A missed line call by Alberta and three pistols from BC's backend see Bottcher needing to be sharp to get his single with his last rock. He is, takes the force, goes into the 9th

all-square without hammer, then seizes that slim chance to go on and win the game – and later, the Brier.

So what lessons can I take away from this pro situation and apply to my level of curling? Be ever mindful of what I'm trying to achieve and what I'm trying to avoid. If my priority is to avoid the steal, don't leave it too late to make the move from set-up to cashing out by addressing shot rock. When the scoreboard dictates that I must score 2 or more, it might be in my interest to go a bit deeper, play one more set-up shot then cash out.

Mickey's Last Word: "Know when it's time to take advantage of a good setup and make the move. Ensure an acceptable outcome at the very least."

Puzzle #30

Darn it. Your Lead has just fired her tick attempt out the back and now the other guys have thrown up the double centre guard. If this were the 90's and we were playing the good ol' three-rock free guard zone, you'd be peeling like a cheap banana on this shot. But sadly, times have changed and so must you. But how? Here's the situation:

- 10th end of 10
- Score is tied
- You're red
- You have hammer
- It's your Lead's second shot
- Five feet of swing on good ice

Come on, Skip, give 'em a shot that shows you know how to avoid the odd banana skin every now and then. What's your call – and why?

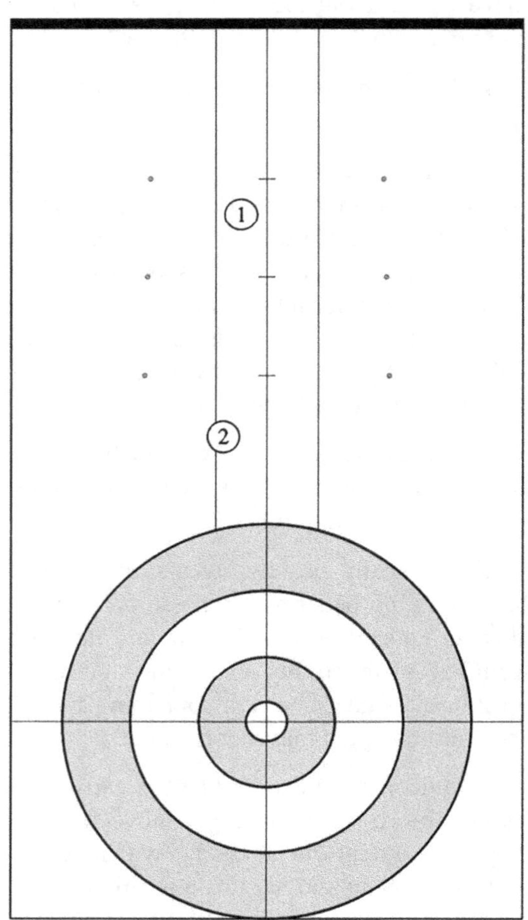

Second Time Lucky?

This puzzle is all about the tick shot and its lurking dark side. We hear more and more how easy it is to make and how the World Curling Federation wants to ban it. (At the time of writing, it was still legal.) It must be so easy to play. Why don't we see it all the time?

"The problem with the tick shot," explains Mickey, "is that if you miss it, you start off the end in a major hole. Your shooter goes out the back and you give the other team a two-rock head start. Sweden (yellow) is obviously going for the steal here so with the missed tick they get a chance to put up two centre guards and clog up the middle before you even get one rock in play. You're playing catch-up right off the bat. I recommend that most club teams not even consider the tick. If you miss it – and if you don't practice it, you probably will – then you've wasted a rock. I'd rather see them play what Kerri called

here. Sit just open in the top four / top eight to be used later if needed."

But why not throw the tick so that, if missed, it ends up on the tee line or back rings at worst, I ask?

"The tick is mostly about trying to open up the centre and make it hard for them to hide one close to the scoring area. But you are also trying to make sure you have a draw into the four-foot with your last. Now if you're playing tee weight, how far do you think the rocks are going to move? Maybe far enough to clog up your draw path and make it hard for you to score?"

I see the problem and silently curse myself for not looking fourteen shots ahead.

"That said," Mickey offers, mostly in sympathy I think, "the top teams are playing this shot with less weight than before. The logic is that almost any contact makes it better, and with back-8 or so, there's no chance of killing the guard regardless of where we hit it. The trick is to make sure we don't nose it and leave them with a centre guard and shot rock back four."

So Canada's Lead, Briane Meilleur, misses her first tick and Sweden throws another centre guard, well-spaced apart and almost in line. That brings us to our Puzzle Shot. So which guard should she go for with her second tick attempt, I ask?

"Well, I suppose it's an option, but I don't like it. Someone who practises it a lot might consider it. If they can tick the tighter guard out to the wings, it's pretty good. But you're rolling the dice. If you miss, Sweden gets to play another free one – maybe a guard, maybe they'll draw under – but they'll have three down the middle and you have none in play. So you just can't allow them to have another free shot. You have to make this one count."

Kerri agrees and calls for the draw to sit top-four on the centre-line, just open. What's with that, I ask? Why sit open? Why not use Sweden's guards, draw around and sit the game-winning shot under the cover on the button? Let's beat them to the punch!

Mickey explains Kerri's approach. "As a Skip, you need to always be asking yourself 'What if?' What if your come-around slides just behind tee and they freeze to it? They'd be on the button, sitting with backing behind two good guards out front. Even if you stopped on the tee-line and they froze to lie shot, you're in a pickle. You would be chasing hard the rest of the end and might not have a draw to win.

"So keep them away from those double guards until you can deal with them. Play this little sitter and that stops them from coming around because we'd have a two-foot runback. And they have to deal with it and take away that runback threat. That keeps them away from using their centre guards."

But isn't playing to the top four-foot just leaving them a nice easy hit-and-roll under?

"Is there such a thing as a nice easy hit-and-roll under?" asks Mickey. "Watch professional curling. Watch the best players in the world play hit-and-rolls and see how many they actually make. They are the lowest percentage shots in our game.

"But as you see in the video, Sweden doesn't play a hit this early in the end. They want a complicated end with lots of rocks in play and hopefully a chance to manufacture a steal. So they play a tap and wait for an opportunity."

So there we are. Canada tries to throw out a sitting duck at the top of the four-foot to keep Sweden occupied and away from their guards. Sweden, on the other hand, plays soft weight to try to complicate things and get under the guards if they can. Eventually, Sweden bumps a Canadian

rock to the button and Canada takes a crack at the double peel to open things up.

But the double peel turns out to be only a single. Is this where they lost it – not peeling two with their first, I wonder?

"Well, maybe. The double was available, but the guards were well spaced, so it wasn't automatic. Whether they made a single or a double peel, Kerri wanted to open things up and make sure she had a route into the four-foot to win. She did that over the last half of the end. The fact that she missed doesn't mean the strategy was wrong."

So what are my Newbie takeaways for a situation in which we just have to score with hammer? First, I'm going to think twice about the tick unless my team is playing at a high level. A missed tick can put me in a hole right from the start.

Secondly, I need to continually be looking at the 'What ifs?' What if we slide deep? What if we grind to halt in the slide path at top-twelve? Then I add in some three-shot window thinking: if I slide back button, she'll follow me down, and then I'll have…what? Looking at the downsides of a slightly missed shot can help me avoid banana skins.

And finally, I'm not playing around centre guards too early. I don't want to let them create a mess in the middle and perhaps get the steal. I'll be playing shots that make it tough for them to get underneath, and then I'll clear out the front as soon as I can. I'll play this whole end for my last shot – and then I just have to make it!

Mickey's Last Word: "If you need to score with hammer and choose not to play the tick, consider putting a rock just open top four instead of buried. It's a great spot. They'll have to deal with it and that keeps them away from using their guards."

Puzzle #31

This is looking nice for you. You're lying shot, with hammer, their yellow rocks grouped together like peas in a pod – nice and tight for easy removal. Oddly, they seem kinda pleased with themselves. No matter – you know better. Now it's time to cash in on your front-end play, use your hammer to score 2, and take a good lead in this tight game. But how? Here's the situation:

- Second end of ten
- Score is tied
- You're red
- You have hammer
- It's your Second's second shot
- About four feet of swing on good ice

C'mon Skip, give us a shot that shows you're at peas with yourself. What's your call – and why?

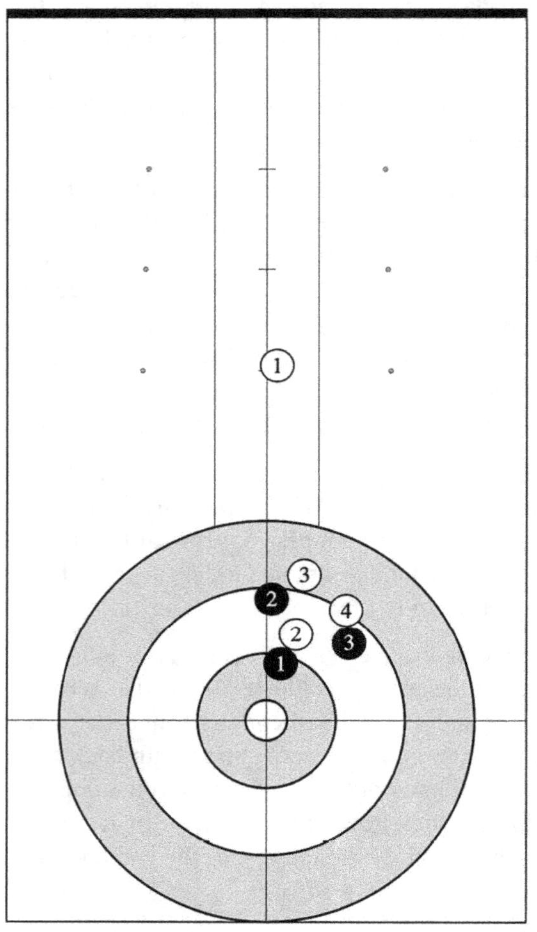

Looking Ahead, Seeing the Potential

"You can see the way the rocks are situated there. The yellows are all frozen to the reds. So the reds are on the backside." – Jill Officer, in the commentary booth, highlighting how Canada (red) is in a precarious situation.

The puzzle makes it sound like red is in control, and a Newbie Skip might think they are, lying shot rock with hammer with only half-an-end to play. But Jill Officer – and Mickey – don't think it's looking so good for you. When the Swiss made two perfect freezes and Brad Thiessen got heavy on his first (cardinal sin: heavy front-end play), the Canadians were left in serious trouble.

As Jill rightly points out, all the reds are on the backside of the yellows, and all the yellows are sitting snugly on top of the reds. That means that with any hit on that group, the reds would tend to go and the yellows would tend to stay. Their rocks are more secure.

Mickey points out that the shape of the situation does not favour a team trying to score with hammer. "Teams with hammer do best by creating an open, well-spaced house so their stones can sit apart and prevent opponents from removing several of their rocks with one shot. And they want a large scoring area with plenty of 'breathing room' so that if things don't work out, they have a path and space to draw for a single and not give up a steal."

Here, the rocks are grouped on top of the four-foot, creating a congested situation. It feels like it's going to get technical in there, a tippy-tappy end where rocks are clustered around the four-foot and it's hard to wedge two in there to score your deuce. In these situations, someone usually scores 1 – and that could be either team. Holding hammer in an early end, Bottcher doesn't want someone to score 1, especially his opponents. He wants 2 or nothing – so he's got to make a change to the shape of the end.

He looks at his first idea – a five-foot runback to pick out some yellows – and immediately recognizes its problems. Runbacks are never nailed-on certainties. His Second might not hit it perfectly and, because the reds are more at risk than the yellows, the result could end up favouring the Swiss.

"I'm worried that if we run something in, we might be in more trouble," Bottcher calls down the ice. With his red rocks on the underside of the yellows, he's right.

If not the runback, then what else?

"Brendan shows a terrific understanding of the angles here, and recognizes two things" explains Mickey, "First of all, he sees that although the reds are vulnerable, it would take a super-precise shot to actually remove all of them from the rings. Based on the set-up, it's likely that Canada's going to be left with one or two in the house even with the best Swiss strike. Had the Y4 curled a few more inches to get into that pocket, it would be a very different story, but it hung out just enough that a hit on Y3 can't easily kill everything.

"And secondly, and perhaps more importantly, he sees that after that strike, all the Swiss yellows are going to be left grouped in the centre. And then we're into the 'grouping of stones' idea. Grouped rocks mean you can usually hit a few at once, so it's a lot easier to clean up a situation if your opponents' rocks are clustered together.

"Brendan's looking at the situation in a rolling 'three shots ahead' window. He sees that if he removes the guard Y1, the Swiss will play some defence, throw a big-weight bomb and try to cut down the number of reds in the rings. And he recognizes that that strike will likely leave one or two of his rocks around the house somewhere and their yellows stones grouped together. And he knows that if their yellow stones are grouped together, then he can blast and change the shape of the situation to favour him – most of the yellows gone, perhaps one or two reds kicking around the edges and a much more spaced-out end with plenty of breathing room. If he can get to that situation, he knows he's very unlikely to give up a steal and might, if one or two of his reds stick around after the Swiss hit, set up a chance to score a multiple."

My head spins. As a Newbie skip, it's the lightning-quick ability to size up the situation and see three shots ahead that is amazing. Maybe it comes with experience. Maybe it's from all that clean living that Brendan obviously does. Whatever the case, he sees the options at an astonishing speed.

So, Brendan calls for the peel, the Swiss throw a bomb that over-curls a fraction, leaving the red rocks spread about the rings and the yellow stones grouped for easy removal. (Top tip: use the spacebar to pause the YouTube video then use the full-stop key to inch forward and see how the angles play out). Within two shots, this end has gone from a congested shape in the four-foot favouring the Swiss to a wide-open, expansive end favouring the Canadians.

So what's the Newbie Skip taking away from this for play at the aspiring club player level? First, I need to recognize when the shape of an end is not favouring me and think about bailing out or changing it in some way. Playing a congested end around the four-foot is risky when I have hammer. I'd like a more open situation with plenty of breathing room for me to draw in and get at least a single point.

Secondly, I need to get better at sizing up the options very quickly and using a rolling three-shot window to plan several shots ahead. I'm going to start with a new regimen of clean living.

And finally, that grouping of rocks principle is repeated over and over again in so many ends. If I can spot when my opponents' rocks are grouped, or encourage them to become grouped, that gives me an edge. In this case, Bottcher used it to bail out of a bad situation. I can do that too.

Mickey weighs in about this play at club level. "I think the peel is a good call at the pro or club level. It gets rid of the opposition guard, makes it likely they will start eliminating reds, and opens up the scoring area. It provides the best chance of achieving your ideal or acceptable outcome."

Mickey's Last Word: "Recognize how the angles are developing and think three shots ahead. If their likely next shot will leave their rocks grouped, that's good for you."

PS. Something to note as the end plays out is the importance of hitting-and-sticking. Again, we think it was Wayne Middaugh who said that if you can hit-and-stick and draw the eight-foot, you too can be world champion. In this end, Moulding's double-and-stick very nearly sets up a 3 for Canada. My personal resolution is to throw only as much weight as needed to remove the rocks – and control my shooter.

Puzzle #32

You'd sure like to win this one. We're into the short strokes in this competition, and your opponent is rowing hard for the line. Luckily for you, your front-end is one of the best in the business and has set you up to float past the other guys and take a memorable win. Victory is at hand with just a few good shots. But how? Here's the situation:

- 10th end of 10
- You're yellow
- You're down by 1
- You have hammer
- It's your Third's second shot
- About a five-foot swing on good ice

C'mon Skip, give us a shot that stops them dead in the water. What's your call – and why?

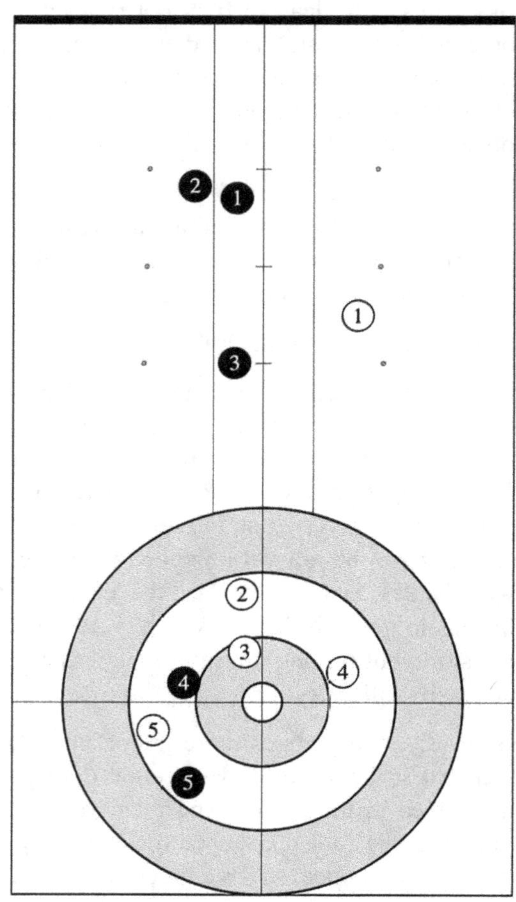

Walk a Mile in the Other Guy's Shoes

Whoever says that front-end players (Leads and Seconds) are there to carry the brooms and fetch the water just doesn't understand curling. Rewind the video and watch the start of this end. BC's Lead and Second (names omitted to protect the innocent) threw a centre guard (R3) a foot wide of the centre line, a tight zone 3 centre guard that landed up high in zone 1 (R1), and a freeze to the four-foot that crashes on a guard out in front (R2). All players making it to the Brier are superb curlers, but for these two nameless souls, this crucial 10th end will not make happy viewing.

Meanwhile, their opponents – the brilliant Karrick Martin and Brad Thiessen – do what Martin and Thiessen do: one superb corner, one excellent come-around, one exceptional tap in the four-foot and one almost-perfect freeze to their own in the top-four. Is it any wonder

that when his front-end signs off, Bottcher's lying three fully buried with hammer? Darren Moulding, Bottcher's Third, could throw both of his shots through and they would still be favoured to score 2 and win the game!

So Leads and Seconds count. They set up the end – or not. They put you in the driving seat – or not. Then they sweep your underthrown draws from hogline to house and make you look good – or not. Without a front-end performing at their peak, you are at a serious disadvantage, and anyone who wants proof of that should take five minutes and watch the 10th from the start.

Anyway, in the puzzle we find ourselves a couple of shots on – we're now in Third's rocks. Alberta (Brendan Bottcher playing yellow) is trying to score 2 and finish this game right now. BC (Jim Cotter playing red) is trying to force or steal. The force doesn't look very likely so now Cotter's going for the steal.

"A key to this call is looking at the game from your opponent's perspective," explains Mickey. "Bottcher sees that BC has two available shots to get one buried on the button and steal the end: the counter-clockwise hit off the side Y4 to roll to the button, and the wide counter-clockwise draw around everything. Alberta talks about this a lot during the timeout before Moulding threw his first rock. It's worth backing the video up and listening to that discussion."

So BC has two options and we can't take away both of those with this shot. I'm thinking that maybe we should just clear the guards, simplify the front, and let BC start hitting. Sure, our rocks are grouped in the rings and they could make some doubles down the stretch. But if we have one still in the rings and a clear front of the house, our Skipper should be able to get us a game-winning deuce. Right?

Mickey's not so sure. "In this case, the problem with clearing the guards is that you just don't know where they are going to go. You have to hit them in the crotch, come off the high R2 and that pushes the lower R1 towards the rings. Anything could happen. It could sit in the gap between Y1 and R3, leaving Cotter another runback rock. Or it could come off the Y1 corner and bounce just across the centre line, setting up staggered guards in the middle. Cotter then loops around the stagger, gets to button and that's very likely the game. Bottcher doesn't want to gamble the game here, especially when his front-end has put them in such a good position. They don't need to."

OK, so we're not clearing guards. That still leaves BC with two good options, but we can only throw one rock with our puzzle shot.

"So again," repeats Mickey, "a lesson in this shot is that Bottcher's team looked at it from the perspective of Jim Cotter. The hit-and-roll is the hardest shot in curling. Line and weight have to be perfect. Throw it a bit narrow at the right weight and it doesn't roll. Throw it dead-on but at too much weight and it rolls too far. Watch the pros. Watch how many hit-and-rolls they don't make. You'll think twice about playing so many at club level.

"What that means is that Cotter would much rather play the wide counter-clockwise draw since it has a much higher chance of success. And that means that Bottcher had to take away that option with Moulding's draw to top-four. This is the right call at any level. You can be a little light or heavy and still get something out of it. And you're taking away the shot they want to play.

"But the real genius here is that his draw also takes away Cotter's hit-and-roll too. Brendan sees how this end will play out for the next three shots. He blocks the draw with Moulding's first and sees that that only leaves Cotter the hit-and-roll. If Cotter makes it perfectly and rolls to the button, then Bottcher taps back our puzzle shot and BC has nothing left.

"So again, we see a top Skip looking at his options in three-shot sequences. I block the draw, he plays the hit-and-roll, I tap him back with the one I just threw. In our game, that's about all you can plan for. Set up shapes and structures and conditions that are likely to help you as the end plays out, but do them in three-shot runs. Don't get too far ahead of yourself mapping out specific shots. It just doesn't work that way, even at the pro level."

We see in the video that Cotter doesn't have much choice but to try the hit-and-roll with his first and misses it by a fraction. Bottcher then blocks the counter-clockwise path with his first and Cotter decides his only chance of stealing or forcing is with a Hail Mary triple runback. It almost comes off but Bottcher delivers a piece of magic with his last to win the game.

To be honest, their front-end's set-up play deserved no less.

What lessons from this pro situation can I apply to my amateur standard of curling? First, I'm going to love my front-end. I'll get two good players and treat them well, carrying their brooms, fetching their water. They're going to set up ends for me, hold the line on my take-outs and drag my draws to the four-foot. Their importance to my team can't be overstated.

Secondly, I'm going to put myself in the other Skip's shoes. What will he play next? What options does he have? When he has two options, I'll take away the easiest.

Finally, I'll practice seeing the game in rolling three-shot windows. Even when watching games on TV, I'm going to try to see what the other Skip has, then plan the next three shots. I should be better for it when I get out on the ice.

Mickey's Last Word: "Be a genius. Put yourself in their shoes, see their options, then find a play that takes them away. Thinking in three-shot increments will help you see those opportunities."

Puzzle #33

Well, you hope this isn't a case of 'the older you get, the better you were'. By any standard, you were a Golden Boy back then and you'd like to think you still have it now. But you're up against another Golden Boy here, and he's got fewer miles on the clock. You need to be sharp and try to take your slender lead into the last couple of ends, wrap this game up and resume your place at the top of the heap. But how? Here's the situation:

- 8th end of 10
- You're red
- You're up by 1
- Yellow has hammer
- It's your Third's second shot
- About a five-foot swing

C'mon Skip, give us a shot that shows you know the difference between fool's gold and the real stuff. What's your call – and why?

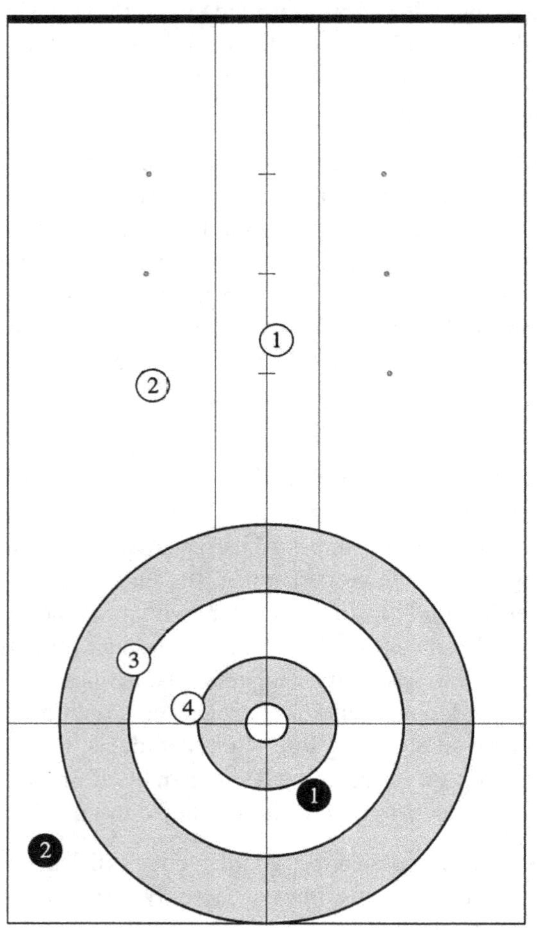

A Master at Work

At club level, sometimes we like to keep our tactics secret from the other team. Maybe they won't see something we see, or maybe they'll be thinking down different lines. Here in the game to determine whether the golden boy from the 2006 Olympics or the golden boy from the 2014 Olympics will represent Canada at Beijing 2022, there are no secrets. Both skips know exactly what's going on and exactly what is required. As does Mickey.

"Brad Gushue's discussion with Mark Nichols lets us hear what he's thinking. He's a Skip who, in 2022, was right at the very pinnacle of world curling and it's great to see him at work. What he's thinking about here is four principles: shapes, the rolling three-shot window, avoiding grouping his stones, and making his opponent play hard shots while he plays easier ones.

Four principles in one little shot? We'd better start with the first ones, shapes and the rolling three-shot window. How do these ideas sit together?

"Well, there's a difference between thinking about specific shots and thinking about general structures. We know what general structures or shapes favour us or threaten us. And as an end develops, we try to manage those. For instance, we often peel centre guards when we have hammer because that shape threatens a steal. And by peeling, we might roll to the side and encourage play out to the wings, which is where we want it. So we generally try to call shots that encourage play in the direction of travel we want.

"So we know the direction of travel we want, and we get there in three-shot sequences. Let's say we have hammer and they have one on the button guarded on Second's last. I know that's not a shape that's good for me and I want this end to head in a different direction. So I make a plan: I'll peel knowing they'll guard again and then I'll peel again to move towards the shape I want.

"But that's about as far as I go because I know that in those next three shots, we might miss our peel. Or their guard might slip into the rings or leave shot rock half-open. Or I might have miscalculated, and they might decide not to guard at all. So after each shot, depending on the results and how the situation has changed, I think about the objectives I'm trying to achieve, the overall type of end I want to play and the shape I want in order to achieve those. Then I reset my window and map out the next three shots. It sounds complicated, but it becomes second nature after a few thousand games, trust me.

"So that's what Brad G is doing here. At 1-up without in the 8th, his ideal outcome is to steal, he'd be okay with a force or a blank, but his third rail here — the one that would fry him — is to give up 2. In general, he wants to play some defence and cut their score and hold them to 1 — and all that's at the back of his mind.

"Then he starts considering the next three shots. You hear him say 'If we roll under, he's bumping it back for a pocket.' You can hear the gears grinding, thinking 'What would our third shot be? And is that a shape or situation I really want?' He doesn't have the rest of the end mapped out precisely, and he's just trying to think three shots ahead and move closer to his obje'tive, Ih at this point looks like a force-not his ideal outcome, but acceptable."

Okay, so I see he's playing three shots forward to build a shape or situation that's more favourable. I get that. What's the second principle he's playing?

"The next is very straightforward. What he doesn't want to do is group his rocks. There are two problems he could walk into if he did that. First, he might leave Jacobs a double to perhaps lie 2 with hammer. And secondly, grouped stones could set up a pocket that Jacobs could use to secure one of his own rocks in there. That could easily set up a 2 or 3-ball and that could be fatal. So Brad's going to play something that keeps his rocks pretty well-spaced and keeps the force alive."

And what's the last principle that Gushue's using to his advantage?

"The last general skipping principle he's using — and you hear him call out it down the ice — is to make Brad Jacobs play hard shots while he plays easy ones. It would be tempting to hit that Y4 and try and get under a guard but the perfect hit-and-roll is the most often called-and-missed shot in curling. He'd rather not play that if he doesn't have to.

"So he looks at the next three shots and thinks 'If we nose, he can't nose because if he did, we'd have an easy double to clean up.' And he sees that if he asks for a relatively straightforward nose hit then Brad J will have no choice but a very difficult hit-and-roll-under. And that suits Brad G to a tee. You hear him call 'I'd rather him play this hit-and-roll to be quite honest, and then we can freeze him.' The unspoken part: it's a hard shot and he probably won't make it. But if he does, we freeze him top button, cut down that scoring area and I think we can hold him to one."

Mickey spots a bonus point to highlight in a drive-by sort of way. "When you want to leave the other guy a tough double, try get your rocks at about a 45-degree angle like Gushue does with his last. Even if his own rock wasn't in the way, Jacobs' double is super-thin one way and he'd lose his shooter the other way. That's the perfect placement."

So what can I apply to my standard of curling? First, I need to think in shapes and three-shot windows. I want to create a structure and move in a general direction and I want to do that using the next three shots. I shouldn't bother thinking much beyond that.

Secondly, I need to be careful about grouping my stones if I'm trying to keep them in the rings or avoid setting up a pocket.

And finally, if I can think of three shots where I'm playing easy ones and force him to play tough ones, that's golden.

Mickey's Last Word: "I'm sure this all seems kinda daunting but keep it in perspective. First, know your objectives for the end — ideal, acceptable, unacceptable. Then know the type of the end you'd like to play to reach those objectives, and keep in mind the general shapes you'd like to encourage or discourage as the end plays out. Finally, let these other more tactical ideas, like avoiding grouping of stones and making him play tough shots, help you when you're thinking three shots ahead. Brad and Brad have been at it for a lifetime. Keep working at it and you'll get there before your final buzzer sounds."

Puzzle #34

Oh boy, you are licking your chops here. This is like an all-you-can-eat at the curling buffet. Time to fill your plate and dig in. You're up against The Kid, who's looking decidedly middle-aged now and maybe a little rusty. And you've got him on the ropes, lying 2 with a pile of shrapnel out in front. You just need to get another one in there and steal a bundle out from under his nose. But how? Here's the situation:

- It's the second end of 10
- You're yellow
- You're up by 1
- Red has hammer
- It's your Third's second shot
- About a four-foot swing on good ice

C'mon Skip, quit your drooling and give 'em a shot to fill their bellies. What's your call – and why?

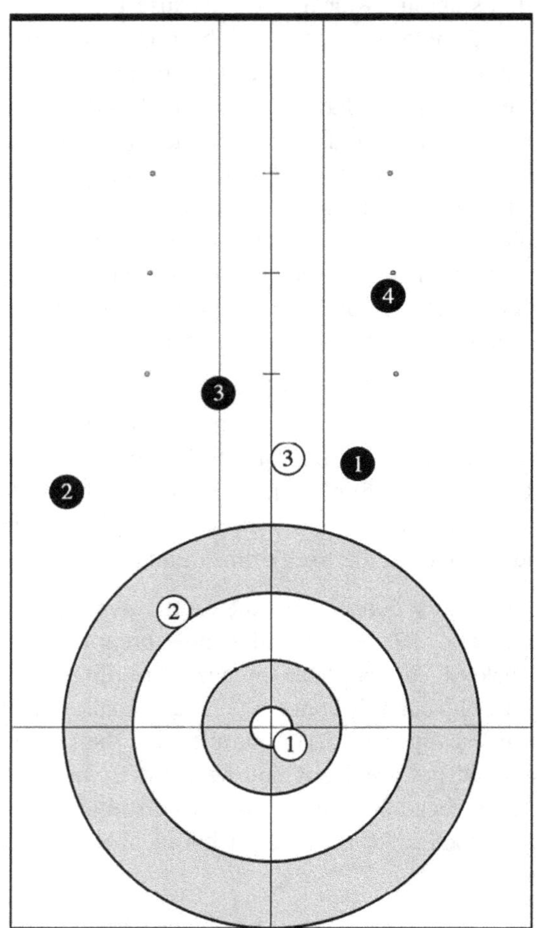

Don't Overextend When Your Goal is Within Reach

It's early in the game, and the Gunner (Jason Gunnlaugson, and yellow) has managed to earn a slim lead. Now he's defending without hammer. If we asked him about his ideal, acceptable and unacceptable outcomes for the end, I think he'd say that a steal is ideal, a force or a blank is acceptable, but giving up a deuce or more is his unacceptable outcome. He doesn't want to give up a big end that puts him behind.

And according to Mickey, he's in pretty good shape as we make our way towards Skip's rocks. "It looks like Jason has won the first two-thirds of this end. He's got shot rock buried in the four-foot, second shot is high in the rings, and all the draw paths are blocked by an assortment of guards. It's looking good for a force anyway, and with a bit of luck, maybe a steal.

"Importantly, he's got no opposition rocks in the rings – where the points are scored. We get kinda carried away with strategy and tactics sometimes, but it's important to remind ourselves that if the reds aren't in the rings, they don't count. So, with no reds in the rings and two yellows spaced apart so they can't be easily removed with one shot, the Gunner's in good shape."

This is where I start licking my chops and dreaming of a steal of 2. I'm thinking to myself 'Let's get another one in the rings behind all that cover and maybe take an unassailable lead right here!' Mickey – and The Gunner – put the brakes on any talk of that.

"It's tempting to loop one more around," Mickey says, "but you need to keep your goal in mind and not get too greedy. You're going for a steal or a force. It's down to Third's last rocks, so James Grattan has to be addressing shot rock and he'll be doing that with runbacks. He's already thrown one so you know more are coming until he digs out your Y1.

"By putting another yellow in the house, you're essentially setting up another catcher for the runback. You'll hear

Jason say 'It makes the runback unmissable' and that's the problem with going for more. If you set up a pocket for him to run his guard into and he sits behind all that junk out front, you've allowed him to go from chasing to controlling. Be patient, be measured, keep your objective in mind. You're in good shape. Don't blow it. Setting up another catcher is how you could blow it."

And maybe by failing to address that powerful red R3 out in front, I ask? I'm starting to catch on to the notion of 'powerful rocks' and even I spot the looming threat of that red guard in the centre. It's fairly close and it's sitting right over the four-foot circle – where the points are scored. When Mickey talks about 'powerful rocks', he generally means rocks that are close to the rings and threaten that four-foot circle by owning that path. They can be used to run back onto opponents' stones, and they can be used to tap back to score. They're dangerous.

"Yes, for sure," Mickey confirms. "That rock is a little way out of the rings but it's still the primary threat to Jason's shot rock, so if you can do something about that now, so much the better."

As an aside, I wonder about rocks behind tee. Aren't they also dangerous and therefore powerful, I wonder?

"They're dangerous and they're useful," Mickey answers, "but I wouldn't call them powerful. They can be used as catchers for the team that's trying to score so you don't want them hanging around if you're defending. But once they're behind tee line, it's pretty hard to move them back into scoring position. Dangerous depending on your perspective, but in my book, not what I would call powerful."

Okay, so it's primarily rocks that hover above the scoring zone that we'll call 'powerful'. But how about at the club level or for teams who don't play with the same precision as the pros? Does that red R3 still have a lot of power?

"At a club level or for a team that maybe isn't yet playing at a highly competitive level, runbacks aren't going to made with a lot of frequency, so that guard might not carry the same power. If you're playing against less precise curlers, the main threat is the counter-clockwise draw, so you might want to go top rings in that gap on the counter-clockwise side (between R3 and Y2), ideally edge-buried under R3 so your opponent can't double out two of your yellows with one rock. That should set you up nicely for Skip's rocks."

So the Gunner does all the things Mickey recommends. He doesn't give Grattan another target or catcher for his runback, and he guards up to take away the power of R3 in front. Jonathon Beuk, the New Brunswick Third, makes a nice runback, Grattan misses his and all The

Gunner has to do is drop a simple guard out front. But are gunners the types of folks known for their touch and feel? Not generally – and not on his last shot.

Anyway, my takeaways from this situation? First, don't lose sight of my goals, get too greedy, overextend, and end up helping the other guy. Once I've won the first half of the end, reinforce my position and make sure I reach my goal.

And second, recognize the other guy's powerful rocks and see if I can't address those.

Mickey's Last Word: "Keep your goal in mind and consolidate when you're within reach. And don't get greedy. Recognize when putting additional rocks in the rings might create offence for the other guy."

Puzzle #35

This is a multi-shot sequence of puzzles. After each situation, we'll discuss the Skip's choice and the shot played – but we'll save the QR code and the Big Reveal until the last puzzle in the sequence, Puzzle 37. If you can hold off and work through each puzzle first, we think you'll get more out of watching the three plays unfold together and see how the front-end shot choices influenced the rest of the end.

Oh no. The Blank Slate. You hate these calls. You could do anything here – guard, draw, tick, peel. Well, you can't peel, of course, not with the five-rock free guard rule. But you know what you throw here will influence the rest of the end, and you want to get it right. If only you could remember what you discussed in the team meeting before the game? Oh well. Here's the situation:

- 1st end of 10
- Tied at 0-0, naturally
- You're red
- And you have the hammer
- It's your Lead's first shot
- About a five-foot swing on good ice

C'mon Skip, give 'em a shot that makes them think you know what you're doing. What's your call – and why?

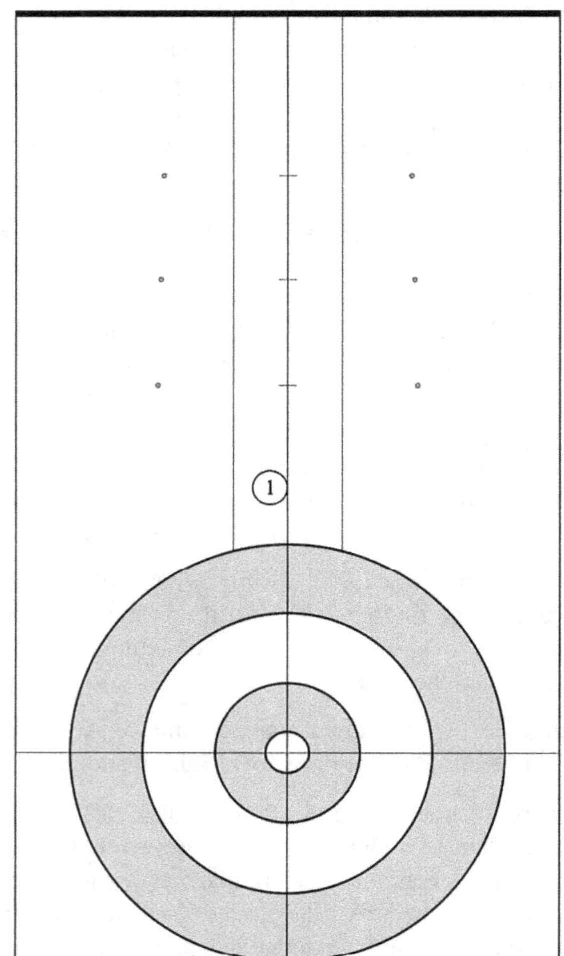

Know Your Options, Know Where They Lead

As a Newbie Skip, I struggle with how to open an end. Fortunately, Mickey's on hand to explain the choices faced by John Epping and Scott McDonald as they battled at the 2021 Brier.

"Scott McDonald has thrown the tight guard, and now John has three or four options available, depending on how he wants the end to play out," says Mickey. "His first option is to come around McDonald's tight guard and try and own that four-foot area. He'd be playing a safe, patient end that says, 'I'm going to get underneath and make you chase me. If I get half-miss or you rub a guard, maybe I get two split in the house and we manufacture a deuce out of it.'

"By calling that shot, John would not be letting rocks build up out front that could generate a complicated end. If both teams play well early on, he'll probably get a few stones grouped in the middle, then someone will run back the centre guard, and we'll have rocks flying about. If he wins the angles in there and the other guy doesn't execute, John might get a chance for a deuce.

"But it's a safe play in the rings that doesn't let a huge amount of junk build up out front so it likely keeps the draw path open later for a single if needed. And it keeps the blank alive since the rocks are all grouped in the middle and can be removed more easily. It might result in offence but should leave a decent chance at a blank or at least a single."

Okay, so that's Option 1. What else could he do?

"Another option here – if you can execute – is the tick shot, ideally pushing them to the side and rolling your shooter to the other side in front of the rings. It's an

"

offensive/defensive shot that takes care of that powerful centre guard and gives you a chance at corner guards that could generate some offence. Even if you roll in, they'll hit, you'll hit, someone rolls out and it's probably a blank.

"Brad Jacobs called this a lot because he liked a patient game – and he had Ryan Harnden, one of the best Leads in the game. But if you don't have Ryan and don't make the tick shot, you've thrown your rock away and handed the advantage to the other guy. They'll play another guard in the centre or draw around their own and put you under pressure within the first two rocks."

So that's also a conservative opening – if you can make that very precise shot. What's the third option?

"The third option is to throw the corner guard, and that's what John does in our game. What he's saying is, 'I know you're going to create a threat by throwing another centre guard or going around to top-four, but I don't care. I'm throwing the guard, then we're going to duke it out in the middle for the next few shots, and I think my guys can out-execute your guys. I bet we'll win the battle of the angles in there and later, once the centre gets cleaned up, I hope I get a chance to make use of that corner and score a few.'"

"John's a naturally offensive player who likes to score big, and in this case, against a team with a new Skip, he decides to go right after them, throw a corner up, complicate the end and try to take advantage of the hammer. He's basically sending a message here, saying 'I'm coming after you right here in the very first end. I'm going to give you a little bit of a head start in the middle, but I'm betting my guys will claw back it back and maybe then we can use that corner and score big.' It's a pretty bold opening."

So that's three responses: the come-around, the tick and the corner guard. What's the fourth option?

"This is a good one for club-level competition. You just throw to the side eight-foot to see if they'll hit it. If you get the miss, draw to the other side and set up your deuce. Or you hit and stick a couple of times. If they roll out, you can peel the centre guard or take your chances and come around with just a few rocks left. But the key is that both teams are spending rocks, playing in the rings without a lot of shrapnel out in front, and it makes for a nice, simple end without much risk.

"This play works if you know you're in over your head and want to apply a little pressure without risking going around the centre guard. We don't see it much at the elite level, but it's OK at most other levels to minimize risk and play patiently, waiting for their miss."

Mickey makes one other key point about your options.

"If you think your team can execute at a higher level than the other guys, why wouldn't you junk it up, get lots of rocks in play and keep shots at a high degree of difficulty? Put the pressure on them and make them perform.

"But if you think they have the better players, I think it's better to keep the game simple with straightforward hits, look for half-misses and take advantage then."

My takeaways? First, with hammer, I have four responses to their centre guard, depending on how I want to play the end:

1. The come-around to top-four – A safer option for a more open end where I can pounce on half-misses. Keeps the single or blank alive.

2. Tick shot – Tricky but a good offensive/defensive shot that eliminates the centre threat and might set up a corner guard to use later. Not recommended for the club player.

3. The corner guard – Gives the other guy a head start in the centre, but I'm hoping we can outplay them over the next four or five rocks and set up a chance to bring that corner into play. Higher risk if my guys don't execute and I get bogged down under centre guards.

4. Finally, draw to the wings to encourage a simple hitting game out there, wait for a half-chance so I can come around or peel the centre guard.

My second takeaway? If I back my team to play better than the other guys, I'm going to junk it up and make them play complicated shots, hack-weighters, tricky freezes and chips, and try and generate a big score. But if they have better skills, I'll keep it clean and simple and make easy hits and straightforward draws. When they make a mistake, I'll try to seize the opportunity to score.

Mickey's Last Word: "Know what type of end you want to play, understand how your first couple of rocks set the tone for the end, and plan accordingly."

Puzzle #36

In this second of three parts, we now find ourselves as Scott McDonald, facing an aggressive team Epping who look like they want to mix it up right out of the gate. Again, you can skip ahead to the QR code in Puzzle #37, or hang tight and put your wits against two of our most aggressive Skips.

Oh no. Team Epping looks like they mean business. And they have the guys to deliver. If I were you, I'd be especially concerned about that Fry-Guy at Third. Anyone who delivers from their belly must be pretty useful. Anyway, they've got the corner up, so they're coming after you right out of the blocks. What to do, what to do? Here's the situation:

- 1st end of 10
- Score is tied
- You are now yellow
- You don't have hammer
- It's your Lead's second shot
- Good five-foot swing

C'mon Skip, give us a call that puts them on their back, not their belly. What's your call – and why?

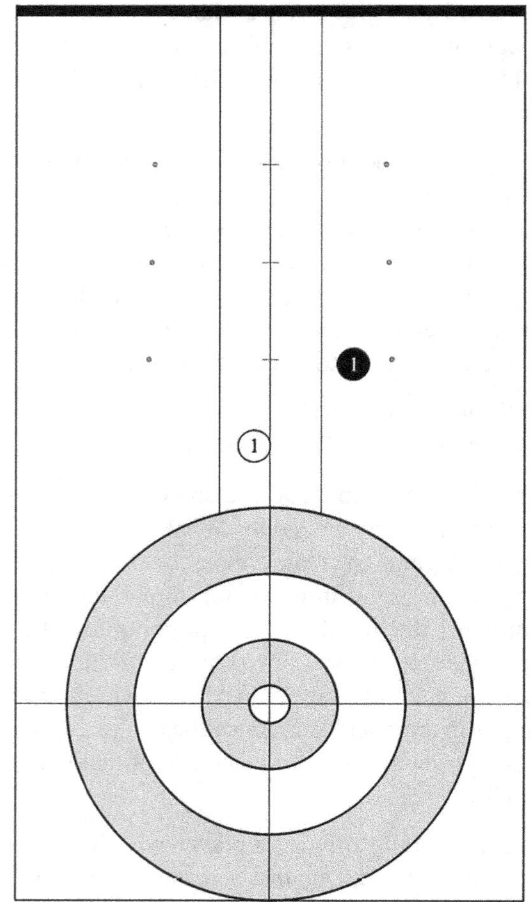

The Hoover Gambit

In this second part of the puzzle, we find ourselves playing as Scott McDonald (yellow), trying to figure out how to respond to John Epping's red corner. Mickey sets out his options.

"McDonald has an interesting decision to make. His first option is to come around his own guard, Y1, try to set up in the four-foot and keep play away from the corner. But his guard is so tight that it's a little bit like the grouping of stones concept. If McDonald goes around, Epping follows him in and sits on top. McDonald then comes around again and freezes. When they finish all that, those rocks are now stacked up just a couple of feet from the guard in front. Matt Camm and Ryan Fry make those short runbacks in their sleep.

"And when they play that runback, everything will be moving, and the winner will be decided by the angles. Maybe McDonald's third shot curls across the nose of Epping's freeze, and the runback would squeeze out Epping's rock. Or maybe Epping's freeze is sandwiched perfectly between two yellows, and McDonald's rocks fly out."

"To McDonald, that's the risk of playing around a tight guard. If Epping gets those angles perfect and then runs the guard in, his rocks might be lying. Maybe he even springs one toward his corner guard."

So if that centre guard were, say, three or four feet higher, would the come-around be a better option?

"Yes, it would, because then the runback isn't so certain. And if the runback is missed, then McDonald can solidify his position in the centre and really start to squeeze this end."

Would this be a different story at club level, I ask?

"That's a good question," Mickey answers. "At club level, even short runbacks aren't automatic, so the come-around might be a better option. It would be the 'get there first' tactic, and you'd hope to sit top-button or four-foot, complicate things and maybe get a steal."

But the guard is where the guard is and McDonald knows the runback is likely to connect. What's another good play he could make?

"Scott's other option – and the one he plays in this puzzle – is to throw a long centre to set up double guards down the middle and drag play back to the four-foot. Set up double centres and in a close game, John really has no option but to go around them – before McDonald gets under them on his next. Epping has to 'get there first'. The only three situations in which John would not go around those guards is (a) if he has a reasonable chance of peeling them both with one shot and rolling the shooter, (b) if he could chip the tight guard and roll into the rings under his guard, or (c) if he is way behind on score and decides to use his corner now. Otherwise, he's gotta beat McDonald in. And that means the play is coming back to the centre and away from that corner, which is exactly what McDonald wants."

That double guard in response to a corner seems like a giant vacuum (in Scotland, we call them Hoovers!) just sucking Epping's next shot into the centre. But there must be a drawback to playing the double centre since not all teams throw it?

"Teams play with different appetites for risk. For example, Bottcher and Jacobs might choose to be more conservative and come around the tight guard, confident they'll make the runbacks and doubles to clean things up.

"Other Skips like Kevin Koe and Jennifer Jones play more aggressively and try to put the other team under pressure. They don't mind lots of guards in play and are willing to take a few more risks. Keep in mind that Scott McDonald is from Ontario, and the Ontario style is the drawing, tapping game. Scott's pretty comfortable risking a couple of guards out front, forcing a technical game in the four-foot and keeping Epping away from his corner.

"But there's no doubt it's a riskier play. You can give up a 3-ender pretty easily when you throw double centres. If you set them up and then get outplayed in the middle of the rings, those centre guards will be hurting you, not them. McDonald's giving Epping the chance to grab that scoring territory first. If he grabs it and McDonald's guys can't get their following rocks into good positions – say they crash on a guard or something – Epping will have a chance to get more rocks in the rings, behind his corner or more in the four-foot, and Scott will be chasing for the rest of the end.

"So if you're not comfortable playing more technical come-arounds and tap backs and freezes, then don't play the high guard. Go around the centre into the rings now and play a simpler end."

What happens? "I love the mind games that are going on right from the start of this game," says Mickey. "John ignored Scott's first centre guard and threw a corner, essentially saying, 'I'm not afraid of you, so buckle up.' And then on this puzzle shot, Scott opts to throw the double centre guard, saying, 'Bring it on, let's go!' It's a lot of fun to watch these guys go head-to-head right out of the gate."

You'll see Team McDonald play a nice guard in the middle, about eight feet above their first, so Epping really has no choice but to draw around to the top of the four-foot and 'beat him in'. McDonald tries to follow but rubs his own tight guard and rolls open. That's where we'll pick this up in the next and final part of this multi-puzzle.

So, what is this Newbie Skip taking away from this situation – a disrespectful opponent ignoring my centre guard and throwing a corner? First, I can play the come-around into top-four. It's a safer play, especially at the club level where runbacks aren't automatic. I'll be seizing the high ground first and making them chase. If they do make the runback when the five-rock rule expires, rocks will fly, and it will likely be an open end where the blank is a more likely outcome.

Secondly, I could play a long centre guard. In a close game in which my opponent won't want to bet the farm by using their corner right away, that pretty much guarantees that they'll come around both of my rocks, and play will come back to the middle where I want it. Of course, setting it up to let them get in first behind double guards carries a few risks, and my team will have to execute and make the rest of our shots in the four-foot. Dicey.

Mickey's Last Word: "Throwing a double centre guard will draw play to the middle. Just be ready to make some tough shots."

Puzzle #37

In Part II of this puzzle, Scott McDonald threw double centre guards (Y1 and Y2) forcing John Epping to draw around to top-four (R2). McDonald tries to follow him down with his Y3 but rubs the tight Y1 guard and rolls open – the risk that Mickey was talking about. In this final part, you're playing as Epping (red) and trying to decide what to do with this gift…

Oh, this looks juicy. You knew your pro guys were going to outplay these part-timers. Now it's time to lower the boom. Of course, there is a little matter of that shrapnel out front, and this end isn't the wide-open shape that usually favours teams with hammer. But come on, lying 1 with a corner and about to throw? This is like shootin' fish in a barrel! Here's the situation:

- 1st end of 10
- Score is tied
- You're now red
- You have hammer
- It's your Second's first shot
- Good five-foot swing

C'mon Skip, give 'em a shot that has them swimming around in circles. What's your call – and why?

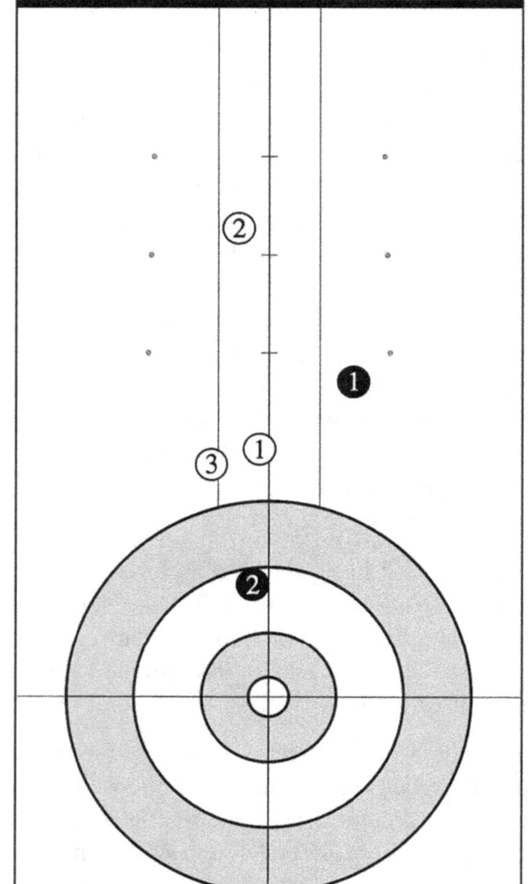

Once Again, If You Play With Fire…

John Epping would love to score a deuce here in the first, but he doesn't want to give up a steal either. Team McDonald has just crashed on their guard and rolled open to Y3. Is the green light now flashing for go, or is the yellow light flashing for caution?

The issue here is whether Epping thinks the opportunities outweigh the risks. Part of him wants to draw for points, but the yellows down the middle can be very dangerous. This is not typically the shape of an end that favours the team with hammer. They would much rather have play moved out to the sides with much, as Mickey calls it, 'breathing room' to spread their rocks around, avoid double takeouts, and if things don't work out, make sure they have a draw to score their single with their last. This end isn't looking anything like that!

But then again, Epping has a corner that can be used, he's lying shot, is about to throw another one in the rings, and has hammer. He can almost see the 3 on the scoreboard.

The risk he's facing is McDonald's two centre guards. If McDonald gets buried under all that shrapnel first, Epping might be done.

"This shot is the turning point of the end," says Mickey. "John can take the path of safety first, decide that the centre guards favour the team without hammer, start to clear them up and make sure he doesn't give up a steal.

"Or, he can leave the front junked up, come in, lie 2 and hope to score a big end. But the risk is that if his team misses a few shots, McDonald's got protection in the middle and if he gets one underneath, John might be hard-pressed to score."

So what exactly are John's options? I suggest the wide clockwise draw around the corner R1. Epping's Lead, Brent Laing, likes that one but Mickey and John aren't buying.

"You could do that, but you've left that centre congestion there," says Mickey. "If you miss – get heavy or rub a guard or something – and McDonald gets under the centre, you'll spend the rest of the end trying to dig him out. You might have nothing but a difficult draw on unknown, first-end ice just to score 1. That's a risky call."

OK, then let's double peel those yellows and open things up.

"The angles are difficult,' Mickey replies. "If you try to peel the Y2 guard across the top of the tight yellow guards, any connection pretty much takes out your shot rock R2. And if you run Y2 straight back, you're leaving your shooter sitting in front and what have you accomplished? Both options aren't that appealing."

Alright then. If in doubt, peel one guard. Matt Camm is arguing for this shot, and John looks at it.

"That's not a bad call," agrees Mickey, "and maybe that's the right call at club level. Your opponent either puts it back, and you do it again, or he tries running one of those front yellows into your shot rock. If he misses, you wrap around your corner, and you've tilted the scale towards a deuce.

"At the competitive level, it might not be the shot. If you peel the high centre guard, then the short runback onto your shot rock – probably using Y1 – becomes open. Good hitters make that for fun. And even if they miss, they'll still have powerful rocks still hovering at the top of the rings. You would have to clear those, go around them, or go around your corner. Clearing them up leads to a blank, going around them lets them run back another at you, and going around your corner allows him to sit another rock in the centre and take control there. None of those paths really lead you towards a deuce."

OK, I ask, what would you and John Epping play then?

"Well, John being John, I know he wants to go all-in here and try and score 3. Lying 2 with hammer behind a bunch of guards is a very juicy proposition, but it is not without risk."

"The shot he plays, and I like it, is the counter-clockwise draw to get fully into the eight-foot at about a 45-degree angle off the corner of their R2 shot rock. It's down a known path that they've been using in their draw-to-the-button before the game started, it's buried, it's a difficult angle for a double, you're lying 2, and the other guy is chasing. It's pretty nice."

The downsides of this play? Brent Laing knows them, and when John Epping suggests it, he calls out, "I don't love that. We're gonna get in trouble."

Mickey explains Brent's concerns. "Well, you're leaving a shape that McDonald wants, a clogged centre that favours the team without hammer. Even after you make this shot – and Matt Camm couldn't have played it any better – McDonald is still pretty happy, with three-quarters of an end to play. If he can get one or two buried under there, then you'll be chasing him, and you'll be in trouble with all that granite out in front."

"So the key point here is that if they stick this rock anywhere in the middle, it's a gamble to leave a shape that McDonald likes. If you don't out-execute the other guys, and they get buried under a ton of granite down the middle, you'll be lucky not to give up a steal."

What happens downstream? Well, Brent Laing was bang on, and it pretty much goes pear-shaped for John Epping from this point forward. McDonald's part-timers out-execute John Epping's full-timers – and steal 3. You can certainly blame poor execution, but Epping chose to take on the risk with the shape of the end he called. This time he got burned.

So what can I take away from this puzzle for use at my level? If I decide to pursue the big end and leave a shape that doesn't favour me, my team had better execute flawlessly, or we risk a bad outcome. If I don't think I can outplay the other guys, I should play simple shots that keep working towards my goals but in a shape that comes with less risk: lots of 'breathing room' with access to the four-foot for my last.

Mickey's Last Word: "If you don't bail when rocks are positioned in the other team's favour, you better make everything. Recognize when an end is shaping up against you.

Puzzle #38

What a racket your guys are making! Sure, it's a delicate moment, with you needing two points to win or a single to take your chances in the extra end. But it's not like you're struggling in this situation. It's almost embarrassing having to choose between the abundance of shots you have available to you. It's just a matter of selecting the best, making it, and wrapping up a memorable win. But which shot? Here's the situation:

- 10th end of 10
- You're yellow
- You're down by 1
- But you have hammer
- It's your Third's second shot
- About a five-foot swing on good ice

C'mon Skip, give 'em a shot that shuts them up once and for all. What's your call – and why?

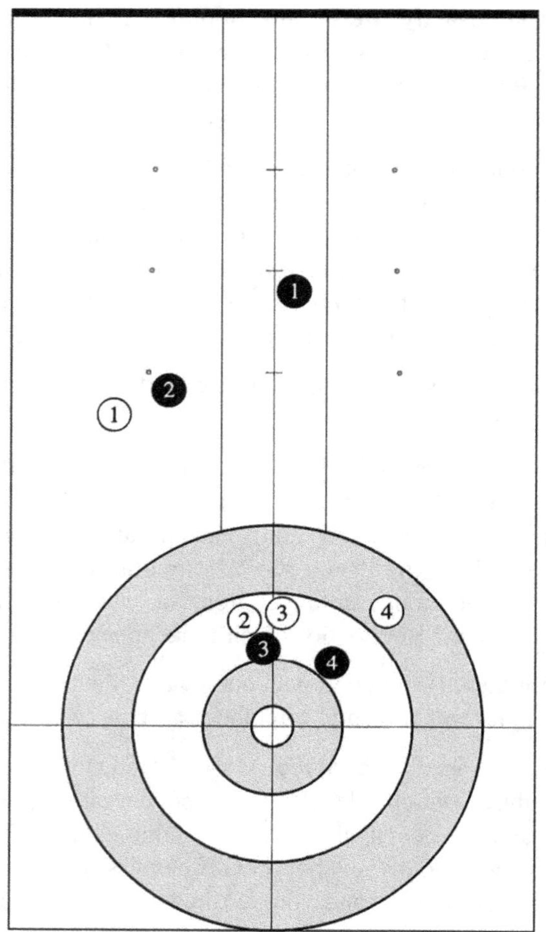

Risk = Chance x Consequence

Puzzles are sometimes like city buses: you wait for one forever, then two or three come along at the same time. And that's the case here as Kevin Koe battles John Epping in the 2020 Brier. Every one of either team's shots – from Colton Flasch's first through to Kevin Koe's last – involved so many choices. For fun, go back to 2:01:00 in the video, make a call before each shot and see how you do. Then try to figure out why they called what they did. What a great end of curling!

When it comes to our puzzle shot, I found it fiendishly difficult to decipher and struggle to weigh up the pros and cons of one shot versus the other. Fortunately, Mickey is here to help.

"First of all, there's not much point in bailing out in this situation. At the pro level, going into the extra without hammer is almost certainly a loss, so Kevin needs to keep pressing for 2 here.

"The problem he faces is that it's late in the end and Epping is lying two reds. Kevin needs to have a definite route to deal with those with his next three rocks – and do that without leaving Epping ways to bury one or kill lots of yellows and force Koe to a single point. If Epping can bury behind a stagger, Kevin might be forced and lose the game in the extra.

"Or if Epping can make a triple and a double, Kevin could be forced. That seems unlikely, but the rocks are grouped, so you never know. Anyway, those are the rules of this situation: don't let Epping draw behind a stagger, and don't leave any triples."

During the time-out, the team looked at two options: the board-weight nose hit on Y2 to deal with R3, and the nose hit on the open R4. Kevin decided to deal with R3 first, but Mickey disagrees.

"If Kevin noses R4 like Ted Appleman suggests, what would John have? There's no triple, and Kevin will always have multiple rocks hovering above the four-foot area to kill any reds in the centre. It's almost an embarrassment of riches. Any one of them could be used to nail anything that John gets in there. I mean, what could John play?"

But Kevin didn't call this seemingly obvious shot. Mickey called him up to discuss his choice.

"First of all, Kevin's tried to put this game out of his mind. He missed a tricky double and lost the game, so he's not too keen to revisit it. I encouraged him to think of it as therapy. When he watched it back, he said, "That should have always been a deuce. I just missed.'

"In general, he thought both the shots they discussed were good options – if they were made perfectly. But he thought the downsides of missing the shot they played – leaving a stagger or grouping his rocks to leave a triple – were less than the downsides of missing the nose on R4.

"The problem with playing R4 is making the hit but rolling away. That would leave John the wrap-around to the back-four to sit second-shot under a guard and a stagger. Kevin might not have a shot for 2."

I'm starting to get it. If risk equals the chances of something happening times the consequences if it does happen, the risk playing that nose hit is quite high. The chances are relatively slim – BJ probably makes that hit and stick nine-out-of-ten times – but if it's the one time he rolls, then the consequences are very high. John draws to the back of the four-foot, and that could be the ball game.

"There's an additional risk with playing the nose on R4," Mickey says, "and that's that it might force John to throw a guard and protect his shot rock R3. Sure, nobody wants to guard one solitary red in a bunch of yellows, but John just might be forced into it. Kevin would have the angle slash on a corner guard (R2 or Y1), but that's a 50/50 shot. Well, for Kevin, it's a higher probability than that, but you get my point. He'd be scrambling a bit. At club level, a guard forcing us to an angle runback could be lethal."

But there are risks associated with the shot he played, I mention. He could cross over the nose, roll onto the corner of R3 and leave a stagger for John to get underneath. And he'll always be leaving some double, if not triple.

"The double is fine. Kevin would still be lying 2 and throwing, so he has a route to a deuce and the win. The stagger could be a problem, but if John gets around it, Kevin can always double it out using R4. Besides, he thinks that by throwing hack weight, his sweepers will be able to control the line. They'd have a very high probability of hitting Y2 on the nose or above, which is precisely what happened.

"So for him, it was just a matter of weighing up the downsides on the two shots. If they miss the hit on Y2 and leave John a wrap-around, they can still use R4 to get out of it. But if they miss the nose hit on R4 and roll away, John can wrap-around, and Kevin probably wouldn't have a shot. As it turned out, Kevin's last two attempts didn't come off the way he wanted, and he lost the game. Execution always matters."

As I watch the timeout, I'm always surprised at Kevin's patience in taking input from his team – even his enthusiastic Lead. Mickey's not.

"I've seen Skips who are so insecure that they're unwilling to accept suggestions from their teammates, thinking it makes them look weak. But really, it's just the opposite. Kevin told me he's totally happy with the discussion by the team and feels that that input is likely to produce a better decision. Kevin is one of the greatest strategists in the game, and if he's willing to stand there on national TV and let his guys suggest what he should play, maybe the Little Napoleons of our local leagues should be willing to do that too. They'd certainly win more games."

So what lessons can I take away from this puzzle and use at my level? First, I need to consider the downsides of an option. It's tempting to consider all the good outcomes of one shot versus another, but sometimes it's best to consider all the bad things that could go wrong. Risk is the likelihood of something happening multiplied by the consequences if it does happen. Something might not be very likely to happen – like BJ rolling away on a nose hit – but if the consequences of a missed shot are really high (i.e. losing the game), maybe that's a shot best avoided.

Secondly, on Third's rocks, I need be thinking about how to cash in on our set-up play, move their rocks out and set up my score. I need to switch into 'Don't leave them a way out' mode.

And finally, I'm going to accept lots of input from all team members at critical decision points. Who knows which player will throw out the best idea?

Mickey's Last Word: "When you have a great setup, choose the shot with the least risk so you don't give away the advantage."

Puzzle #39

Woohooo, down by just 1 in the Brier semi-final, up against one of the Biggest Beasts in the curling jungle. Surely you can see this through. Make him score here, and this could work out. Sure, you'd be 2-down going into the final three ends, but you'll get the hammer in the 8th and then (hopefully) again in the 10th. A force-deuce-force-deuce books your spot in the final. This could be the moment you take control. But how? Here's the situation:

- 7th end of 10
- You're red
- You're down by 1
- Yellow has hammer
- It's your Lead's second shot
- About a five-foot swing on good ice

C'mon Skip, get ready to use one of your hammers to bop the Big Beast on the head. What's your call – and why?

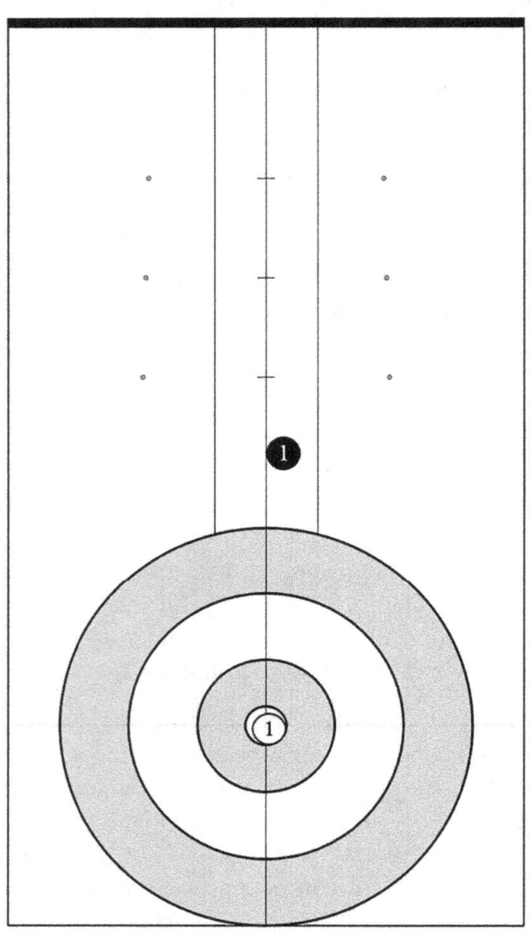

Half-In, Fully Out

"It's an interesting end because Newfoundland knows what Saskatchewan's plan is. They're going to leave rocks in play and try to force....which gives Newfoundland an opportunity to score a big end." – Cheryl Bernard in the commentary booth, setting up the 7th end.

I think it's fair to say that the commentators were not keen on how Matt Dunstone attempted to force here in the 7th end of the 2020 Brier semi-final. Mickey is in complete agreement.

"At 1-down, Saskatchewan really wants to force Newfoundland here in the 7th end, so they get the hammer back in the 8th and ideally in the 10th. Newfoundland knows that, and they want to keep their options open, jumping on any opportunity to score a deuce but also ready to knock some rocks around and take a blank into the 8th.

"Gushue comes around the Saskatchewan tight guard with his first, Y1, wanting to own the top four. That shot works for Brad in a couple of ways. First, he gets there first and forces Saskatchewan to make some quality shots if they want to steal. And secondly, it could lead to a cluster of stones behind a tight guard. Brad's thinking he can run the guard back later into the group and perhaps get a blank to take hammer into the 8th and then hopefully the 10th too.

"So, Matt has a couple of options after Brad's come-around. But the problem is that he doesn't really commit here," explains Mickey. "He knows that throwing the long guard may be the best way to avoid the blank. He'll create a pile of granite out front, and there will be rocks in play. And it might even create an opportunity to steal if they outplay Gushue.

"But of course, it adds risk. Using his Lead's second to set-up a double centre lets Gushue put another into the four-foot to lie 2 fully buried, with hammer. Matt decides the risk is too great and follows Gushue around the tight guard.

You can pretty much hear the commentators slowly deflate. "I thought Saskatchewan would throw up a second centre," says Russ Howard. "If it gets dicey here, they only have that one rock to get out of jail." Russ is referring to the lonely R1 to give them cover in the middle.

One shot later: "Here goes the last guard." – Russ, as Brett Gallant blows everything up.

"A couple of centre guards would have made that tougher." – Cheryl.

"Ya, you either go for it, or you don't, right. And they kinda went half-in." – Russ, preparing to fill the next five minutes of airtime as the two teams play out a blank.

Mickey shares their puzzlement. "The conventional way of setting up a mess in the middle to get a force or a steal is to throw another centre guard, well-separated and lined up so they can't be peeled off in one shot without leaving the shooter.

"Faced with two good guards, Gushue could try to tick – but that could put corners in play and make it easier for Matt to hide one later and take away Gushue's blank. So Brad will likely loop his second shot around into the centre – and then Matt would have his nice, complicated end going in the four-foot behind two good centre guards. Both teams would be forced to tip and tap, and that often leads to someone scoring 1. For Saskatchewan, either team scoring 1 is a good outcome."

I point out that Matt uses his third shot to tap a rock back, trying to get the guddle going and build a pocket. Pockets keep rocks in play and can make a mess of an end. And it might mean some of Saskatchewan's reds are in the paint when Gushue's Second and Third finish blasting. Maybe he can split the rings and get his force that way, I suggest.

"Both approaches can work," Mickey replies. "It's just a matter of how badly you want it and how much risk you are willing to take on. Leaving only one guard out in front and using your shots to set up a pocket might get rocks in play and might get you a force. Throwing the double guards puts up a pile of granite out front and is more likely to create the force. But the risk with that is, as the saying goes, that you might force them to 2 or 3 if you don't execute.

"But the upshot is that if you play an end around a tight guard and the other guy wants to clear it up, well, that's pretty doable – especially at this level. It takes Brett Gallant one rock to blow the whole thing up, and the blank is almost a certainty after that.

"At club level, where five-foot runbacks aren't usually made, I like Matt's call of coming around the guard. Get the congestion going and see if you can't get superior rock positions to the other team. Maybe you even get a steal out of that. But at this level, those rocks are grouped together under a tight guard, and it's just too easy for Gushue to clean that up."

The funny thing about how things worked out: Gushue got his blank here in the 7th end. In the next, Dunstone threw up two centre guards as everyone suggested – and forced Gushue to 1.

But sadly for Saskatchewan, Newfoundland was now scoring in the even ends. Team Dunstone scored a deuce in the 9th to level the score, leaving Gushue needing just a single to win in the 10th. Had Dunstone gone harder and got the force in the 7th instead of the 8th, he would have had hammer in the evens going into the last three ends, and Brier history might have been different.

My takeaway for my level: If I need a force or steal at club level, I can go around a tight centre guard and take my chances. At the competitive level, where guys can clean up with a tight guard, I need to set up well-separated, in-line guards, create a mess in the middle, and be prepared to outplay them in the centre.

Mickey's Last Word: "Against a team that can make five-foot runbacks, playing around a tight guard will not get you the force or steal if they don't want it. You have to go all-in and get messy."

Puzzle #40

Hmmm. That other guy didn't clear out your reds hovering at the top of the twelve-foot and played another guard (Y4) instead. Does he know what he's doing? Maybe his gold medal was a fluke. Then again, maybe your run at this year's Brier has been the fluke. After all, you haven't thrown a rock for donkey's years. But you're calling a good game and making your shots. Maybe a donkey year isn't that long after all. Anyway, he's throwing guards and leaving your dangerous rocks, so it's probably time to lower the boom on him. But how? Here's the situation:

- 2nd end of 10
- You're red
- You're down by 2
- But you have hammer
- It's your Third's first shot
- About a six-foot swing on second-end ice

C'mon Skip, don't make an ass of yourself. What's your call – and why?

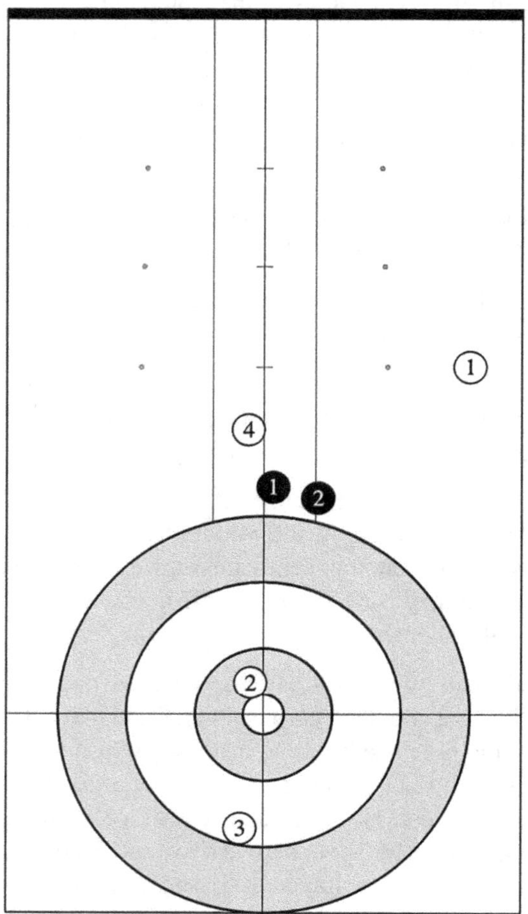

All or Nothing

This puzzle finds Brad Gushue (Olympic gold medallist, world champion, and yellow) putting the heat on Wayne Middaugh (not a donkey, also a world champion, and red) in their matchup at the 2021 Brier. Before we get to the puzzle shot, let's figure out what Brad's doing when he left those two reds and threw another guard. Why isn't he playing safe, Mickey?

"This whole situation is set up by the quality of Geoff Walker's shot (Y2) to top button. First, it's stayed in front of the tee line so Wayne can't freeze his way out of trouble. And secondly, because it's top-button and not top-eight/top-four, it's shrunken that scoring area so much that it's tough for Wayne to get behind it to score 1, let alone 2. So just by having his Lead go top-button rather than top-four or top-eight, Brad threatens a steal instead of a force. That's a huge lesson for Leads and Skips when you want to threaten the steal."

OK, great point. But the reds, Mickey, the reds. Why is Brad throwing a guard and not clearing out those dangerous rocks hovering above the rings?

"If they were easily removable, I think Brad would have played safe and cleared them out. Sitting up there they would usually have a lot of power, especially for guys who make six-foot runbacks on a regular basis.

"But the reds aren't level or cornered on each other so a double to clear them out isn't automatic. It would be easy to hit the high R1 a little fat, push the low R2 into the rings and spin his shooter up to the corner. Wayne would come down, make a play on shot rock and sit two in the rings with hammer. Brad doesn't want to take that chance so he's not hitting.

"But what he does is use some three-shot thinking here and sets up staggered guards. He sees that if gets Y4/R1 overlapped, Middaugh will have only R2 angle runback to deal with shot rock. If Middaugh calls it and misses, then Gushue could throw another centre guard and make it really hard for Wayne to avoid the steal. Even if Middaugh's team kills shot rock but doesn't stick it, Brad could loop another around to button under the staggered guards that are left and Wayne's still in trouble. So when Brad sets up the stagger and Wayne calls out, 'It's all or nothing' by playing the R2 runback, this is what he's talking about. If Scott Howard doesn't stick it, Wayne could easily give up a steal. Setting up the stagger is a nice little play by Gushue."

So if not the all-or-nothing play, what are Wayne's other options? Scott Howard suggests the paper-thin triple takeout, but nobody agrees with that. Too easy to miss.

"Think about Wayne's unacceptable result for the end," Mickey instructs. "He definitely doesn't want to give up a steal. A deuce is great. A blank or force is okay. But no steals. Steals lead to losses.

"The threat he sees – what could lead to a steal – is that stagger. Staggered guards – use them or lose them, right. So he'd like to deal with the danger and make sure he can always get his acceptable outcomes, a single or blank."

Cheryl in the booth and Tim on the ice like the idea of tapping the crotch of the two reds (R1 and R2), killing the stagger, spilling them into the rings and setting up multiple options for a runback into shot rock with your next. Russ initially likes the call but comes back to it later, calling that shot 'all or nothing' too. I don't quite follow that comment and ask Mickey about it.

"Russ is concerned about tapping R1 not far enough and leaving another stagger with Y4/R1," explains Mickey. "Wayne wouldn't really be in any better position if that '*what if*' played out."

Wayne seems to agree and settles on the hit-and-flop on Y4, clearing the stagger, opening up the front while trying to shimmy R1 into the rings. What's with the shimmy, I ask? Why not make super-sure you clear up?

"Wayne does err on the side of safety by calling peel-weight and icing a bit tight. But – and this is important – he knows Gushue's unacceptable result, and that's giving up a 2. Knowing that, Wayne expects that Gushue will hit it any red that rolls in and not set up another stagger. That will let Wayne clear out the shot rock, and the danger will be over. If Gushue gets a little crazy and plays the stagger anyway, then Wayne will have a red in the rings to work with. It's a little two-for-one play that might just lead to a deuce."

Mickey's not so sure about this play for less precise players. "At the club, I might just get rid of Y4 and see if they can make a perfect guard again. Maybe I'll get a bit easier situation later, but we need to acknowledge that the middle is getting messy and we need to address it if we want to score."

As you see in the video, curling is not a game of perfect. The peel-weight shimmy doesn't work, Gushue tries to get another stagger going, and the rest of the end is played attacking the button. Perhaps a few donkey years ago, Wayne would make his last.

But what are the lessons I can use at my level? First, if I'm thinking steal, have my Lead throw top-button. Top-four/top-eight lets them get in behind and back tee allows them to freeze on top. Top-button leaves a scoring area about one foot wide.

Second, I need to think about the downsides – the *what-if's* – of a nominated shot. Sure, the angle run using R2 would be great and Cheryl's double split could create some opportunities. But get either of those wrong and they could set up my unacceptable outcome.

Third, I need to be aware my opposition's ideal, acceptable and unacceptables for the end. Seeing the end from their point-of-view will help me anticipate their next play. His unacceptable is giving me a deuce. If I roll one in, he's gonna hit it and that will let me clear shot rock. A three-shot sequence using his point-of-view. Nice.

And finally – and most importantly – I need to spot danger, be ready to give up on my ideal outcome and pivot to my acceptable. If the stagger could lead to a steal, I need to bail out, clear it up and get my single. I'm constantly amazed at how top skips see danger and don't hesitate to clean it up. Wayne sees it – those staggered guards – and acts to take his unacceptable outcome out of play. Me? I'm playing too often with my unacceptable outcome still on the table, going deeper and deeper into an end, trying to get my deuce, and leaving myself no apparent path to get out of trouble. I need to smell the danger when it's in front of me and deal with it sooner rather than later.

Mickey's Last Word: "Bail before you get cooked. Steals lead to losses. If something sets up your unacceptable, fix it and make sure you get your acceptable."

Puzzle #41

You're one of the sharpest shooters in the game, but your opponents just don't care. They just keep going and going and going, like the Eveready Bunny. They. Are. Relentless. And now you're scrambling, trying to manufacture some offence and score a deuce to level things up. But how? Here's the situation:

*   5th end of 10
*   You're red
*   You're down by 2
*   You have hammer
*   It's your Lead's second shot
*   About five feet of swing on good ice

C'mon Skip, give 'em a shot that makes the other guys hopping mad. What's your call – and why?

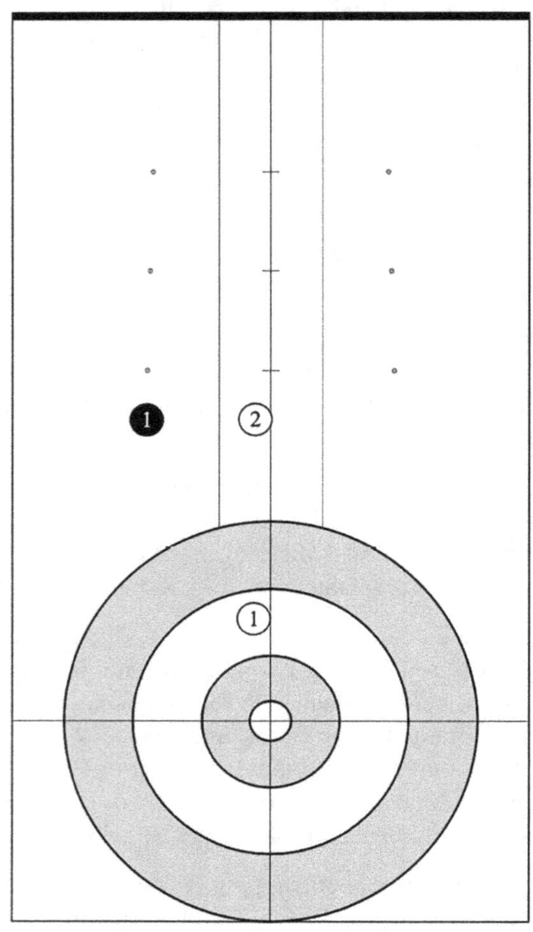

Delayed Corners & One in the Bank

Generating offence is supposed to be easier under the five-rock rule, but I'm not so sure. There seem to be so many complicated options. Fortunately, Mickey spelled them out for us in the Hierarchy of Offence in the Fundamentals section. Here, we get to see Matt Dunstone put them to work. What's he up to, Mickey?

"Newfoundland (yellow) is trying to avoid giving up 2, so they're setting up a structure in the centre and trying to drag Saskatchewan (red) into the four-foot for a tippy tappy end where someone scores 1. Geoff Walker set up two beauties in the middle to try to keep play focused there.

"After Walker threw his first into the rings (Y1), Saskatchewan could have played the Delayed Corner tactic we discussed in Puzzle #12. It's a good play and a call more club teams should consider. At this level where they have the hitters to clean things up, it's too safe though – you'll need to complicate things a bit if you want to score a multiple, especially this late in the game."

Okay, that's the Delayed Corner. I like it at the club. Clean, simple, safe. Might get a crack at 2. Gonna file that one away for future reference, but it's too safe at the elite level.

Dunstone didn't play the Delayed Corner. And he didn't play Chicken Little by drawing around their centre guard (Y1) with his first.

But with his second, he could have played Corner-n-Freeze by drawing around Newfoundland's next (Y2) and freezing to Y1. But that's not his choice. Presumably, Matt's playing a little more aggressively by playing One-in-the-Bank?

"That's right, that's the shot Dunstone asks for – the draw around his corner guard to put one in the bank right away. The play is basically to put one in scoring position right off the bat and try to bring it in to play later, an appropriate gamble at this level down 2.

"But of course, there's a risk that your opponents might just throw another centre guard. Now you're spending most of the end digging them out just to avoid giving up a steal. Or if they can see your rock in the bank, they might choose to keep it simple and chase you, as Newfoundland did in this end. If they miss, you address their centre rocks, then work to get two in the paint, and you can see how a deuce can develop from there."

Mickey makes an additional drive-by point. "Watch how Saskatchewan drew around their corner," adds Mickey. "You'll see that it over-buried and was poking out the outside edge of the guard. I like erring on this side for a couple of reasons. First off, think about the distances that rock will have to travel to leave the rings. Because it's poking out the outside edge, it has to get across about twelve feet of rings to not sit in the paint. If it were poking out the inside, they would just have to move it two or three feet to kill it. Considering that Newfoundland will likely be throwing a down-weight shot to get some curl and clear the guard with room to spare, you'd rather have them move it twelve feet instead of three.

"Secondly, what if they if they clip your guard when chasing around the outside? They'd send yours into the rings, towards their shot rock. Good things can happen when they chase that side. Alternatively, if your rock was poking out the inside of the guard and they rub it, their shooter rolls into the rings. So, over-burying isn't bad. Under-burying is a risk."

That's a good point. Also filing that one away for future reference!

For me as an aspiring curler, the essential lesson of this puzzle is that there are multiple paths of risk and reward, and the opening shots of the end dictate which path I'm going down. If they go into the rings on their first – like Walker did – I can play the Delayed Guard to get a simplified end with a sniff at offence. If they throw a guard first, I can play any one of the shots in the risk/reward progression outlined in Puzzle #4 in the Fundamentals section. I can play Chicken Little, Corner-n-Freeze, One-in-the-Bank like Dunstone did here, or even Double Guards if I'm feeling really lucky – or even a bit desperate.

In any event, I need to be clear about the different risk/reward paths available to me and, given the score and game situation, throw the set-up shots that lead to the path I want to take. If I get a good set-up, then hopefully I can carry that through the decision phase and the finale and get the result I want. A hierarchy of risk vs reward paths – that's the essence of this puzzle for me.

Mickey's Last Word? "Know which type of set-ups lead to which type of results and agree with your team how you want to play ends given your objectives. And when coming around or guarding, err on the side of showing them the outside of the rock in the wings, not the inside. Good things could happen."

Puzzle #42

Well, your opposition might be part-timers, but they are good. And they're keeping things pretty cagey here, getting one buried in the four-foot and putting you under some pressure. But you've got one biting the rings, buried under a corner. You just need to build on that and make hay while the sun shines. But what to play? Here's the situation:

- It's the third end of ten
- You're yellow
- You're down by 1
- You have hammer
- It's your Second's last shot
- About a four-foot swing on good ice

C'mon Skip, give us a shot that doesn't sell the farm. What's your call – and why?

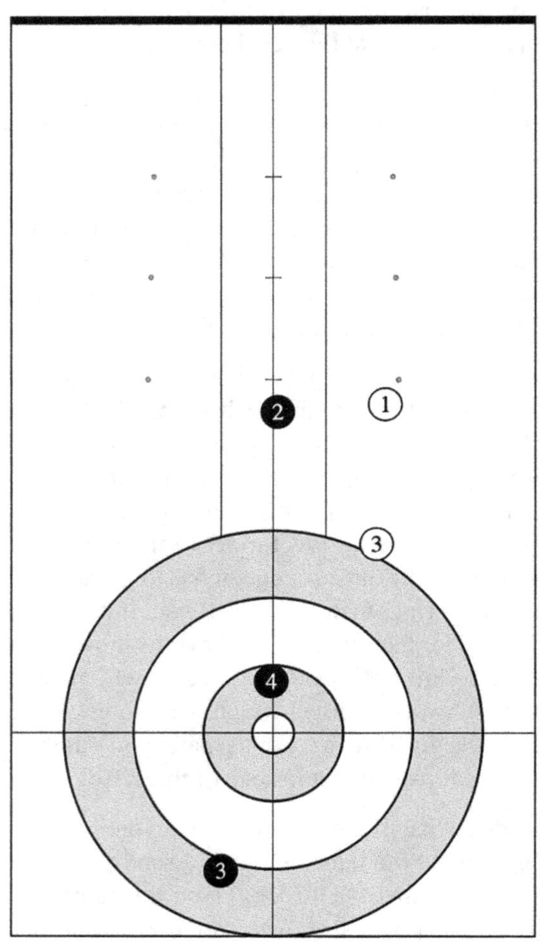

One-on-One

This puzzle is a great example of setting up – and then taking advantage of – a one-on-one situation. Let's see what it's all about.

The end shapes up as the superb part-timers of Team Krista McCarville (Northern Ontario and playing red) try to keep play down the centre by throwing their first to top-four. Kerri Einarson and Team Manitoba (yellow) are down by 1 and looking to score. They throw a corner, Y1.

Northern Ontario's Lead's second shot is slightly offline, leaving shot rock exposed opening the door for Manitoba. (In my efforts to stick names on situations and make them more memorable, I'm going to call this situation when the Lead doesn't cover their rock in the rings the 'Exposed Shot Rock Conundrum'. No really, I am.)

Kerri, looking ahead three shots, sees that the Exposed Shot Rock Conundrum sets up a golden opportunity. By chipping shot rock, she has an opportunity to limit McCarville to one single, solitary centre guard out front. If Einarson chips shot rock and sits open, McCarville will hit to eliminate the Manitoba rock and try to roll under her centre guard. But…she won't be throwing another centre guard.

And if Einarson's chip rolls under her corner (or even out), she sees that McCarville will draw under the single centre guard to try to bring play back to the middle and away from the corner. But again, only one centre guard.

So when Northern Ontario's Lead left shot rock open on her second, Kerri saw that she could get them into a situation of guarding one rock with one rock – a situation kinda like the Delayed Corner set-up. One rock covering one rock is always going to be tricky for the defending team, and Einarson can now make hay. But how? Mickey is on hand to spell out the options for us.

"One call is to go all-in and put one around Y1 and Y3. However, it's a precise shot with those narrow guards.

More importantly, it's too late in the end. Sure, she might get one rock buried under cover to work toward her deuce, but she risks letting McCarville throw up another centre guard or just come around R2 again. Northern Ontario would be creating a fortress in the middle with just a few rocks to go, and the steal – Einarson's unacceptable outcome here – would be in play.

"Another call is to come around R2 and freeze on Northern Ontario's R4. It's less risky – Einarson would be frozen on top of a Northern Ontario rock and would have backing. Hopefully, she'd win the battle of the angles from there and have a chance to score 2. If things don't work out, rocks grouped in the middle can be more easily removed and she would have a chance to blank or at least score her single.

"Of course, it doesn't always work out like that. Sometimes you create a mess in the centre, they outplay you, you can't escape, and they end up stealing 1. No play is without risk and trade-offs in our game.

"The third option – and the one that Kerri plays – is to peel the guard and wait. She's got her opponent into a position of guarding one rock with one rock. If she can see the shot stone, she's going to seek it, chip it and try to roll under her guards. But if shot stone is too well hidden and with the five-rock rule expired, she's going to peel the centre guard, ideally roll for a corner, and make her opponent throw a replacement.

"And Krista will have to make that replacement perfectly – time after time, for the rest of the end."

In our puzzle, that's exactly what happens. Kerri peels the centre R2 and rolls to the opposite side to set up another option for her chip-and-roll. McCarville, seeing that she can't peel three corners, hides shot rock with another centre guard. If it's the perfect line and depth, Einarson peels again.

But if the guard is too high or it's slightly offline, Kerri can use the swingy ice to chase shot rock, chipping it away and trying to roll under cover on one side or the other. Mickey points us toward a key skipping principle.

"It's a rule of thumb that guarding one rock with one rock, especially on 4-5 feet of curl, is not easy. A few inches offline or a few feet light leaves shot rock exposed.

"It's also accepted that making a perfect come-around that can't be chased is also very difficult on swingy ice, especially if the guard is a bit long. In this situation on this ice, it's going to be hard for Krista to line up her guard and her shot rock time after time. Kerri will very likely get her chance."

McCarville hides for a cycle or two, but eventually leaves her shot rock a hair exposed on the right. Einarson chips and rolls under. On her last, Krista leaves it a hair exposed on the left, and Kerri chips for her Skip's deuce. Krista had to be perfect to guard one rock with one rock – especially on her last. She played a great end but she wasn't perfect, and Kerri was able to chase on this swingy ice and get her 2.

"Of course, there's always a bit of risk for the chaser when chasing," cautions Mickey. "If you flash wide and miss both shot rock and the guard, your opponent throws on a second centre guard or a second counter and now you have a problem.

"And, if your opposition gets one absolutely dead buried on their last, there won't be an option to peel. You're going to have to out-draw it to not give up a steal. In our puzzle case, Northern Ontario's last rock was pretty good, but sweepers made the chip for the Kerri – as they so often do – and Manitoba scored 2."

But at club level, peels aren't always automatic. What would you recommend in that situation?

"At the club, these ends often become a congested mess. Instead of peeling, the Skip often calls the come-around to shot rock, they follow you in, and they can't see daylight by the time the Skip gets to throw. Perhaps instead of throwing the peel, you throw the chip on shot rock with a nice easy-to-throw weight, say back-ring or hack weight. But here's the key: ice it a bit tight. If they're wide, you get the chip. If they're tight, you end up moving the guard out one way or the other."

So what's my takeaway from this situation? When the opposition Lead fails to line up their guard and shot rock on swingy ice – setting up the Exposed Shot Rock Conundrum – I've got an opportunity to set up a one-on-one: one rock guarding one rock. I immediately chip. Whatever happens, they're playing their next rock in the rings, and now I've got a situation I can use to score. If their shot rock is open, I chip and try to roll under cover. If their shot rock is totally underneath, I peel their guard and make them replace it. Over and over again. I'll likely get a miss and can hopefully make a chip-n-roll to score a few.

Mickey's Last Word: "Guarding one rock with one rock several times in a row is difficult. If you're playing patient offence, peel a few times to see if you get a chance to get rid of shot rock, chip and set up a multiple score."

Puzzle #43

What to do, what to do? You're one of the leading lights in the curling world, but you're up against someone who just might be brighter. And she's making life difficult for you. Sure, some might argue that her best days are behind her, but on any given day she can summon the curling gods and spray sunshine all over the end to score a bundle. You'd like to arrange things so she can't do that here. But how? Here's the situation:

- 1st end of 10
- Score is naturally tied
- You're red
- Yellow has hammer
- It's your Third's last shot
- About 5-feet of swing on good ice

C'mon Skip, give us a shot that throws some shade all over this bright star. What's your call – and why?

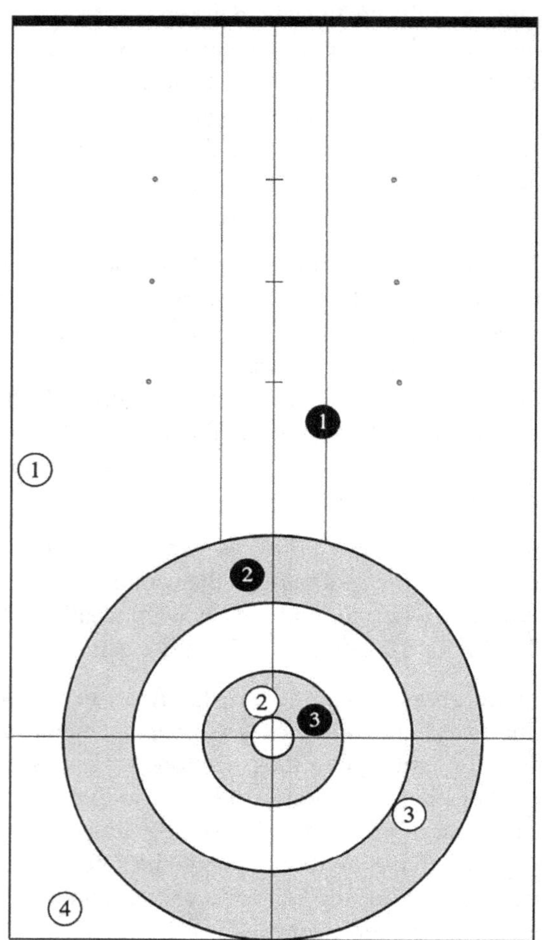

See the Whole Picture – And Be Patient

These shots on open rocks constantly befuddle me. Why the heck would Rachel Homan hit a rock lying third shot out in the weeds instead of going after that shot rock and making it hard for Jennifer Jones to score?

According to Mickey, this one illustrates not one, not two, but four key principles:

- Timing
- Putting yourself in your opponent's shoes
- Grouping of stones
- Limiting an opponent's potential score

Oh boy. Where do we start?

"Both teams are down to Third's last rock," says Mickey. "So timing comes into play. Rachel needs to deal with that Y2 shot rock pretty soon. She could ask her Third (Emma Miskew) for the short R2/Y2 runback, but it's the first end and Rachel might not really know the ice yet. Or there could be fresh pebble, making it harder to be precise. If Miskew, well, miscues and even slightly misses the runback, Jones could be lying 2 or 3 with hammer after her next shot. Rachel knows she needs to be patient."

But Mickey, surely Jones will kill R2, a powerful opposition rock hovering above the four-foot. Homan won't get a chance to play it!

"Not so fast," Mickey replies. "It's getting late in the end with just three of your shots to play. And while Rachel's feeling the heat, she puts herself in her opponent's shoes and knows that Jennifer is feeling it too. Jen needs to deal with that dangerous R3 on her Third's last so she doesn't risk giving up a steal. Jones can't try the R2/R3 double because she might stuff it onto her own, so she has to go straight after R3 and leave R2. Rachel anticipates all this and knows that R2 will be sitting there for her to use later."

OK, so Rachel leaves R2 for the moment. How does that make the situation better for her, I wonder?

"This is where the grouping of stones comes in," Mickey explains. "When stones are grouped together, it's much easier to remove multiples than when they're far apart. After Jen plays something on R3, Rachel expects Jones' yellows to be close together so she can remove a couple with her next shot."

You hear Cheryl in the commentary booth say "I don't know where Manitoba [Jones] goes." And Russ agrees. "Even if the red (R3) is moved, there's probably a double or a run double."

"At the club," says Mickey, "and maybe even for some competitive teams, I don't mind the guard between R1 and R2. It almost guarantees the force, and if they mess things up a bit, I might get a chance to get rid of Y2 and steal. But these elite teams take a different approach."

Of course, we don't know where Jones' next will end up exactly, Rachel doesn't know and Russ and Cheryl don't know. But everybody knows it's going to end up in that four-foot area, close to the other yellow and grouped together.

Well, everybody knows they're going to end up close together – except the curling genius that is Jennifer Jones! After Homan elects to leave the centre as it is and hits the wide open Y3 to limit her opponent's potential score, Jones asks Kaitlyn Lawes to throw a nice hack-weighter to tap Y2 back and push R3 out the back. Her yellow rock is actually feathered away from the scoring area so her stones aren't grouped. "Oh fantastic," purrs Russ up in the commentary booth.

How does the rest of the end play out? Homan makes her runback with R2 now, dead stuffing her rock and leaving it sitting open in the four-foot. Jones hits that and, notably, rolls under the R1 guard.

"Now I think Jennifer Jones may very well be the greatest woman curler of all time," Mickey confides, "but she got that wrong. She calls for the roll under and I don't think she should have done that. Getting it edge-buried would have put her yellows at a 45-degree angle, enough to take away any double from Homan yet still leave it available if Rachel hit the open yellow and rolled under on her last – just like she does. Jones could have used that exposed rock to dig out Homan's stone and score her 2."

So what are the key lessons I can take from this pro puzzle and use in my game? First, it seems to me that Rachel's call comes from her ability to put herself in Jennifer's shoes. She looks at the rocks, knows where they are in the end, and sees that Jennifer has to get moving on R3. And she sees that Jennifer can't play the runback double with R2 – it's just too risky. So, she anticipates that Jennifer will go straight after R3 and that will (probably) leave Manitoba's rocks grouped and easy to take out…on the next shot. It's that ability to look at the situation from my opponent's view – and not be so focused on my own immediate problems – that seems so valuable.

Secondly, I'll watch for grouped stones. Avoid grouping mine. Manoeuvre things to group theirs.

And finally, an edge-buried rock is often more valuable than a fully buried one. I'm not going to be so keen to get rocks completely underneath guards.

Mickey's Last Word: "Think three shots ahead. Anticipate how the situation will develop, and if it's to your advantage, be patient, remove one of their potential counters – and wait."

Puzzle #44

Are you one of these guys who used to think you were decisive – but now you're not so sure? You must have seen this situation about a dozen times this week and yet you're still scratching your head and asking your team what to do. Why exactly do you make the big bucks? And why do the TV guys always want to speak to you? Maybe they should try your Third – he seems to know what's he's doing. Anyway, the clock is ticking so you'd better make up your mind. Here's the situation:

- 9th end of 10
- You're red
- You're down by 1
- You have hammer
- It's your Lead's second shot
- About 5-feet of swing on good ice

C'mon Skip, give us a shot that shows you're sharp like tack, not like bowling ball. What's your call – and why?

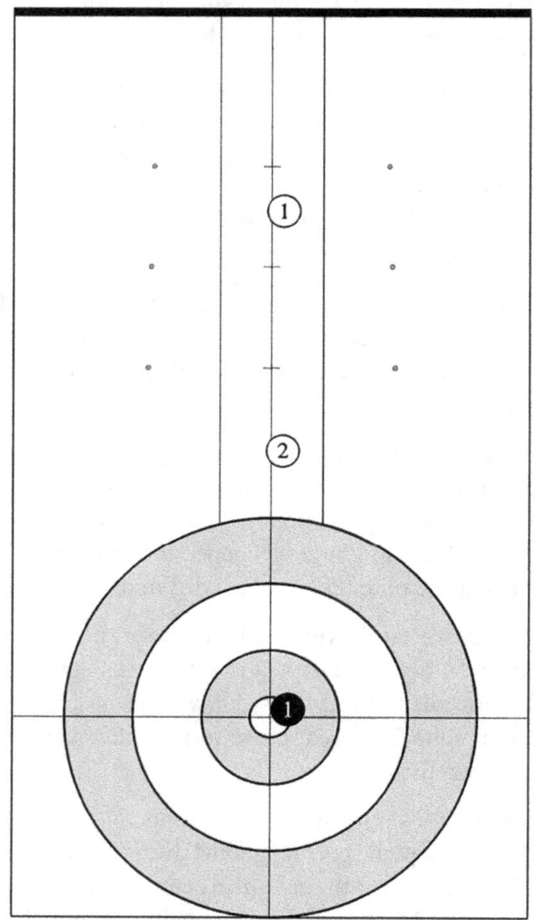

Lies, Damn Lies & Statistics

I like these puzzles where a simple situation causes hesitation for even the best players in our game. Both teams are dancing around here in the 9th, trying to seize the advantage before heading into the last end. CurlingZone.com has tracked thousands of elite games and know that the chances of winning going into the last end are:

- Up one without hammer – 60%
- Down one with – 40%
- Tied with – 75%
- Tied without – 25%
- 2-down with – 15%

So Jacobs (red and down-1 with) would be delighted to score 2 (to get to a 60% chance of winning) and would accept a blank (40%). What he doesn't want is to get forced and be all square without in the last (25%). And he naturally doesn't want to give up a steal to go 2-down with hammer (just a 15% chance).

On the other hand, Gushue (yellow and 1-up without) would be delighted to force and go all-square with hammer into the last (75% or higher). And he doesn't mind blanking (60%) or can even live with giving up 2 (40%). What he really can't do is go all kamikaze, let Jacobs score 3 and go 2-down himself.

But I'm puzzled. If Gushue doesn't want to give up a big end and go down in flames, surely he wants a nice clean sheet and low scores. What's he doing throwing two guards? And what's Jacobs up to by going around them into the four-foot? This must be a situation made for ticking centres into corners and generating a deuce or even more. Mickey tries to help me understand the tactics in play.

"In this scenario, the team without hammer (Gushue) throws first and dictates where and how the end will be played. He wants a congested end in the four-foot, freezes and taps, moving rocks around, trying to win the battle of the angles in the hopes that someone scores 1. So he throws the long centre guard to draw play to the middle. To get that force or a steal, he's willing to accept the risk that comes with having rocks in play. After all, he could give up 2 and still be in okay shape."

You hear Team Jacobs discuss the tick in the video but, at the urging of Marc Kennedy, settle on the come-around. As a Newbie, I'm all for Jacobs ticking here. Open the four-foot, avoid the steal, set up some corners, try and get a deuce and have a chance in the last. What's going on?

"Marc's concerned about the downsides of the tick shot," suggests Mickey. "Yes, it moves play out to the wings and spreads things around, and it can set up a chance for a deuce.

"But it's most often played in the last end when the team with hammer just needs to score 1. To Jacobs though, scoring 1 to go all-square without into the last is almost as bad as giving up a steal (25% vs 15% victory rate). He wants 2 or nothing, but not 1.

"One risk with the tick is you're setting up corner guards in a situation where a blank is a good outcome. If you set up even one decent guard and Gushue gets around it late in the end, you're blank is gone and you could very well end up getting forced to go all-square without in the last. So ticking for corner guards in this situation is a risk. You have to remain conscious of your acceptables and unacceptables.

"Anyway, Jacobs didn't throw the tick on his first and now he faces double centre guards. If he changes gears and ticks on our puzzle shot, Gushue's next play is probably the freeze on shot rock under a long centre to try to get the tippy tappy end he wants.

"But look at Ryan Harnden's first rock (R1). It's sitting a foot or two deep. To increase his chances of scoring 2-plus, Jacobs wants as big a scoring area as possible. Ideally, that Lead rock (R1) would be top-four and, after your tick, Gushue's freeze would be sitting in the eight-foot. The end would start to develop in the eight-foot circle, and you'd have all sorts of area to score your deuce later. But with R1 sitting so deep, the end will develop inside the four-foot, and it might get hard to score 2 later.

"Here's an important point: a key to punishing the other guy when he's dragging you into the centre is getting good rock positioning with your set-up stones. Think about if Ryan had gone top-four with R1, then Gushue throws his second guard, and then Ryan goes top-eight. Now Gushue has three bad options with his next.

"First, he could try to bury under Jacobs' rocks but would likely end up back-four or back-eight or something and would just provide a catcher for Jacobs to use later. Second, he could freeze to the pile, but the freeze will

be in the twelve-foot, leaving a nice open territory in the centre. And finally, he could try to bump them back, but it would be super tough to get around his guards and move them. If he did, he'd be sitting in the twelve-foot, could get chipped by Jacobs' next, and suddenly Northern Ontario might be sitting a couple with hammer. So, if you're wrapping around a centre guard with hammer, getting your Lead rock positioned just a foot or two higher means all sorts of good things could happen."

"So I agree with Marc that you need to beat them in now. Maybe they'll get a miss and be able to set up their deuce or, with grouped rocks, get a chance to clean up for the blank later. They can live with either of those."

"This is even truer at the lower levels. You've got a chance to sit two double-buried, and you'll be making them chase you. Sure, the end might get all tippy tappy and someone scores 1. But when the other guy throws two in the free guard zone, you don't have much choice. And ticks aren't usually in our arsenal at club level, making the choice even simpler. Keep your Lead rocks at top-four and top-eight and you'll have room to score."

Phew – what a puzzle! I used to think that Skip's shots were the most important. The more I do these exercises, the more I realize that an end can easily be won or lost by my Lead. I need to take better care of him, maybe even buy him a beer sometime.

What is the essence of this puzzle that all of us aspiring curlers can use to our advantage? First of all, I need to be crystal clear about my acceptable and unacceptable outcomes. Here, a deuce or a blank is fine; a force or steal is not.

Secondly, a tick for corners is not only a risk because it's a low-percentage shot at my level. It might also give my opponent a way to force me.

And finally, if the other guy is determined to force me to the middle for a tippy tappy end, I can call his bluff, beat him in, keep my Lead rocks high to maintain a nice big scoring area, and make him sweat.

Mickey's Last Word: "Lead rock positioning is the key to so many ends. Here, we see that the way to punish an opponent throwing centre guards is to go top-four and top-eight. Keep that Lead rock at the perfect balance point – deep enough so it's hard to get around yet high enough to set up a large scoring area – and you'll win more ends."

Puzzle #45

You're one of the most aggressive Skips out there. What's the point of just knocking rocks out of the rings and scoring ones or even zeroes, you ask yourself? Surely the way to win is to chuck a bunch down into the house and then clean things up later. But maybe you need to start thinking about that cleaning up part of that plan. Your opposition (red) is lying shot under a ton of granite, and it's a tight game. You need to get a move on. But how? Here's the situation:

- 7th end of 10
- You're yellow
- You're up by 1
- You have hammer
- It's your Third's first shot
- About a 5-foot swing on good ice

C'mon Skip, maybe a bit less passive and more aggressive here. Give 'em a shot that cleans things up and scores a few. What's your call – and why?

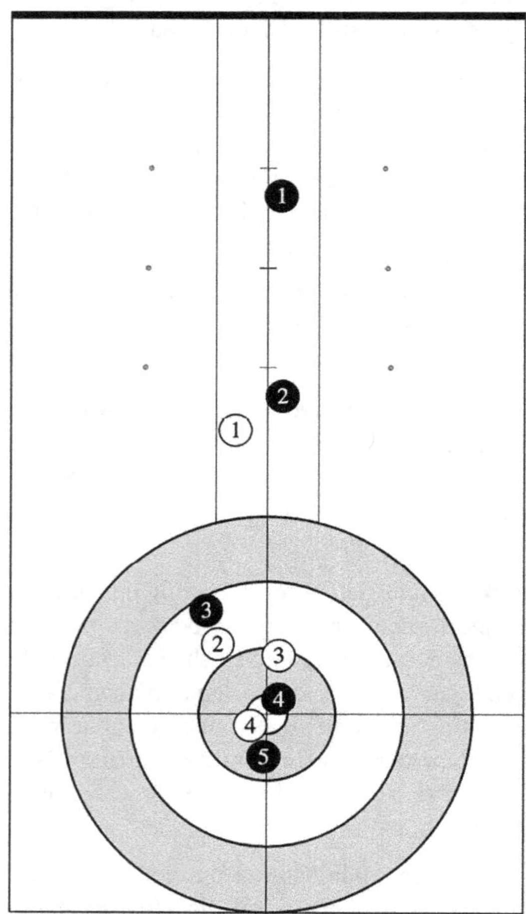

Getting Them a Hundred Ways (or At Least a Couple)

This end should be in every workshop and training camp just for the quotes alone.

"There's that tap, and they are the shot rock!" – Vic Rauter

"Think it gets it, Brent?" – Bennie Hebert

"Do we need to right now? It's kinda lined up pretty nice." – Marc Kennedy

"If we can tap this so it goes on the inside of his red, he's in a world of hurt." – Brent Laing

"Now that's a golf shot. We got him coming and going now, boys." – Brent Laing, after Marc makes a beauty

"He's got us a hundred ways here." – Brad Gushue

Well, maybe not a hundred, but it turns out to be enough! Team Koe goes on to score 3 and effectively win the Brier in 2016. So what's going on here, Mickey?

"This puzzle is all about patience and not worrying about shot rock too soon. Vic thinks shot rock is important. But with half-an-end to play, Team Koe isn't concerned about that yet. They decide to play one more set-up rock with Third's first to get Gushue from both sides, and as soon as it's made, Gushue knows he's cooked."

A couple of aspects of the rock position are important to this puzzle and don't favour Gushue. He's got two reds almost on the button – including Vic's shot rock – but they're low men on the ladder. All the yellows are sitting on top of them, so any contact means that reds go and the yellows stay. He's lost that Battle of the Angles we discussed in the Fundamentals.

The second rock situation that favours Koe is the R3/Y2 combo on the left-hand side of the sheet. Benny asks whether it would, in fact, drag and kill the red R4 shot rock, and Brent Laing confirms that a quarter-rock slice would get it. It's an important point because that sets up Team Koe to have them from the left side.

For many of us in this situation, our natural inclination is to get shot rock at the first opportunity. The way to do that here is to play that R3/Y2 raise and lie 3 or 4 with hammer. Mickey suggests that that is not always the best approach as we aim to improve our tactics.

"As they sit right now, yellow owns that position on the left side. R3 can't be used to make things better for Gushue, but the Y2 can be used to improve things for Koe. The yellow has all the power.

"But as soon as Koe plays that raise, the red gets unlocked, and it becomes powerful. It can then be chipped in or blasted into the pack or whatever. Gushue can't use it right now, but if Koe unlocks it, he can. So Koe decides to leave that situation alone."

Their deliberations move on to their Y1 above the rings, the one Bennie left when he was short on a come-around attempt. (Leads – be light not heavy.) It sits there hovering above the four-foot for the entire end, holding a lot of power and ready to be used by either team.

Team Koe talk about raising it back into the bunch but are afraid about changing the angles. "You don't want to jiggle those two," says Kevin, talking about their R3/Y2 money-in-the-bank setup on the left.

Finally, they decide to do one more set-up shot on the right side. "This is the classic 'be patient' play, adding one more set-up shot with Third's first," says Mickey. "As soon as they throw that, they have an option from either side to deal with shot rock, and they're in the dominant position."

They make their move on the next shot, move Gushue's R4 shot rock off the button and bring the end home, if ever so slowly. Scott Pfeifer, Team Koe's coach, who makes the long walk for the time-outs, seems to be getting more exercise than anyone else in this end!

Brad Gushue and his Third, Mark Nichols, play an ingenious 'reverse freeze', trying to tuck one under their shot rock to shore up its position. It doesn't quite come off.

And Brad has an in-off that might have rescued the situation. But those hit-and-rolls are tough, he hits it fat, and Team Koe cashes in on all that set-up work to score 3.

So what can us Newbies take away from two of the best teams to have ever played the game? One good lesson for me is to quit always worrying about shot rock. Be patient, build my end, look for ways to get better positions where I can't be removed and they can – and then bring it home with my last few shots.

And the second lesson for me is that once we have them pinned down on one side, I should look for opportunities to get them from the other. Good things will happen if we can get them from both sides. This applies at club and pro levels.

Finally, I liked how the team walked out to the hog line and looked at it from the shooter's perspective. I've lost bonspiels by not looking at the situation from the top of the rink. My team muttered some memorable – if unprintable – quotes then too.

Mickey's Last Word: "Be patient. Don't get too fixated on who has shot rock too early. Try to get things set up two ways.

"And remember, it's not only about what you make. It's also about what you leave for the other guy."

Puzzle #46

You love playing against this guy. Both of you like lots of rocks in play and high-stakes, aggressive curling. And y'know, this is starting to look pretty good for you. You're up by 1 with just two ends to play, you've got a bunch lying down the centre, and you're lying shot. Of course, the other guy has hammer, but that's usually a minor inconvenience for a team of your calibre. You just need to pin him down, get a steal to go 2-up, and you're probably home and dry. But how? Here's the situation:

- 9th end of ten
- You're red
- You're up by 1
- Yellow has hammer
- It's your Second's first shot
- About five feet of swing

C'mon Skip, give 'em a call that makes mincemeat out of his high-stakes. What's your call – and why?

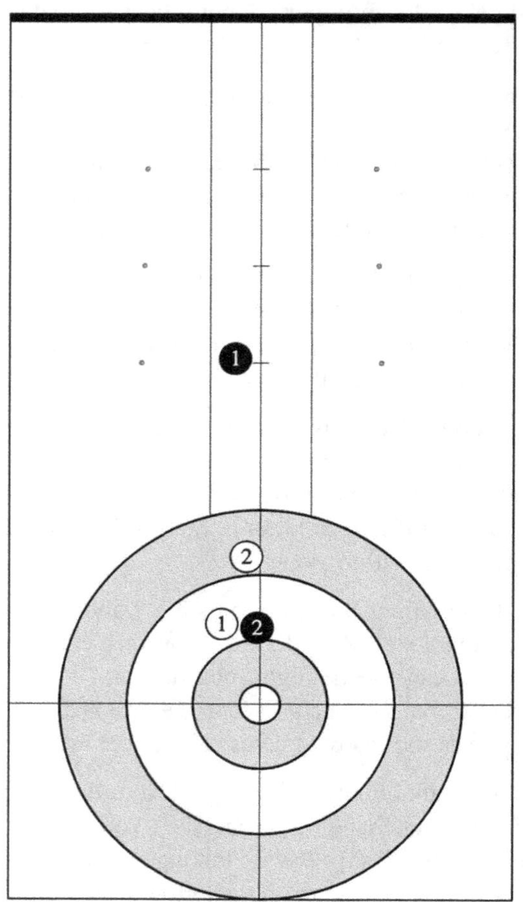

Fish or Cut Bait?

This puzzle is about two Skips knowing what they're trying to get out of the end and what they're willing to risk to achieve it. What's going on here, I ask Mickey.

"It's a one-point difference very late in the game. Both skips will know the odds of winning given various scores, so they know their ideal, acceptable, and unacceptable outcomes. And they'll know what the other guy is after and willing to risk to get it.

"John Epping is trying for a force to get it back to all-square and have hammer in the 10th. But he's happy enough with a blank, thinking he'll force in the 10th and win with hammer in the extra end. He just doesn't want to give up an easy deuce and let Kevin Koe take the lead.

"On the other hand, Kevin Koe at 1-down would love a deuce, but he's happy enough with a blank to keep hammer into the last end and try his chances there. He doesn't want to get forced and he definitely doesn't want to give up a steal.

"The key thing is that neither of them want to lose it here by going too hard for their ideal outcome. John's not throwing double centre guards to go for the steal but leaving Koe a chance to get around behind and score a bunch. And Kevin's not throwing double corners for his deuce and opening the door for John to create a fortress in the centre. Both Skips are going to keep it pretty cagey.

"And that means they're going to keep everything tight in the middle with not many rocks out front, with either team ready to blow it up if they need to. Epping will limit the number of rocks in play and make sure Koe doesn't get a head of steam going. Koe's happy enough to keep things bunched in the centre. If he gets a miss from Epping, maybe he gets a soft deuce but otherwise, the rocks are grouped so he can run some rocks in and avoid the force and get his blank."

And that's where the puzzle finds us – rocks grouped in the centre, both teams trying to get a miss or half-shot from the other guys. John had asked Brent Laing, his Lead, to freeze R2 onto Y1, get some backing and wedge it in there. But the team swept it, kept it a foot heavy, it rolls off Y1 and becomes backing for Koe's next rock (Y2). As it stands, R2 is the low man on the ladder and is easy to remove any time Koe wants. That's not so good if you're trying to keep one in there, get a guddle going in the four-foot and get the force.

"So now John has to decide," explains Mickey. "And the question is 'Given the rock situation and given that it's the 9th, is it worth sticking another one in and persevering for the force, or is it better to bail now, clear out some yellows and probably get a blank?'"

We see in the video that he blows things up – but why such a pessimistic decision, I wonder? Why not try one or two more rocks and see where it goes before you pull the ripcord?

"They look at a couple of options," Mickey replies, "including going right around the back to get under cover and get some congestion going in the four-foot. But they don't look at that for very long! Looking ahead, Kevin would follow him down, sit on top of it, and yellow would have another in the rings – with backing. The yellows would be adding up, and all the reds would be exposed. A couple of hits and the reds could go while the yellows all stay. So that's too risky a play for Epping at this stage of the game."

The other option they consider is to try to get one across the nose of Y1, almost into the crotch of Y1/R2. 'If you ever got across nose, it's amazing,' you hear Ryan Fry say.

"In the end, they just think it's too low percentage and quite dangerous," says Mickey. "If they roll off, Koe will have an easy hit-and-roll out to the eight-foot to sit three in the rings, with hammer. And if it ended up on the nose, Koe has a board-weight angle raise with Y2 to probably remove that rock and keep three yellows in the rings, well-spaced out and within sight of a 2 or 3."

Matt Camm likes his chances of making the precise Y2/Y1 double better. They risk peeling their guard, which wouldn't be great; Koe would put three in the rings, and Epping would have to make two doubles with his last five rocks. But the chances are that Y1 and Y2 will be somewhat close together, so getting those doubles is fairly doable at the Brier level – maybe less so at the club.

Which makes me wonder, which option does Mickey like at my amateur / improving level? We don't make a lot of quarter-rock doubles and we're not great at precise across-the-nose freezes either.

"The club shot might be to go behind everything, make that scoring area as small as possible and let them try to follow you down. If you get deep, it's probably best to sweep it to back-eight, hope they freeze on you. Then you freeze on them to cut that scoring area and lie 2.

"The other good club option is to throw a guard and protect shot rock. You might get them drawing around into the four-foot, and then you're creating a mess in the middle and you're halfway to your force."

In any event, Epping plays safety first. Killing the two yellows means Koe won't be able to build an end and construct a chance to score 2 or more. Camm makes it perfectly, Koe throws in the towel, peels the guard, and the blank is virtually on the scoreboard before the Thirds start to throw. Everybody ends up kinda not unhappy.

So what can I learn from this pro situation to apply at my level? First, it seems to me that John Epping knew precisely what he was playing for – a force or a blank – and what he wasn't willing to consider – a deuce or more. I need to let the Three Guiding Questions, well, guide my skipping decisions.

My other takeaway is to always be sizing up the situation and recognize when the shape of the end favours the other guy achieving his goals and not me achieving mine. Here, Epping sees his rock is low man on the totem pole and is at risk. In contrast, Koe could get two or three good ones in the rings – well spaced out or with a bit of backing and with hammer. In this tight contest and late in the game, John decides to bail at the first sign of danger. I need to be aware when I'm at risk and be ready to bail too.

Mickey's Last Word: "After Lead's shots, and definitely after Second's shots, be aware of how the end is shaping up for you. If the structure or set-up is pointing towards the other guy achieving his ideal outcome and you getting stuck with your unacceptable one, don't be afraid to cut bait, work towards your acceptable outcome, and fish for better results next end. Early in the game, you might let it go another shot or two. If it's tight and late in the game, be ready to bail early like John did."

Puzzle #47

Oh no. Oh no, oh no, oh no. What a time for your team to go walkabout! The ninth end of the biggest game you have ever played – maybe you will ever play – in your lives. But your Lead got slightly offline and left an easy double peel, and your Second – your dependable, awesome Second – has hogged a guard. Ever helpful, your Third just informed you that you're in trouble. What insight! Anyway, it's time to rescue the situation. But how? Here's the situation:

- 9th end of 10
- Score is tied
- You're yellow
- Red has hammer
- It's your Skip's first shot
- Five feet of swing on ice that's going just a hair fudgy

C'mon Skip, give 'em a shot that shows your Third he's not the only guy who understands the situation. What's your call – and why?

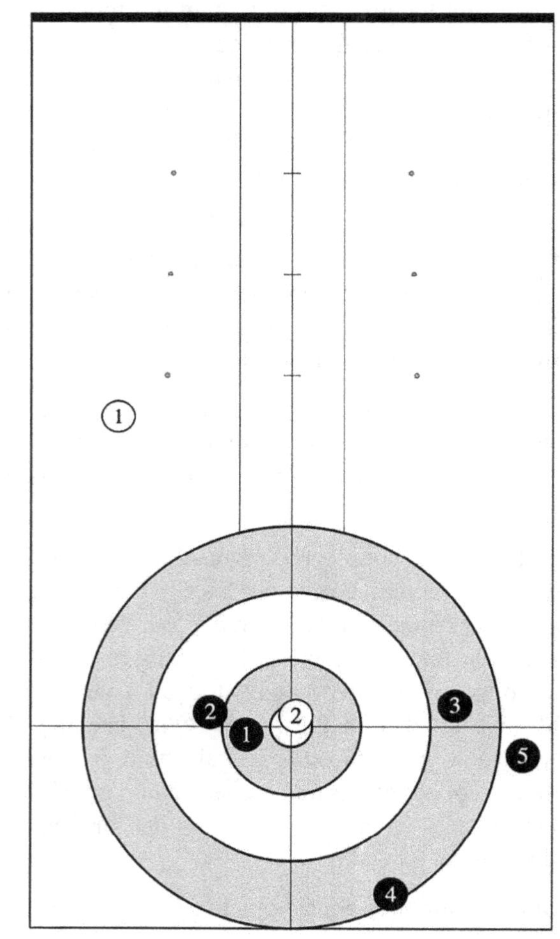

The Fifteen-Minute Timeout

"I remember seeing this live and I didn't disagree at the time," says Mickey. "But watching it back with the benefit of a fifteen-minute timeout to study it here at home, I think there may have been a couple of better options than the freeze that Scotland played on their Skip's first. Of course, I'm not out there on the ice with thirty seconds to decide, so it's a different ball game. But with the benefit of time, maybe there's something we can take out of this."

It's a situation I find myself in all the time – a couple of my players didn't quite execute the way I'd hoped, and now I have no usable guards and the other team has a pile of rocks in the house. I can't hit them all out. What the heck do I do?

"This is Bruce's first and I liked it when he called it, but obviously, it didn't work out. It over-curled slightly,

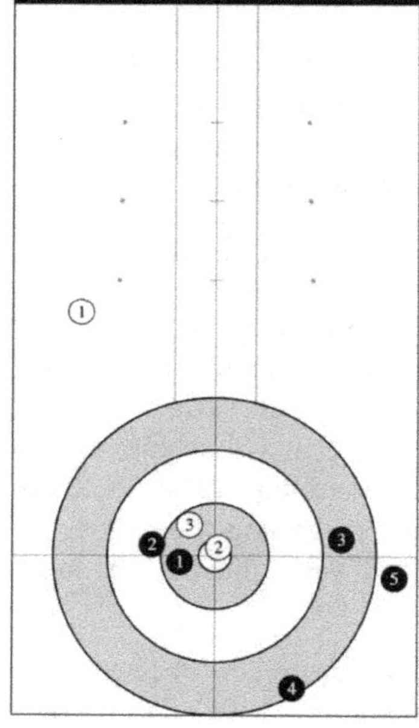

tapped Y2 an inch instead of freezing low side on R1, and that was enough to give up a 5 and the World Championship.

"But what if we look at it this way: what if that freeze was Bruce's last shot and Edin only had one more to come? Even when Niklas blasts it through an opening that doesn't seem to exist, Scotland still lies 1. So if Bruce plays that freeze into the pocket with his last, he steals.

"So now the question is, 'What does he do with his first?' I think there are two options that might have worked, although they both require things to go your way.

"The first spot (opposite) is just about a foot short of the pocket in position Y3. It's really the same as the freeze he called but miss it a foot light instead of an inch heavy. Nik wouldn't be able to leave those yellows there, so he'd have to hit and get rid of one. If he chooses to nose Y2, it might leave us a pocket or a freeze-tap. He might have a shot for two, but at least we're in the game.

"Or he might try and blast and open things up by running Y3 into that group of stones. So Y2 goes and R1 goes and so does his shooter. But your Y3 stays, biting the button or somewhere close to it. You could guard that, or you might have some type of hit-and-flop on R2 to sit two rocks with no double. You'd need the stars to align and have your last rock flop out to the edge of the eight-foot, perfectly even with your Y3. But that would leave him no doubles, and you might get out of this mess with a force. Maybe."

Okay, I like that. It's got a chance of working out better than what actually happened. What's the second option for Bruce's first shot?

"The second one needs a little more gumption. What happens if you guard your shot rock just biting or a foot short of the twelve-foot, around where Y3 is in our second diagram at right? Nik might peel it to leave himself something on his last, and that would leave us Bruce's freeze that he plays on his first shot. We'd be guaranteed a steal."

But Nik's a pretty smart guy, I point out, and he's played a bit. Would he be likely to walk into that bear trap?

"No," replies Mickey, "he wouldn't. He would try and play the Y3/Y2 runback double on the yellows. And he probably misses that once or twice a year – but this could be the one. And even if he makes it, you could freeze perfectly into the R1/2 pocket and hold him to 1 or 2.

"What you're doing here is setting up a tougher play for him than by freezing now. And by doing that, you just might get the miss and an opportunity to keep your hopes in this game alive."

Thinking about playing at my level, both options are pretty good. Sitting in that pocket just short of R3 will leave us options on our last. They hit shot rock (Y2)

and I guard to force him to 1, maybe 2 if he's drawing like a pro. I'm still in the game!

But I kinda like this second option – guarding up – better. It requires less precision on my part and more on my opposing Skip's part. After all, what are the odds of a six-foot runback in my Monday night league? If the other guy misses, he leaves his shooter somewhere out in front, I guard again, and maybe I get out with a steal. That's not a bad plan.

Mickey brings me back down to earth. "At your level, that could work. At the pro level though, we'd expect to make contact with that runback say eighty or ninety percent – so you're really grasping at straws."

What can I take away from this? First – and I'm starting to sound like a broken record – I need to learn to operate in a three-shot window, and all the more so when it comes to Skip's shots. All the set-up is done, and now it's Tic Tac Toe. If I do A, then he does B, then I do C, and he's left with D. But if I do A, and he does B, and I'm left with not very much on C, then I think I had better look at A again.

Mickey's Last Word: "Bruce called an incredibly precise shot and missed it by an inch. But if they'd taken a moment to look at another option or two that required less precision, it might have worked out better. Maybe they should have used their timeout on Skip's first, not on their last when it was a bit too late."

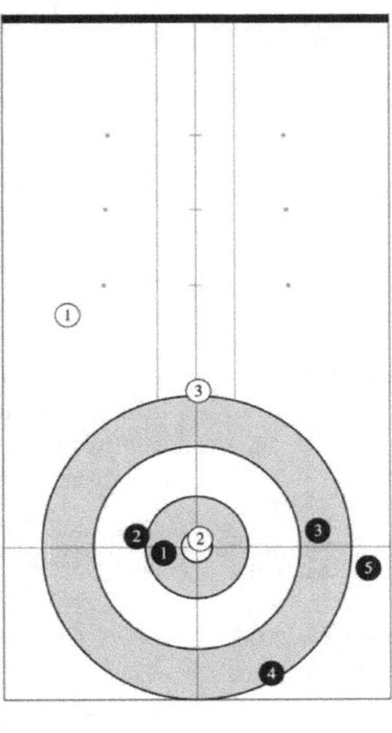

Puzzle #48

It's never easy going to a big competition for the first time. Sure, you're holding a good two-point lead and lying shot rock, but those other ladies can play a bit. And they've been here before. They're hoping to win, and you're just hoping to not fall over on your first slide! Still, if you could engineer a steal now, you would have just two more ends to bag yourself a memorable win. But how? Here's the situation:

- 8th end of 10
- You're red
- You're up by 2
- Yellow has hammer
- It's your Third's second shot
- About four feet of swing on good ice

C'mon Skip, give 'em a call that's not completely unbalanced. What's your call – and why?

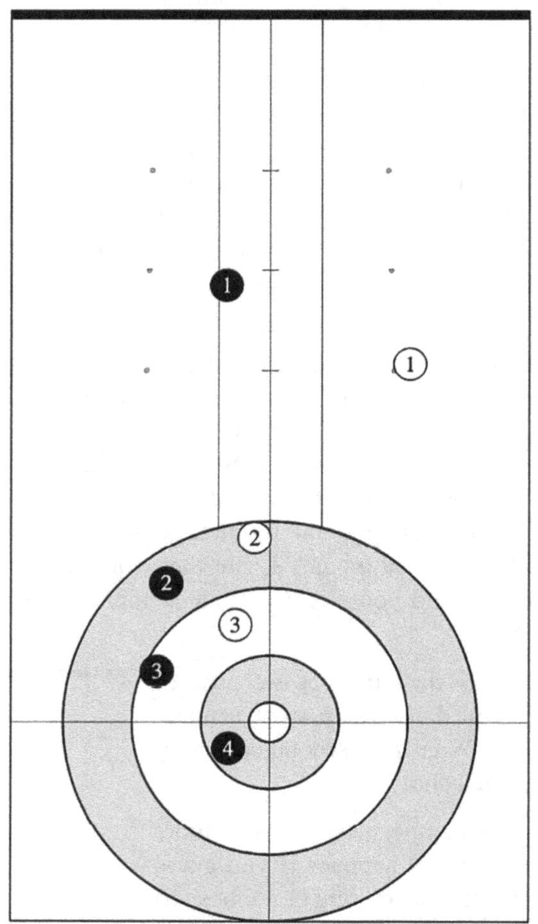

Sometimes You Just Gotta Make the Shot

I'm not sure that you could ever call Kerri Einarson and her team unbalanced, but they are up against some stiff competition in the form of Anna Hasselborg and her 2018 Olympic gold-medal winning team from Sweden.

I'm sure that ninety percent of readers will have called Canada to play the clockwise come-around to freeze on the R4 shot rock and try to take this end away from the Swedes. And that's what Mickey and commentator Melissa Soligo, Scotties winner and Olympic Silver medallist, also called. But that shot is not what Kerri Einarson played. What's up with that?

Mickey weighs in. "At 2-up in the eighth, Canada's looking to force and get the hammer back going into the last two ends. Maybe they should have been going for the steal since things are looking pretty good for them.

But they're playing conservatively and cautiously here in their first World Championships – up against a European team who represents their country every year – so they don't want to make a blunder that costs them the game."

What's the blunder they could make, I ask? They're lying one fully buried under a gaggle of guards, some of them staggered. Surely the force or steal is just around the corner. How could they go wrong?

"They're concerned about three potential risks," Mickey answers. "First, they look at drawing down and freezing to their R4 shot rock. Melissa up in the commentary booth likes that and so do I – at both the pro and club level – because it takes away the path Sweden wants to use.

"But it seems like Val Sweeting, Kerri's Third, is concerned about rubbing off or sitting out wide and letting Sweden double out their shot rock, maybe even using their Y1 corner to run in. Anna has the ability to make that shot. So, if Sweden were to double out R4, they could have three in the paint with a makeable double on R2/R3. Canada would be in a precarious position with just a couple of rocks to play. So they're understandably a bit nervous about that call."

OK, I'm getting better at this stuff, and I kinda saw that. (No really, I did.) What's the next risk that Einarson and company are worried about?

"You hear Val say she doesn't want to leave a pocket, and what she's talking about is freezing to her own and leaving a couple of catchers for Sweden's Y2/Y3 runback or maybe that corner Y1 runback. At one point, Val points to the two yellows and says, 'She's got so many options….' They're worried that if they come in first, they're grouping their rocks and maybe making them easier for Hasselborg to remove with one good shot."

Okay, I get that too. Honestly. But what's the last risk?

"The last concern comes with throwing a guard to cut off the Y2/Y3 runback onto their shot rock R4. The runback is a precise shot – but it's makeable. And here at the Worlds, you have to assume that the other players are likely to make it, so Kerri and her team are right to be concerned.

"But by guarding it, they might be setting themselves up for problems later. Sweden would go around to button. If Canada follows that but misses with their Skip's first – say they crash on a guard or slip deep or something – then Sweden could loop another around. They could be lying two with hammer with a pile of shrapnel – including that guard that you threw – out in front.

"Or say you throw the guard and Sweden slashes the R2/R4 double to sit first and third under your guard and R3 wide open. The point is that by throwing a guard, Canada are cutting off their ability to bail with their Skip shots, and they're not so keen on that.

"Plus there's an unwritten rule about guarding the other team's rocks. If you do that and they manage to get rid of your shot rock, you now have to deal with the guard you threw. That play never makes for comfortable conversation in the bar later with the wags behind the glass."

Never a good idea to cut off your own escape route, I guess. But I'm a little confused now and point out that the shot they played carried some risk too. They're going way out in the weeds to make it, and it could end up anywhere. You see Kerri point out the dangers of over-curling and getting it half-sandwiched between Y2 and Y3. In the end, they left it high where Sweden could use it to blast Y3 into the four-foot – which they did on Anna's first a couple of shots later.

"I'm not saying this is the shot I would have played," says Mickey. "Since I can't get inside their heads, I'm guessing a bit here, but I think what happened here is they got mentally zoned in on the force, not the steal, and figured they could put this somewhere safe without disturbing a pretty good situation. They thought Anna would freeze down to their shot rock – which she did with Third's last– and then they could freeze down to that and get an easy force without too much risk.

"The problem is that they decided on a precise shot that had a couple of downsides, and it left Anna with a much more makeable shot – the come-around – than the Y2/Y3 combination or the long Y1 runback that she would have had if Canada had drawn down to shot rock first. Like Melissa in the commentary, I thought the clockwise come-around was much more makeable and had options, which are nice to have at any level. They could have left it in several spots from the top eight-foot to fully frozen. It had some tolerance for error. The shot they played didn't."

What is my takeaway from this situation? When faced with no 'perfect' option, choose the one which is more makeable for me and leaves them the not-quite-as-makeable options. That is, play easy shots that make them play harder shots.

Mickey's Last Word: "If you're going to beat the best, sometimes you just have to make the shot even if there's some risk involved."

Puzzle #49

Like John Travolta strutting down the street in a pair of jeans three-sizes too small, you're feeling just a little uncomfortable. It's Saturday night, your team's a tad feverish and the young whippersnappers you're up against seem to have all the moves. Still, you were down by 4 and have clawed your way back to 3, so you're stayin' alive, stayin' alive. But how deep is your luck? You need to do something quick – but what? Here's the situation:

- 8th end of 10
- You're red
- You're down by 3
- You have hammer
- It's your Skip's first
- About 4-feet of curl

C'mon Skip, quit your jive talkin' and give us a shot. What's your call – and why?

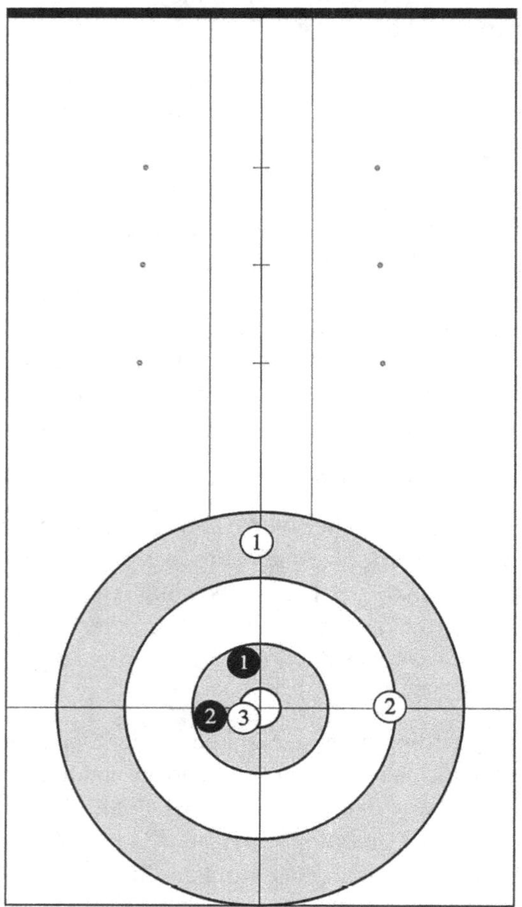

Stayin' Alive: Risk vs Reward

Well, it's not Saturday Night in New York. In fact, it's very likely Sunday afternoon in Halifax – but why let facts get in the way of a good intro! I'm claiming artistic license and going with my finely crafted allusion to the 70's mega-hit, Saturday Night Fever.

Of course, Jeff Stoughton is about as far from John Travolta in attitude and disposition as you could get. Yet he's the guy in the tight pants here, feeling the pinch as he tries to scramble his way back into this game. Mickey gives us his perspective on the problem.

"This one is about three lessons," he says. "First, there's the idea of thinking in a three-shot window. I play A, he plays B then I have C. We talk about this idea a lot, but it's useful to notice here how Jeff and his whole team are thinking about the remaining sequence of shots here, not just their first.

"The second is about making sure the risk doesn't outweigh the potential reward. The team identifies a choice between a makeable shot to score 2 and stay alive at 1-down in the 9th (the hit-and-flop that he plays), or an unlikely shot to score 3 and get to all-square (the freeze to nose of R1). If he can make that come-around freeze that Jon Mead's talking about, then maybe Jeff could have some type of tricky shot for 3.

"But in 2005, the ice didn't swing like it does now, and the sweepers hadn't figured out directional sweeping yet. It looks kinda ludicrous to see guys hammering on the wrong side, but that's the way a lot of teams swept back then. We didn't know any better!

"So the freeze to nose is the unlikely shot – it's much harder and uncertain. In fact, it's odds-on not to work. For instance, instead of freezing to nose, Jeff could easily sit it on the corner of R1 and leave Brad an easy hit to clear two of his reds and sit shot. (See diagram opposite). Jeff would be struggling just to score 1. If he goes 2-down without with just two ends to play, there's almost certainly no way back. His Olympic dream would be over.

"But make the hit-and-flop that they play, leave Gushue a double, score the deuce and he's probably still alive to play the 9th and 10th. It's a much easier shot, he sets up a way to get to shot rock on his next and leaves Gushue no shot that is likely to clear all of his reds. With a bit of luck, he might force a young, inexperienced Gushue to a nail-biter in 10 or maybe even get to the extra end."

So lesson #2 is all about weighing up whether the additional risk warrants the potential rewards. Here, Stoughton judges that it doesn't. The freeze could end his Olympic dream right here, right now. Perhaps if it was a shot for a 4 and probable victory, Jeff might have taken it on. But here, he opts for safety first – and he stays alive.

Mickey likes this call for the club / aspiring level too. "This logic holds true at all levels. You need to remove Y1 so you can score with your last. You might not make the perfect hit-and-roll at your level, but even if you just open up that situation in the four-foot, they have to make something pretty special not to leave you a shot for 2."

Okay, so that's the second lesson. What's the third?

"The third idea is about leaving yourself several ways in. Jeff knows that by hitting and flopping, he almost certainly has a shot for 2. If he rolls a bit wide, Brad hits the open R2. At worst, Brad will have stuck his shooter and Jeff will have an easy double for 2. If Brad's shooter has rolled away, Stoughton has the unmissable R1/Y3 runback for his deuce.

"But if he flops just a bit (as is the case), Gushue will be trying to kill as many reds as possible, and almost certainly won't make the angle triple (as is the case.) Stoughton makes an easy hit for 2.

"The point is that as long as Jeff left it hovering somewhere around the top left of the rings as we look at it, he was going to have two options. Either was good enough for him."

So, a pretty fiendishly set of what-if's with just three shots to play. It takes my Newbie brain a bit of time to walk through all those combinations, something Stoughton and team do in about thirty seconds.

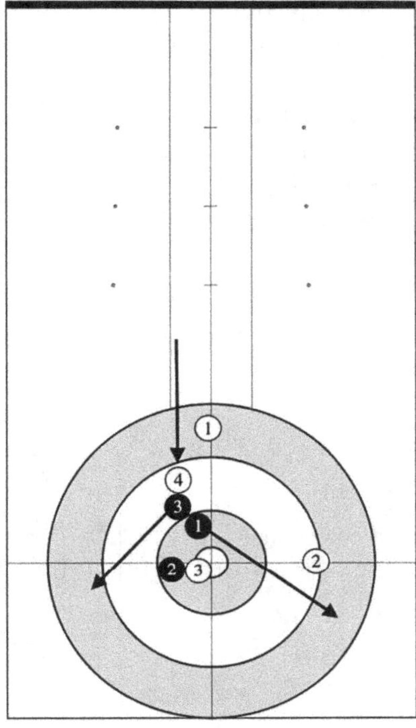

But what principles can I apply to my standard of curling? First, I need to think in three-shot sequences. I do A, he does, B, we do C. I really need to visualize that sequence for each option.

Second, in some situations, the potential return doesn't justify the additional risk. Sometimes it's better just to stay alive and try again next end.

And finally, I need to look for ways to leave myself options on my last. Don't leave myself just one option that they can block or take away. Give myself two so I'll always have one after their last rock.

Mickey's Last Word: "Try have two ways in whenever you can. And be realistic about what you can get from a situation. Don't shoot for the moon unless you really have to."

Do things work out for Stoughton? Yes – and no. He stays alive and takes it to a measure in 10. But, as we all know, he lost that, and Brad Gushue and team started their march to win Olympic gold. In Torino, on a Saturday Night.

Puzzle #50

Well, you're pretty cooked here, Skip. You've already coughed up a 4 in the second end and the third's not looking a whole lot better. Clearly, all those tactical tips in the preceding forty-nine puzzles haven't worked. Is it too late to get your money back? [Ed note – It is.] Anyway, you've got to find some magic here and see if you can't find some way to climb back into this. But how? Here's the situation:

- 3rd end of 10
- You're red
- You're down by 4
- You have hammer
- It's your Skip's last shot
- About a five-foot swing on good ice

C'mon Skip, it's not too late to put the first forty-nine puzzles to use. What's your call – and why?

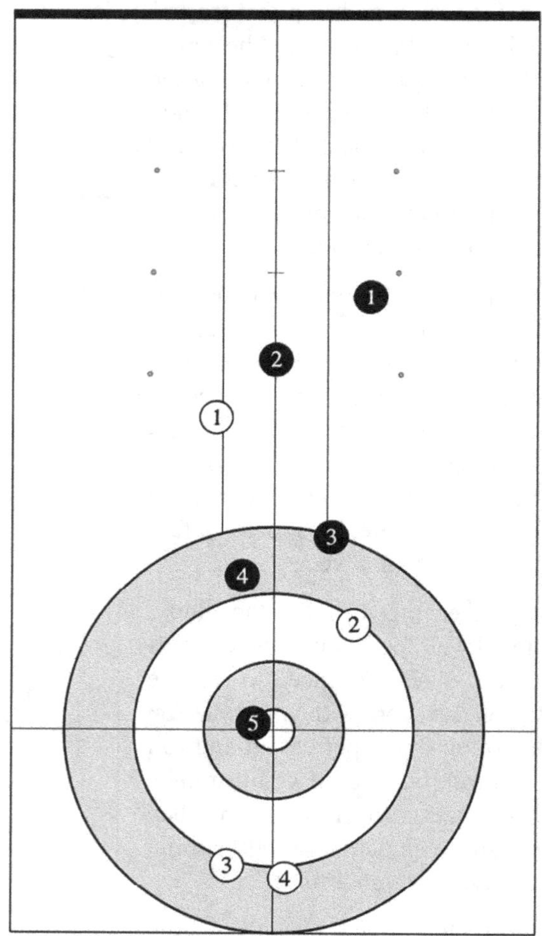

Just Insane

"This is one of the best shots you're ever going to see." – Mickey Pendergast

"That has to be the best shot I've ever seen in curling. Johnny didn't even see it." – Cheryl Bernard

"That's insane. Just insane." – Russ Howard

Well, there are almost no tactical implications in this puzzle, aside from scoreboard management, but we're sticking it in anyway. It's just the perfect way to end this book – one of those shots that has to be watched and admired over and over and over again. Stay with the video into the next end and hear two of the most seasoned veterans in the sport continue to wax lyrical over this play.

And what better guy to walk us through it than Mickey, Kevin Koe's old Skip. Kevin (ten Brier appearances, eight finals, four titles…and counting) played for Mickey when he was first breaking through in Alberta, so Mickey's got a pretty good insight into Kevin's thinking on this one.

"First of all, he's down by 4 so he's gotta take some chances. A lot of people would go for the wide come-around and try for their relatively simple deuce. I say relatively because it's not a certainty anytime you go out that wide and try to come around to the eight-foot. Bottcher just played it and slid a little deep. In the third end, it's probably pretty fresh pebble out here, so you don't know what you're going to get.

"And in Kevin's mind, there's not that much risk to the shot he plays. Listen to the chat when he and Johnny Morris are sizing it up. He says 'We're gonna get something' and 'It's just as easy as the wide draw.'

"He sees there's some margin for error. If you throw back ring weight, something's gonna go into the eight-foot – either the R2 that gets raised or the R4 rock it hits. He's recognized that he's got a 3-4 inch wide target to make a deuce, so that's not too risky at this level. But of course, to get a 3 out of it, he's got a much smaller target and a much smaller window for the weight.

"You could throw this a hundred times and not make it and not be surprised you didn't make it. But if the Skipper's seeing it and feeling it, then you gotta let him throw it, especially if it's Kevin."

"At the club, I don't think anyone sees it, let alone throws it, let alone makes it. At club level, it's probably best to try the wide draw around, take your deuce and hope for some better ends down the stretch.

"But at Kevin's level, given he's likely to get the deuce – same as he would if he went wide – it's worth the gamble. And making this shot is mentally a very big deal. He makes this and now it's a ball game. Bottcher's been leaning back, thinking he's totally in control up by 4 and happy holding Koe to a deuce. Then Kevin pulls this out of the hat, makes a spectacular 3-ball and now it's a one-point game. Sending a message to your opponent might make this shot worth more than 3."

As a Newbie, I'm taking away a two basic points. First, rocks in the top rings or short can be promoted. And when I need points, I need to put rocks in play and leave myself something to work with.

Mickey's Last Last Word: "For me, I like the vision that Kevin demonstrates, seeing the shot in the first place. And I like the risk calculation that goes into it. He was as likely to get a 2 by playing this as he was by going out wide. And by playing this, you just might get a 3. Especially if you're Kevin Koe."

www.ingramcontent.com/pod-product-compliance
Lightning Source LLC
Chambersburg PA
CBHW080302030726
47593CB00009B/2592